Health Psychology in Action

Edited by

Mark Forshaw and David Sheffield

Ⓦ WILEY-BLACKWELL

A John Wiley & Sons, Ltd., Publication

This edition first published 2013
© 2013 John Wiley & Sons, Ltd.

Wiley-Blackwell is an imprint of John Wiley & Sons, formed by the merger of Wiley's global Scientific, Technical and Medical business with Blackwell Publishing.

Registered Office
John Wiley & Sons Ltd, The Atrium, Southern Gate, Chichester, West Sussex, PO19 8SQ, UK

Editorial Offices
350 Main Street, Malden, MA 02148-5020, USA
9600 Garsington Road, Oxford, OX4 2DQ, UK
The Atrium, Southern Gate, Chichester, West Sussex, PO19 8SQ, UK

For details of our global editorial offices, for customer services, and for information about how to apply for permission to reuse the copyright material in this book please see our website at www.wiley.com/wiley-blackwell.

The right of Mark Forshaw and David Sheffield to be identified as the authors of the editorial material in this work has been asserted in accordance with the UK Copyright, Designs and Patents Act 1988.

Wiley also publishes its books in a variety of electronic formats. Some content that appears in print may not be available in electronic books.

Designations used by companies to distinguish their products are often claimed as trademarks. All brand names and product names used in this book are trade names, service marks, trademarks or registered trademarks of their respective owners. The publisher is not associated with any product or vendor mentioned in this book. This publication is designed to provide accurate and authoritative information in regard to the subject matter covered. It is sold on the understanding that the publisher is not engaged in rendering professional services. If professional advice or other expert assistance is required, the services of a competent professional should be sought.

Library of Congress Cataloging-in-Publication Data applied for.

A catalogue record for this book is available from the British Library.

Set in 10.5/13pt Minion by Aptara Inc., New Delhi, India
Printed in Malaysia by Ho Printing (M) Sdn Bhd

1   2013

Health Psychology in Action

Contents

About the Editors

Mark Forshaw is a Chartered and Registered Health Psychologist and Chartered Scientist. He has worked variously at the University of Manchester, Coventry University, Leeds Metropolitan University and Staffordshire University. He has a specific leadership role in external liaison and consultancy, holds some national positions in professional body work, and is the author of a number of books and articles across a wide range of psychological research themes and issues. Outside work, he is a film 'buff', an avid traveller, a poet, a painter of 'semi-abstract' work, and a number of other things he doesn't have enough time for. He tries very hard not to take things seriously, most of all himself.

David Sheffield is the Associate Head of the Centre for Psychological Research at the University of Derby. He is a Health Psychologist with the UK Health Professions Council and a Chartered Psychologist with the British Psychological Society Division of Health Psychology. Following a PhD at Glasgow Caledonian University, he worked in the United States for 6 years in cardiology divisions; there he was supported by grants by the National Institutes of Health to examine the role of psychological factors in the perception of pain in cardiac patients and the effects of mental stress on ischaemia. Returning to lecture at Staffordshire University in 2001, he helped to develop the first Professional Doctorate in Health Psychology in the United Kingdom that provided Stage 2 training. As well as contributing to doctorate, masters and degree programmes, he has supervised 13 doctoral students to completion. He moved to the University of Derby where his research extends to stress and cardiovascular responses, positive psychological interventions to improve well-being, pain and mathematics anxiety.

List of Contributors

Sarah Baker is a Chartered Psychologist and Associate Fellow of the British Psychological Society. She obtained her PhD from the University of Plymouth in 1995 and was a Lecturer in Health Psychology at Keele University before making the move into the field of Dentistry in 2005. She is currently a Senior Lecturer at the University of Sheffield in the School of Clinical Dentistry. She is based in the Unit of Dental Public Health, which consists of an interdisciplinary team of clinicians and academics at the forefront of patient-based research in relation to oral health.

Amy Baraniak is a trainee health psychologist at Staffordshire University. Amy worked for a number of years in primary health care with a varied role involving oversight of the implementation of the Quality & Outcomes Framework (QOF) and a number of enhanced services before taking on additional responsibility for providing smoking cessation and computerized cognitive-behavioural therapy interventions. Amy moved to the University of Derby in August 2009 where she lectures in Health Psychology with a focus on the application of health psychology within a primary health care setting.

Julian Bath is a Consultant Health Psychologist based at the Health Psychology Department of Gloucestershire Royal Hospital. He is the manager of the Gloucestershire Cardiac Rehabilitation Psychology Service and manager of the Gloucestershire Community Psychology Research Team. He also manages clinical, counselling and health psychologists providing services to renal medicine and adult diabetes. He has a broad range of experience working clinically with groups and individuals in cardiac rehabilitation, renal care and diabetes and a wealth of research and consultancy experience. He has numerous publications including the recent Wiley-Blackwell book, *Cardiac Rehabilitation: A Workbook for Use with Group Programmes*.

Sheila Bonas works in private practice as a Health Psychologist and Counsellor, and also has a part-time academic post in Clinical Psychology at the University of

Leicester. She has worked as a registered Health Psychologist in the National Health Service (NHS) in pain management and a cystic fibrosis service. In her academic experience she has enjoyed working at the interface where psychology interacts with the practice of medicine and health-related behaviour. Her research interests include work on research methodology, medical education and health professional–patient communication, and she has been increasingly drawn to use qualitative methods, especially phenomenology.

Neil Coulson is a Chartered and Registered Health Psychologist. He has worked previously at the University of Exeter, University of Plymouth, University of Derby and University of Nottingham. He is currently based at the Institute of Work, Health & Organisations (IWHO) at the University of Nottingham where he has been the Deputy Director of IWHO for the past four years. He is currently the Course Director for the Professional Doctorate in Health Psychology programme. He has held and continues to hold a number of positions on committees and boards of professional bodies such as the British Psychological Society. His research interests focus on the role of online support communities in helping patients manage long-term illness.

Lorna Dodd is a Health Psychologist working as a Senior Lecturer in Psychology at Newman University College, Birmingham. Lorna lectures on a number of undergraduate and postgraduate psychology modules, is involved in developing new and exciting programmes to align with current psychology trends and engages in scholarly work and health psychology research. Lorna has a Doctorate in Health Psychology from Staffordshire University and is a member of several professional bodies. Lorna's area of research falls within the umbrella of health behaviours and health-related lifestyles of young adults, in particular, a student population.

Darren Flynn is a Chartered Psychologist. His PhD investigated the psychological aspects of idiopathic scoliosis. He was previously a Research Fellow, a Lecturer in Psychology and a Senior Lecturer in Research Methods. Currently he is a Senior Research Associate with the Decision Making and Organisation of Care Group in the Institute of Health and Society at Newcastle University, working on the development of decision support for thrombolytic treatment in acute stroke care. He has co-authored a book on the influence of nonmedical factors on medical decision making and articles on subjects such as prostate cancer, dementia, gastrointestinal disorders and idiopathic scoliosis.

Claire Hallas is a Practitioner Psychologist with the UK Health Professions Council and a chartered psychologist with the British Psychological Society Division of Health Psychology. She has a PhD from the University of Liverpool, and postgraduate training in Cognitive Behavioural Therapy from the Oxford Cognitive Therapy Centre. She has spent the last 15 years delivering psychology services in a variety of UK National Health Service trusts specializing in the psychological care of cardiothoracic and oncology patients. She held a Consultant Health Psychologist post and was the Deputy Director of Rehabilitation & Therapies Services from 2004 to 2008 in a London tertiary care trust. She has worked as a Consultant Health Psychologist at the Department of Behavioural Medicine, Sultan Qaboos University Hospital in the Sultanate of Oman where she developed health psychology clinical services and teaching on the medical education programme. She is the author of a number of book chapters and research articles on the subject of mood disorders with respiratory and cardiovascular disease and the neuropsychological outcomes of cardiovascular surgery.

Jennifer Lunt is a Principal Health Psychologist at the Health and Safety Laboratory (HSL), which is an agency of the Health and Safety Executive (HSE), the independent watchdog for work-related health, safety and illness in the United Kingdom. Jennifer has a Professional Doctorate in Health Psychology from Staffordshire University, and is a Chartered Health Psychologist. When completing her doctorate she drew on her experiences in applying health psychology to health and safety. As a technical lead she has responsibility in assuring the technical quality of projects that relate to this area through a team of experienced occupational and health psychologists and health scientists. Her portfolio of work ranges from behavioural change and worker engagement, to disease reduction barriers and enablers, risk communication, retention at work, sickness absence and work-related well-being. Prior to joining HSL, Jennifer worked as a trainer and research psychologist for a human factors training consultancy, and has previously worked in the NHS delivering occupational stress management interventions.

Tim Moss is a Reader in Health Psychology at the University of the West of England (UWE), Bristol. He is registered with the Health Professions Council, the regulatory body for psychology in the United Kingdom. He leads the MSc Health Psychology programme, and is former programme director of the professional doctorate in health psychology programme at UWE, as well as contributing to other MSc and undergraduate programmes. He is the supervisor of several PhD students in the field of psychosocial adjustment to differences of appearance. Tim is the co-ordinator of the Derriford Appearance Scales project (www.derriford.info), providing measurement tools, advice and consultancy in the field of appearance and visible difference in the United Kingdom, Europe, Japan and the United States, amongst others. Tim is a member of the BPS Health Psychology Training Committee, and a BPS Assessor for the Stage 2 qualification in health psychology. He is a former Visitor for the Health Professions Council, involved in the evaluation of professional training programmes in psychology. From 2010, Tim has represented professional psychology training on the Advisory Board of the Psychology Network. He is also a fellow of the Royal Society for Public Health, and maintains an interest in public health applications of psychology. In 2011, Tim was appointed as Associate Head of Department of Psychology at UWE, with the Research/Knowledge Exchange portfolio.

Michael Murray is Professor of Social and Health Psychology and Head of the School of Psychology at Keele University, Staffordshire. Prior to that, he held appointments at other universities in England, Northern Ireland and Canada. He has published over 100 journal articles and chapters and (co-)authored and edited several books and collections on critical and qualitative approaches to health psychology including *Qualitative Health Psychology: Theories and Methods* (with Chamberlain, Sage 1999), *Critical Health Psychology* (Palgrave, 2004) and *Health Psychology: Theory, Research & Practice* (with Marks, Sage 2010). He is the Associate Editor of the *Journal of Health Psychology* and of *Psychology & Health* and sits on the editorial boards of several other journals including *Health, Psychology & Medicine, Health Psychology Review, Arts & Health* and *Subjectivity.* His current research interests include the use of participatory methods to engage communities in various forms of collective action.

Felix Naughton completed his PhD and Health Psychology BPS Stage 2 training at the University of Cambridge in 2010. His general research interest is in changing health behaviours, particularly smoking, and he is specifically interested in the use of new technologies in health care and health promotion.

Shilpa Patel is a Registered Psychologist and an academic researcher. She is a member of the British Psychological Society and Division of Health Psychology. She has a Professional Doctorate in Health Psychology from Staffordshire University and currently holds two posts, clinical and academic. She works clinically as a Health Psychologist in pain management at Milton Keynes NHS Foundation Trust and academically at Warwick Medical School, where her research focuses on musculoskeletal pain. Shilpa is a successful investigator on NIHR-funded research and has published and presented in the field of pain and pain management.

Sue Peacock is a Consultant Health Psychologist and registered with the Health Professions Council. She has a PhD from the University of Leicester, and currently works in the Pain Management Department at Milton Keynes Hospital NHS Foundation Trust and in private practice. She is the author of a number of research articles mainly relating to chronic pain. She has served on various committees within the British Psychological Society and currently is the psychology representative and secretary for the British Pain Society's Pain Management Programme Special Interest Group.

Karen Rodham is a registered and Chartered Health Psychologist and Associate Fellow of the British Psychological Society. She has a PhD from the University of Portsmouth and currently divides her work time between her academic and practice duties. She works four days a week as a Lecturer in Health Psychology at the University of Bath and one day a week as a practising Health Psychologist at the Royal National Hospital for Rheumatic Diseases. She is a qualified mountain leader and has a deep and enduring love for the mountains. She cherishes the time spent alone walking and clambering about in the outdoors, but also enjoys her voluntary work with young people completing their expeditions for the Duke of Edinburgh Award.

Katja Rüdell is a Chartered Psychologist. She has a PhD from the University of London, currently works in the Patient Reported Outcomes Centre of Excellence in the Primary Care Business Unit at Pfizer Ltd and has an honorary lectureship at the University of Kent. Her clinical health psychology background is in smoking cessation and her research interests are in development of patient-reported outcome measures for evaluating health care interventions, patients' perspectives on illness and cross-cultural health psychological research.

Harbinder Sandhu is a Registered Psychologist and member of the British Psychological Society and Division of Health Psychology. She has a Professional Doctorate in Health Psychology from Staffordshire University and is an Assistant Professor in Health Psychology at Warwick Medical School, University of Warwick and Health Psychologist in Chronic Pain Management, Milton Keynes NHS Foundation Trust. Harbinder is the author of a number of research articles in the area of clinician–patient communication. She is also the recognized UK trainer for the Roter Interaction Analysis System, an internationally valid and reliable tool used in health care communication skills assessment and analysis.

Rachel Shaw is a Health Psychologist registered with the Health Professions Council and a Chartered Psychologist of the British Psychological Society (BPS). She is Honorary Secretary of the Qualitative Methods in Psychology Section of the BPS. Rachel completed her PhD at De Montfort University in 2001. She currently works as a Lecturer in the School of Life and Health Sciences at Aston University. Her research interests include illness experience, health management, media framing of health issues, metasynthesis of qualitative evidence, interpretative phenomenology and reflexivity. Rachel has publications in health psychology and qualitative methods in psychology journals. She is also author of several chapters in qualitative methods textbooks.

Veronica Joan Thomas (commonly known as Nicky) is a registered health psychologist with the HPC. She obtained a PhD from London University Goldsmith's College. She is currently working as Consultant Health Psychologist in the Department of Haematology and Haemophilia at Guy's and St Thomas' NHS Foundation Hospitals Trust in London. She is also an honorary Lecturer in Health Psychology at the Institute of Psychiatry, Kings College London. She has held a variety of clinical, research and academic Health Psychology posts within Kings College, London and University College London Medical Schools. She has considerable experience in psycho-oncology and has worked in the Cancer Research Campaign department teaching communication and counselling to senior physicians and nurses working in cancer care. She has undertaken numerous research projects and is the author of a number of articles and chapters in academic books.

Preface

Mark Forshaw and David Sheffield

What is health psychology? One early and oft-used definition comes from Matarazzo (1982); 'Health Psychology is the aggregate of the specific educational, scientific and professional contributions of the discipline of psychology to the promotion and maintenance of health, the prevention and treatment of illness, the identification of etiologic and diagnostic correlates of health, illness and related dysfunction, and the analysis and improvement of the health care system and health policy formation' (p. 4). However, nearly every book on the subject seems to have a slightly different definition, something discussed in some detail, for example, in Forshaw (2002). Not much has changed since then, except that we probably have even more definitions than we had before. Of course, developments come in two ways: top-down and bottom-up. Proclaiming that health psychology is X, Y and Z, and then expecting all health psychologists to devote themselves to X, Y and Z, is a top-down approach, and is very valuable at times, especially, we would argue, in the middle stages of a profession. We believe we are moving out of the middle stages. The bottom-up approach involves looking to see what people who view themselves as health psychologists are getting up to, and defining the subject based on that. Health psychology is what health psychologists do. In our view, this is what happens in the earliest stages of the development of a profession, and again in the latter stages, to allow for some rejigging before the formula is mostly complete. In the earliest days of health psychology, groups of people were doing certain kinds of work, and they saw that they had things in common, and that those things weren't adequately captured by the professions in existence. Health psychology thus emerged, from the work of those people, defined organically. That set of topic areas rapidly became what health psychology was defined as, for sensible reasons. It was a guide to new generations of health psychologists and other interested parties. Division 38 of the American Psychological Association formed in 1978, after many years of hard work setting up and lobbying by numerous individuals, notably Stephen Weiss. It took the health psychologists in the United Kingdom a little longer to convince the British

Psychological Society of a need for a Section, which became a full-fledged Division in 1997, after being in existence as a Section from 1986. In BPS structures, Sections are groups of people with academic or political interests, and Divisions are reserved for recognized professions. Once a Division was inaugurated, a training model was needed, and this was first established in 2001. Benchmarked around postgraduate-level descriptors, and competence based, it rolled out firstly in the form of BPS-run Qualifications and shortly thereafter as courses in higher education institutions. Stage 1 of the qualifications is the MSc-level component of the training focusing on knowledge, which is then followed by Stage 2, at D-level, which is practice oriented. At the time of writing, we are currently experiencing the second version of this Stage 2 training, revised and streamlined following extensive consultation. Although British health psychologists lagged a little behind their US counterparts in the earlier days, there has been a tremendous rush forward in recent years. We, as a professional community, are very proud of our achievements in the last 25 years, and equally proud of the trainees who have made their way through the system in the last decade, some of whom have contributed to this volume. We have an eminent past, a vibrant present and an assured future. At times of global uncertainty, and academic unrest in the United Kingdom, it is comforting to know some things are in good hands.

However, we are always open to change, which is precisely what should happen in a relatively modern, developing profession. It is time to take stock, and to reconfigure somewhat. New people, with new ideas, new theories and new ways of working, have entered our profession, and started to stretch the boundaries, and to toy with the emphasis. We welcome that, just as one welcomes a child outgrowing its clothes. Our view is that it is time to ask what health psychology is, all over again, and this book is that very survey laid bare. This book is the new bottom-up. If you want to know where the latest research is heading, we have journals for that. It is much more difficult to discover where real health psychologists themselves are heading, in their careers, in their thinking and in their views on the profession itself. You can talk to some of them at conferences, perhaps, but that is by no means an ideal way to get opinions, reflect on them and compare them to a range of other ideas from diverse professionals. We have done our best, in this book, to draw together that diversity and present a version of reality that we believe captures modern health psychology, mainly from a UK standpoint.

You will find, in this book, those who mostly regard themselves as 'academics', those who primarily regard themselves as 'practitioners' and everything in between. To some extent, this distinction is disingenuous, since most people take an academic, evidence-based approach to their work, and most academics are practitioners in that they teach and train and help to build the theories than underpin the practice. There's more to academia than the ivory tower, and there's more to practice than client work. Realizing this is one of health psychology's most valuable gifts. Health psychology is where academia and practice meet, and the same cannot necessarily be said for all areas of our discipline, which still maintain marked separations.

Naturally, we cannot lay claim to this book being entirely representative, although we have made every effort. Quite simply, we could not approach every single health psychologist, even though between us we possibly know most of them in some capacity or another. We tried to strike a balance between different career stages, and different working environments, and to give a flavour of the vast range of health issues to which we apply ourselves. However, we have aimed to give readers an idea of where health psychology is heading, so there are more early-career psychologists than might be found in many texts. This has enabled us to show the remarkable spread of health psychology across training, practice, industry and academic environments, and the impressive talents of our authors, reflecting the talents of health psychologists more widely.

We are delighted to be able to set out a vision of health psychology both present and future, and we are pleased that this Noah's Ark of a book is now ready to set sail. We are proud to present to you *Health Psychology in Action*.

References

Forshaw, M. (2002). *Essential Health Psychology*, London: Arnold.

Matarazzo, J.D. (1982). Behavioral health's challenge to academic, scientific and professional psychology. *American Psychologist, 37*, 1–14.

Acknowledgements

General

The editors would like to thank the contributors for their patience in the process, and their timely responses to our demands and queries. This is a team effort, and we would like to express our pride at being part of the virtual UK health psychology team. In addition, thanks to the entire staff at Wiley-Blackwell for their understanding and for believing in us that this book was fit for publication, even from day one of the proposal stage. In particular, thanks to Karen, Andy and Andrew.

Mark Forshaw

Thanks to the friends and colleagues across the health psychology community who helped me to become the health psychologist I am. In particular, thanks to Sandra Horn, for recognizing I had something to give. For me, following in your footsteps to chair DHPTC was a radical moment in my development. My gratitude also goes to BPS office team members, past and present, including Alex, Angie, Bethan, Helen, Kajal, Lucy, Rupal and Wilfred. Last but not least, thanks to Amanda Crowfoot for her patience and constructive ideas every time I have said something like 'You'll never guess what's happened now'. It's the sort of thing I say a lot.

David Sheffield

I would like to thank to all my colleagues at the University of Derby and my former colleagues at Staffordshire University. I am also grateful to Doug Carroll and colleagues at Glasgow Caledonian University for getting me started. Thanks to my students past and present who have maintained my enthusiasm. Finally, love and thanks to Sarah, Isaac and Phoebe.

Applying Health Psychology to Dentistry: 'People, Not Teeth'

Sarah Baker

Introduction: Why Dentistry?

I originally intended to become a sociologist but got unwittingly sidetracked into doing a psychology degree, which I began in 1987 at the University of Plymouth. I was not one of those people who knew what they wanted to do aged 10, so I fell into doing a PhD at the same institution. My thesis was on the psychophysiological indices of stress and a great amount of time, thought and energy went into devising ways of making people stressed. Once this was achieved, the rest of the time was spent in a dark soundproof room, my polygraph and I, stressing people and measuring their sweat. Three years later, I embarked on a research assistant job whilst writing up my thesis. Following years in a darkened room with a polygraph, this job, investigating psychophysiological reactions whilst playing video games, was rather fun. However, after a year I clearly could not put it off any longer; a responsible job was needed. I got my PhD and took up a postdoctoral research fellow position in the Department of Psychology at the University of Surrey. The Wellcome Trust–funded study on the psychophysiological and behavioural correlates of social phobia had much in common with the previous 5 years; I spent much of it in a small darkened room measuring the responses of socially phobic individuals whilst they had to interact with others. I realised a number of things early on; in order to spend time with people rather than a large machine (aka a polygraph), to get a bigger room (with lighting) and have job security, I would have to apply for lectureship positions. Given my anxiety of public speaking at the time, this was not something I warmed to. I duly became a Lecturer in Biological Psychology at Coventry University in 1997, followed by a Lecturer in Health Psychology at Keele University in 1998, where I stayed until

Health Psychology in Action, First Edition. Edited by Mark Forshaw and David Sheffield.
© 2013 John Wiley & Sons, Ltd. Published 2013 by John Wiley & Sons, Ltd.

2005. The position in the Psychology Department at Keele was where I really learnt my research skills; particularly the importance of theory and methodology. However, I was also forming the opinion that research in health psychology, that is *applied* research, needed to move out of psychology departments into 'the field'. I wanted, in the old cliché, to 'make a difference' through research; to make it useful and relevant to patient populations. I could only do that by putting my job where my mouth was. Moving to medicine was the obvious choice – there were now quite a few psychologists working in medical schools – but why have the route already mapped for you? I opted for Dentistry. I left the Psychology Department and travelled to the Dental School in Sheffield in 2005. There are 16 dental schools in the United Kingdom, including Sheffield, and I can count the number of psychologists working in these on one hand. Inevitably, 'What is a psychologist doing in dentistry?' or its alternative 'So you do dental anxiety then?' have been asked many times by dental undergraduates, dentists and even psychologists. It was an interesting, in some ways an impulsive choice but, most certainly, the right choice.

What's a Psychologist Doing in Dentistry?

Why would a psychologist be employed in a dental school? The cynical answer is that all such schools have to be accredited every 6 years and the teaching of behavioural science is a part of the undergraduate Bachelor of Dental Surgery (BDS) curriculum. However, many schools simply ask already employed clinicians to do this teaching because 'Psychology is just common sense, isn't it?' When psychologists are employed, it is generally because someone in a senior position has the foresight to understand the potential contributions a psychologist can make to teaching, research and service in dentistry.

This was so in my case. I joined a growing team in Dental Public Health consisting of clinicians (paediatric dentists, orthodontists and dental public health specialists) and two social scientists (sociologists). We are one of four departments in the School of Clinical Dentistry, alongside Oral and Maxillofacial Surgery, Oral Pathology and Adult Dental Care. The School itself is linked, physically and in terms of both teaching and research, with the Charles Clifford Dental Hospital. The dental hospital is one of five hospitals which make up Sheffield Teaching Hospitals NHS Foundation Trust, and provides casualty services and specialist diagnosis, treatment and management for adult and child dental patients. These specialties include restorative dentistry, oral and maxillofacial surgery, paediatric dentistry, orthodontics, cleft lip and palate services, craniofacial implant surgery and trigeminal facial pain.

As the only psychologist in the School and Hospital, my overarching goal through my work has been to shift colleagues' thinking to 'people, not teeth'. So whilst my specialist contribution is the application of the theory, method and techniques from the discipline of psychology to oral health, my role is much broader and diffuse. Essentially it is as an advocate for the biopsychosocial paradigm. This may seem very basic to a psychology reader. However, dentistry is about teeth, gums and the oral cavity – the 'bio' – and it lags some way behind medicine in its consideration of and the importance placed on either the 'psycho' or 'social'. Much of my work is therefore about building a bridge between the clinical and social science disciplines. As such, collaboration and interdisciplinarity are the key.

Interdisciplinarity

Interdisciplinary research is a mode of research by teams or individuals that integrates information, data, techniques, tools, perspectives, concepts and/or theories from two or more disciplines or bodies of specialized knowledge to advance fundamental understanding or to solve problems whose solutions are beyond the scope of a single discipline or area of research practice. (National Academy of Sciences, 2005)

Health is multifaceted and complex; key questions go beyond the expertise of one clinician or one academic and require the efforts and inputs of different disciplines. All of my research involves collaboration with individuals from outside of psychology in order to advance understanding in ways that would not be achievable by one discipline alone through the sharing of ideas, or integration of concepts, methodology or theory. As in all interdisciplinary work, I have to be both a generalist and a specialist. My job is to render the specialist expertise of a psychologist intelligible and relevant to dentists. This requires the skills to be able to analyse, evaluate and synthesise information from different areas of psychology in order to develop and address the pertinent research questions about particular phenomena in dentistry.

Inevitably there are conflicts and difficulty in achieving a way forward. The balance has to be found between the expertise you bring and shared decision making. The decision cannot be 'made' by one person. Interdisciplinarity therefore involves the 3 Cs: cooperation, conflict and compromise! Over time working in many interdisciplinary teams, I have come to appreciate that it is a skill, learnt like others through trial and error; the skill to speak your opinion and be confident enough to differ. You have to enjoy having different perspectives, listening to others and seeking a 'third way'. In a way you are both representing and promoting a discipline; you are educating fellow academics and clinicians on what psychology is and what psychologists do.

The Importance of Theory

One of my key contributions to these teams has been putting forward the importance of a theoretical framework in which to guide research. Theory has not generally been seen as important in dentistry or in dental public health. Theory, however, is important for a number of reasons. Theory helps to address the *what, why and how?* questions; what is the problem? Why does it happen?

What are the contextual influences? What can we do about it? Theory therefore provides the framework to help develop appropriate research questions, identify key variables, establish relationships, interpret findings and design and evaluate interventions.

Oral Health–Related Quality of Life

One of my primary research areas is the testing and development of theoretical models in the field of oral health–related quality of life (OHRQoL) through the use of structural equation modelling (Baker, 2007, 2009, 2010; Baker *et al.*, 2007, 2008, 2010). OHRQoL is a multidimensional construct that refers to the extent to which oral conditions disrupt a person's normal functioning. OHRQoL has, over recent years, become an important focus for assessing the impact of a range of oral conditions on quality of life and well-being (e.g. Gift *et al.*, 1997) together with the outcomes of clinical care such as the effectiveness of treatment interventions (e.g. Awad *et al.*, 2000). Research in the field has largely been descriptive and atheoretical; there have been few studies that have assessed the range of psychosocial factors that influence OHRQoL or attempted to explicitly test the direct and mediated linkages between key variables within a theoretical model.

Why is providing answers to such questions important? Firstly, the validity of OHRQoL as an outcome measure in clinical trials is partly dependent on understanding the causal processes linking oral conditions to patient-reported outcomes. In order to understand the pathways underlying such effects, any proposed model needs to be valid and empirically tested (Shrout and Bolger, 2002). Secondly, developing knowledge of key pathways will help facilitate the design of intervention strategies by, for example, guiding clinicians as to where to most effectively intervene, with whom and in what way.

One model, which explicitly conceptualizes the relationship between clinical factors and quality of life, is that of Wilson and Cleary (1995). This model has become one of the most well-established biopsychosocial models used in a variety of health contexts including cardiovascular disease and HIV/AIDS (Wettergren *et al.*, 2004). My research has been the first to test the validity of the model in relation to chronic oral health conditions, notably xerostomia (Baker *et al.*, 2007) and edentulousness (Baker *et al.*, 2008).

Xerostomia is a common chronic health condition, affecting one quarter of adults and 40% of elderly people, and is a side effect of over 400 therapeutic drugs (e.g. antidepressants). Xerostomia is also seen as a sequela of damage to salivary glands in autoimmune (e.g. rheumatoid arthritis), and other systemic diseases (e.g. multiple sclerosis); and as a consequence of radiation for treatment of head and neck cancer. Symptoms can often be severe and debilitating with a reduced ability to speak, chew, swallow, taste and sleep (Pankhurst *et al.*, 1996). To date, nearly all research in the area has been clinical in nature; yet, in the absence of a curative treatment, the overriding therapeutic goal is long-term management. As such, where treatment is not about cure but increasing patient comfort, there is a strong case for understanding the impact of the condition on patients' everyday lives.

The aim of our study was to test an integrative conceptual model to provide a more comprehensive picture of the impact of xerostomia on the daily lives of patients. The study was a secondary analysis of data collected as part of a randomised control trial of a device for the management of xerostomia (Robinson *et al.*, 2005) using structural equation modelling (SEM). SEM is a powerful statistical technique that allows simultaneous testing of complex interrelationships between variables specified within *a priori* models (Kline, 2005). As such, it is currently the best technique for assessing and modifying theoretical models.

Our findings supported Wilson and Cleary's conceptual model of patient outcomes as applied to xerostomia and highlighted the complexity of (inter-) relationships between key clinical and psychosocial variables (Baker *et al.*, 2007). The results, together with our other SEM studies with both patient and general populations (Baker, 2007, 2009, 2010; Baker *et al.*, 2008, 2010), have a number of important theoretical and clinical implications. Firstly, modelling indirect and mediated effects has helped reconcile why systematic observations between clinical and subjective measures found in previous (oral) health research have generally been weak. Secondly, they re-emphasize the importance of patient-reported outcomes (e.g. OHRQoL) being routinely assessed, alongside traditional clinical indicators, disease-specific symptom measures and wider well-being, in both research and clinical practice. Thirdly, interventions aimed solely at the biological-clinical level, which do not take into account patient experiences of their symptoms, will not be fully effective.

The Impact of Oral Health on Children, Adolescents and Their Families

Disfigurement to the face, hands and body affects about 400,000 people in Britain. These visible differences can arise from congenital craniofacial anomalies or be acquired as a result of trauma, or dermatological conditions. Cleft lip and/or palate (CL/P) is the most common congenital condition of the head and neck region affecting between 1 in 600–700 babies. Treatment requires multiple surgical procedures from birth through infancy, childhood, adolescence and into adulthood, and frequent clinic attendances to deal with problems related to impaired facial growth, speech impairment, hearing difficulties and dental anomalies. As such, CL/P can bring a range of additional life stressors which may impact not only on the person but also on the family unit.

To date, as with much of the appearance literature, the vast majority of research on CL/P has explored this from a perspective of how negative and psychologically damaging the experience is. Yet, in the wider stress literature, it has become evident that people who experience major life stressors can find benefit from such events, often reporting a range of positive outcomes co-occurring alongside negative ones (Folkman, 1997). In our research, we have been working within a stress resiliency framework to explore the factors influencing how families 'adjust well' to having a child with CL/P (Baker *et al.*, 2009) or dental trauma (Porritt *et al.*, 2010). The framework we have been using is the resiliency model of family stress, adjustment, and adaptation (Danielson, 1985), which explains the family's response to a life stressor such as chronic illness, and the individual and family resources that influence coping and, in turn, adjustment.

Findings from our CL/P study indicated that whilst there were many impacts of a child's condition on the family, negative outcomes (e.g. family impact and psychological distress) were not high. On the contrary, parents reported high levels of positive adjustment or 'stress-related growth' as a result of their child's condition. Examples of positive outcomes involved better self-understanding and treatment of others, greater personal strength and optimism, more effective ability to regulate emotions and a greater sense of belonging and religiousness. Such positive adjustment is in line with the three major types of stress-related growth reported in the literature, (1) better social resources, (2) better personal resources and (3) new or improved coping skills (Schaefer and Moos, 1992).

As with the study discussed in this chapter, most of the research I am involved in is about developing an evidence base. This may be in relation to CL/P, or the impact of dental trauma on families and children (Porritt *et al.*, 2010), whether craniofacial conditions influence children's transition to secondary school (Marshman *et al.*, 2009), the influence of cultural factors on meanings of appearance and appearance-altering surgery (orthognathic surgery) (Stocker *et al.*, 2010) or the psychosocial factors which influence adolescents' oral health status and quality of life outcomes (Baker *et al.*, 2010). Each of these studies is designed to build an evidence-based case that has the potential, in the longer term, to contribute to the development of clinical services which are sensitive to the psychosocial needs of patients, children and their families (i.e. 'people, not teeth').

For example, in our most recent work (Baker *et al.*, 2010), we found that it was not clinical status (decayed and missing teeth) that was important in terms of adolescents' health and general quality of life outcomes but psychosocial factors, primarily sense of coherence (SOC). Having a greater SOC – that is, perceiving the world as more comprehensible, meaningful and manageable – was linked prospectively to fewer symptoms, lower functional impacts, better health perceptions and a better overall quality of life. Such findings, the first in relation to oral health, are in line with Antonovsky's (1979) salutogenic theory. Such a salutogenic approach has been advocated in recent health promotion initiatives (Eriksson & Lindstrom, 2008), and it may be that enhancing SOC could be an important 'psychological flu shot' for longer term inoculation against oral ill health. To this end, we are currently carrying out a feasibility study of an SOC school-based intervention for improving oral health–related quality of life in children.

Improving Communication Skills of the Dentists of Tomorrow

In their classic study of dentist–patient communication, Wanless and Holloway (1994) audiotaped consultations between general dental practitioners (GDPs) and 132 adolescents aged 10–17 years. They found that only 56% of consultations involved a verbal greeting to their patient, only 19% involved a preliminary explanation of what the aim of the session was and what was going to happen, and only 4% involved a summary of what the session had achieved.

In medicine, significant developments have been made in the training of general practitioners in patient communication. Few such developments have occurred in dentistry. Yet, we know there are problems. The 1998 Adult Dental Health Survey found that 64% of respondents were nervous of some sort of dental treatment and 49% were anxious of going to the dentist (Kelly *et al.*, 2000). Dental anxiety has been found to be the highest in those who perceive their relationship with their dentist to be poor. Conversely, we know that effective communication increases the quality and amount of information obtained from the patient which, in turn, leads to more accurate and efficient diagnoses. Further, effective communication increases the likelihood of patient adherence to recommendations and treatment, and leads to better health outcomes for patients, greater satisfaction for both patient and health care professionals and a reduction in the level of patient complaints and litigation (Silverman *et al.*, 2005).

The General Dental Council (GDC), the professional body which regulates dental professionals in the United Kingdom and accredits all undergraduate dental courses in the United Kingdom, has recently made communication one of the required competencies of the undergraduate dental curriculum (GDC, *The First Five Years*, 2002). Partly as a result of these changes, the Dental School at Sheffield wanted to significantly enhance its provision within its new leading-edge curriculum to be implemented in 2007. I was given the role of developing and implementing a new communication skills component for this curriculum.

Given the minimal evidence base in dentistry, I decided to adapt an existing communication skills framework developed for medical consultations; the Calgary-Cambridge Framework (CCF) (Kurtz *et al.*, 2005; Silverman *et al.*, 2005). The rationale underlying the CCF is that communication is a core clinical skill rather than an optional extra.

The CCF summarizes the five key stages of a consultation which are the basic tasks that need to be accomplished in everyday clinical practice; initiating the session, gathering information and patient interviewing, the physical examination and treatment, explanation and closing the session. The framework therefore helps the dentist with structure (where am I in the consultation and what do I want to achieve?). It also helps with specific skills (how do I get there?) by providing 71 (yes 71!) different communication process skills that can be used in different stages of the consultation (e.g. the use of open and closed questioning, and relating explanations to the patient's illness framework). Lastly, it helps with phrasing or behaviour (how can I incorporate these skills into my own style and make it work for me?). All of the skills incorporated within the CCF have emerged from research and practice as being of value to communication in health care settings.

The communication skills course that I developed is taught within the first 3 years of the 5-year undergraduate BDS programme. In the first year, prior to students working with patients, the aim is to simply increase their awareness of the importance of communication skills in dentistry, develop their understanding of core communication skills and appreciate the patient-centred approach – the CCF. This may seem straightforward but there are often a number of barriers: students may perceive that their communication skills are good and they will not learn anything, that communication skills are in some way innate and cannot be taught or that their clinical skills are more important and that is where they should therefore invest time and effort. Getting past these barriers – facilitating self-reflection – is the challenge.

The second year is about developing students' core communication skills and for them to begin to apply these skills in patient management. In the small-group sessions, we use trigger tapes as a means of analysing the consultation. The tapes can be used to identify, label and critique skills and to discuss more or less effective skills. On the clinic, students complete both peer and self-assessment exercises of actual communication skills ability, which are then reflected upon in small-group work. In the third year, the aim is to consolidate core communication skills and begin to apply these to specific communication issues and challenges (working with children, elderly people, persons with learning disabilities, cultural and gender issues, and people with dental anxiety and fear). We use role-play of different scenarios in small-group sessions, with student actors taking the role of the patient. Following this, at the end of the year, students' communication skills are formally assessed by way of an Objective Structured Clinical Exam (OSCE). OSCEs comprise short (5–10-minute) stations in which candidates are examined individually by two examiners with real or simulated patients, and are often used in health services (medicine, nursing, dentistry) to exam clinical skill performance and competencies.

The first two years of the course have now been successfully implemented, and evaluations are being carried out. The results will be published and used to inform the evidence base in dental education for the design and implementation of theory-led communication skills courses in dentistry. In addition, I am currently modifying the material into short CPD (continuing professional development) courses for GDPs to use in their everyday clinical practice.

Professional Service, Development and Supervision

Supervision

A great deal of my time is spent giving supervision. Some of this involves for-mal supervision on a range of undergraduate and postgraduate courses; from the elective projects fourth-year undergraduate dental students have to complete when on outreach (education and practice in the community), to oral health promotion projects on the Diploma in Hygiene and Therapy programme, to dissertations on the Masters in Dental Public Health course. Each of these has very different aims, vary greatly in their educational level and require distinctly different depths of psychological theory and methodology input.

In addition, I supervise between four and seven PhD students at any one time. These students may be either psychology graduates who have an interest in applying a psychological perspective to key areas in oral health (e.g. dental trauma and orthognathics); or, alternatively, they are qualified dentists largely from other countries (e.g. Malaysia or Thailand) who are paid by their government to complete further postgraduate study. These students do dental projects (dental screening, oral health promotion and oral cancer screening) which incorporate some aspect of psychological theory. All students are supervised in interdisciplinary teams, comprising myself and relevant clinician(s).

Hand-in-hand with the importance of theory in psychology, is the emphasis placed on research methods. This is in stark contrast to training received in undergraduate and postgraduate dental courses, in which research methods get barely a look in. This has meant that, in addition to formal supervision, I also provide a great deal of advice on research methods and statistics to consultant clinicians carrying out their own research, to specialist registrars in paediatric dentistry, orthodontics or restorative dentistry who have to carry out projects as part of their training, to academic colleagues, and through the development of my Research Methods in Clinical Dentistry module on the Masters in Dental Public Health course.

Given the lack of research methods training in dentistry, the methodological soundness of much of dental research leaves a lot to be desired. In regard to this, I view one of my key professional contributions to dentistry as being the editorial and review work I do for dental journals. I am currently section editor for behavioural sciences for the journal *Cleft Palate-Craniofacial Journal*. This journal is the official publication of the American Cleft Palate-Craniofacial Association and is directed to a multidisciplinary readership of clinicians and academics interested in craniofacial anomalies, including cleft lip and cleft palate. This is an important role as the number of submitted manuscripts which incorporate what might be (very) loosely termed a 'behavioural' measure is increasing; primarily because of the shift in emphasis within clinical research to the inclusion of patient-reported outcome measures (PROMs). I am also a member of the editorial board for the pre-eminent journal in the field of dental public health, *Community Dentistry and Oral Epidemiology*. The journal serves as a forum for research in community dentistry, which means that its scope is broad, encompassing epidemiology, behavioural sciences and health services research.

Both of these roles require an ability to judge a manuscript's originality, validity and relevance from a purely scientific point of view as well as a practical clinical perspective. Both roles are immensely interesting but time consuming, for which there is little direct reward! Again, I am often the only non-clinician in these roles and have to find a line between rigorous academic standards, maintaining credibility and incorporating a psychological perspective. At the same time, it is hugely gratifying that my training in psychology can be useful to other academics and clinicians, often with a very biomedical perspective, as well as to wider scholarship in dentistry.

Development

Minority influence is a form of social influence when the majority are being influenced to accept the beliefs and behaviour of the minority (Moscovici *et al.*, 1969). Initially, a minority of one was thought to be the most influential (Moscovici and Nemeth, 1974), although recent research suggests that two people may be more influential because they are less likely to be viewed as strange and eccentric (Maass and Clark, 1984)! Minority influence is increased by the minority being part of the 'in-group' as their ideas are viewed as more acceptable than those from the 'out-group' (Maass and Clark, 1984).

What does this mean for the application of health psychology? Health psychologists may find they have greater influence if they are located with the 'in-group' (i.e. employed in medicine/dentistry/NHS rather than in psychology departments). Health psychology will gain more credibility in medicine and dentistry if the minority is greater than one and growing. In line with this, I view capacity building within dentistry as a key part of my professional contribution to psychology. At an individual level, this occurs through my supervision of Stage 2 Health Psychology trainees, encouraging psychology graduates to do PhDs in psychology as applied to oral health, and furthering postdoctoral careers for psychology PhD students who are located in dentistry.

On a wider level, this involves getting colleagues together who work in social science as applied to oral heath to develop collaborations and network. In this way, the social science minority, if we remain consistent (!), will, over time, gain credibility and a growing influence. Myself, together with sociology and psychology colleagues, recently organised a successful day in which we brought together all social scientists working in oral health in the United States to discuss where we are now in terms of a social science agenda and how to move this forward. The day acted as both a networking opportunity (being a minority of one can sometimes be a little lonely) and an academic exercise (what areas can we best collaborate in? In what ways? How can we proceed?). In June of this year, we also saw the first issue of the journal *Social Science and Dentistry*, which will act as an important forum for developing a social science agenda and, hopefully, act as a spur to further professional development.

Service

Most of my professional service comes from consultancy work. Over the last three years, myself and colleagues within the Dental Public Health unit have carried out extensive work for the consumer health care division of GlaxoSmithKline (GSK). GSK have a number of leading oral health care products, one of which is for dentine sensitivity. Dentine sensitivity is the sensation felt when nerves inside the dentin of the teeth are exposed to the environment. Pain is the major symptom of the condition. Studies of patients' experiences have largely been restricted to ratings of pain, typically in the laboratory; there has been little consideration of the impact of the condition on a person's everyday life. In the light of this, we carried out an extensive qualitative study which explored the daily experiences of people with dentine sensitivity (Gibson *et al.*, 2010). The findings showed the depth and complexity of pain experiences associated with sensitivity, impacts on functional status and everyday activities such as eating, drinking, talking, tooth brushing, social interaction and also more subtle impacts on emotions and identity. Leading directly from this work, we have developed a patient-centred measure of dentine sensitivity quality of life (Boiko *et al.*, 2010). The measure has begun to be validated as an evaluative measure in clinical trials. Whilst the application of such patient-centred measures in randomized controlled trials is relatively new, our research suggests the prospects for such a measure to capture improvements in pain and other impacts are very high.

Challenges and Joys

Challenges

Any challenges I face are primarily concerned with interdisciplinary working and being a social scientist in a biologist-dominated field. There are common misconceptions or prejudices about one another (aka 'Psychology is just common sense, isn't it?'). Often we do not have a shared 'language'. Moreover, bringing together a team of people each with their own beliefs, attitudes and ways of working means there are inevitably conflicts and difficulty in achieving a coherent view or way forward. Every member of the team has separate obligations and duties which are based on their skills and discipline which come together within the team. Because everyone within the team has different strengths, the aim if the team is to successfully work together is to facilitate the expertise and insights of each member in order to address the problem or question at hand. There are therefore obligations – ethical obligations – of mutual respect within the team. As each person is representing a profession, professionalism is the key – respect for others, which means listening to others and acknowledging their viewpoint. There has to be a willingness to appreciate differing perspectives and methods; interdisciplinarity cannot work if members of the team are stuck in disciplinary attitudes (e.g. someone who advocates the 'rigour' of an RCT design might think qualitative research is the plural of anecdote). In my experience, the willingness to appreciate differing perspectives and methods is stronger in some people than others!

Joys

The enjoyment of working in a non-traditional setting far outweighs any barriers. Sometimes it may lack having another psychologist to have discipline-specific discussions with, although I have found that this can be alleviated by working with others from the psychology department or other social scientists. I have found dentistry to be uncharted territory. I can make of it what I want. There are many, many questions of relevance to oral health that psychology can help address. What dentistry gives is the potential to ask these interesting psychological questions in a different context. The change from dentists treating teeth to treating people is slow, painfully slow at times, and often infuriating, but something health psychology can contribute. This makes working within dentistry hugely interesting, academically stimulating and a challenge.

The sharing of knowledge and skills within interdisciplinary teams has allowed my own development through a critical reflection on my own beliefs and attitudes. I have learnt much from others within these teams; not only explicit things but also about implicit values and beliefs. I have learnt a great deal from others on professionalism, the nuances of conducting research in applied settings, methodologies and, in turn, what health psychology can offer by way of applied research, teaching and professional services. Most importantly, I have learnt how to work successfully as part of a team – something which is typically paid lip service to.

This all condenses into the opportunity to be a promoter for the discipline of health psychology. The sense of achievement and value you get when you have facilitated a patient-centred perspective ('patients, not teeth') in clinical practice, or in your own or others' published research or in the mission or strategy of an academic school is immensely gratifying and rewarding.

Key Debates in Health Psychology

Health Psychology and Public Health – Bridging the Gap

The title above was that of an editorial of a special issue in *Journal of Health Psychology* (Vinck *et al.*, 2004). The special issue was devoted to furthering a public health psychology (PHP) agenda, originally advocated by Tanabe (1982), in order to bridge the gap between health psychology and its focus on *individuals*, and public health's level of analysis, *populations*. To date, social and behavioural science within public health has focussed largely on individual health-related behaviours ("lifestyles"). As such, only a limited range of psychological theories and knowledge have been utilized; most notably, social cognition models such as the theory of planned behaviour. Whilst small to modest changes in health behaviours can be made with carefully designed interventions based on such models, whether these changes are long-lasting or translate at the population level is questionable. Yet, health psychology has huge potential in helping realize public health agendas; that is, creating supportive environments, developing healthy public policy, increasing personal resources and strengthening community action (World Health Organization (WHO), *Ottawa Charter*, 1986). As contributors to the special issue note, in order to realize this potential, health psychology needs to move beyond restricted interventions targeting individual behaviours to incorporate a broader ecological approach which incorporates individual (e.g. health knowledge and actions), social (e.g. interpersonal relations), structural and environmental factors (health and public policy e.g. pricing of alcohol and healthy food). This is not to suggest that health psychologists should become social epidemiologists but rather a call for understanding and integrating both upstream (population-level) social factors and downstream psychological and biological processes, all of which influence health. Furthermore, at a professional level, health psychologists need to start working not just with individuals or target groups but also with systems and those with control over environmental determinants (e.g. local communities and politicians). To further this agenda, PHP needs to encompass and synthesize many different theories, from both psychology and public health, and adopt multilevel approaches and methodologies. Rather than being individual- *versus* population-based approaches to prevention and health promotion, we should be aiming for 'and'. The subdiscipline of PHP is fundamentally an interdisciplinary field; collaboration across health psychology and public health – rather than each discipline attempting to encompass all levels of analysis in 'their' own field. In my opinion, this is the next phase for health psychology, understanding the individual in context, multilevel approaches and interdisciplinary research and practice. By so doing, health psychologists will be better placed to address fundamental questions in relation to the *complexities* of health.

References

American Dental Association. (2011). Dentistry definitions. http://www.ada.org/495.aspx

Antonovsky, A. (1979). *Health, stress and coping.* San Francisco: Jossey-Bass.

Awad, M.A., Locker, D., Korner-Bitensky, N., & Feine, J.S. (2000). Measuring the effect of intra-oral implant rehabilitation on health-related quality of life in a randomised controlled clinical trial. *Journal of Dental Research, 79,* 1659–1663.

Baker, S.R. (2007). Testing a conceptual model of oral health: a structural equation modelling approach. *Journal of Dental Research, 86,* 708–712.

Baker, S.R. (2009). Applying Andersen's behavioural model to oral health: What are the contextual factors shaping oral health outcomes? *Community Dentistry and Oral Epidemiology, 37*, 485–494.

Baker, S.R. (2010). Socio-economic position and oral health: comparing proximal and distal indicators. *Social Science and Dentistry, 1*, 5–10.

Baker, S.R., Mat, A., & Robinson, P.G. (2010). What psychosocial factors influence adolescents' oral health? *Journal of Dental Research*. doi:10.1177/0022034510376650

Baker, S.R., Owens, J., Stern, M., & Willmot, D. (2009). Coping strategies and social support in the family impact of cleft lip and palate and parent's adjustment and psychological distress. *Cleft Palate-Craniofacial Journal, 46*, 229–236.

Baker, S.R., Pankhurst, C.L., & Robinson, P.G. (2007). Testing relationships between clinical and non-clinical variables in xerostomia: A structural equation model of oral health-related quality of life. *Quality of Life Research, 16*, 297–308.

Baker, S.R., Pearson, N.K., & Robinson, P.G. (2008). Testing the applicability of a conceptual model of oral health in housebound edentulous older people. *Community Dentistry Oral Epidemiology, 36*, 237–248.

Boiko, O.V., Baker, S.R., Gibson, B.J., Locker, D., Sufi, F., Barlow, A.P.S., & Robinson, P.G. (2010). Construction and validation of the quality of life measure for dentine hypersensitivity (DHEQ). *Journal of Clinical Periodontology, 37*, 973–980.

Danielson, C.B. (1985). *Families, health and illness: perspectives on coping and intervention.* Baltimore: Mosby.

Eriksson, M., & Linstrom, B. (2008). A salutogenic interpretation of the Ottawa Charter. *Health Promotion International, 23*, 190–199.

Folkman, S. (1997). Positive psychological states and coping with severe stress. *Social Science and Medicine, 45*, 1207–1221.

General Dental Council. (2002). *The first five years – a framework for undergraduate dental education* (2nd ed.). London: General Dental Council.

Gibson, B., Boiko, O.V., Baker, S.R., Robinson, P.G., Barlow, A., Player, T., & Locker, D. (2010). The everyday impact of dentine sensitivity: personal and functional aspects. *Social Science and Dentistry, 1*, 11–20.

Gift, H.C., Atchison, K.A., & Dayton, C.M. (1997). Conceptualising oral health and oral health-related quality of life. *Social Science and Medicine, 44*, 601–608.

Kelly, M., Steele, J., Nuttall, N., Bradnock, G., Morris, J., Nunn, J., Pine, C., Pitts, N., Treasure, E., & White, D. (2000). *Adult dental health survey – oral health in the United Kingdom 1998.* London: The Stationery Office.

Kline, R.B. (2005). *Principles and practice of structural equation modelling* (2nd ed.). New York: Guildford Press.

Kurtz, S., Silverman, J., & Draper, J. (2005). *Teaching and learning communication skills in medicine.* Oxford: Radcliffe Publishing.

Marshman, Z, Baker, S.R., Bradbury, J., Hall, M.J., & Rodd, H.D. (2009). The impact of oral conditions during transition to secondary education. *European Journal of Paediatric Dentistry, 10*, 176–180.

Maass, A., & Clark, R.D. (1984). Hidden impact of minorities: fifteen years of minority influence research. *Psychological Bulletin, 95*, 428–450.

Moscovici, S., Lage, E., & Naffrechoux, M. (1969). Influence of a consistent minority on the responses of a majority in a color perception task. *Sociometry, 32*, 365–380.

Moscovici, S., & Nemeth, C. (1974). Social influence 11: minority influence. In C. Nemeth (Ed.), *Social psychology: classic and contemporary integrations* (pp. 217–249). Chicago: Rand-McNally.

National Academy of Sciences. (2005). *Facilitating interdisciplinary research.* Washington, DC: National Academies Press.

Pankhurst, C.L., Smith, E., Dunne, S.M., Rogers, J., Jackson, S., & Proctor, G. (1996). Diagnosis and management of dry mouth. *Dental Update, 23,* 56–62.

Porritt, J.M., Rodd, H.D., & Baker, S.R. (2010). Quality of life impacts following childhood dento-alveolar trauma. *Dental Traumatology, 27,* 2–9.

Robinson, P.G., Pankhurst, C.L., & Garrett, E.J. (2005). Randomised controlled trial: Effect of a reservoir biteguard on quality of life in xerostomia. *Journal of Oral Pathology Medicine, 34,* 193–197.

Schaefer, J.A., & Moos, R.H. (1992). Life crises and personal growth. In B.N. Carpenter (Ed.), *Personal coping: Theory, research and application.* New York: Prentice.

Shrout, P.E., & Bolger, N. (2002). Mediation in experimental and nonexperimental studies: New procedures and recommendations. *Psychological Methods, 7,* 422–445.

Silverman, J., Kurtz, S., & Draper, J. (2005). *Skills for communicating with patients* (2nd ed.). Oxford: Radcliffe Publishing.

Stocker, Y-O., Thompson, A., Baker, S.R., & Gibson, B. (2010). Experiences of living with orthognathic conditions: an exploratory qualitative interview study with individuals self identifying as being from an ethnic minority population. Paper presented at the Appearance Matters 4 conference, Bristol, UK, June.

Tanabe, G. (1982). The potential for public health psychology. *American Psychologist, 37,* 942–944.

Vinck, J., Oldenburg, B., & Von Lengerke, T. (2004). Editorial: Health psychology and public health – bridging the gap. *Journal of Health Psychology, 9,* 5–12.

Wanless, M.B., & Holloway, P.J. (1994). An analysis of audio-recordings of general dental practitioners' consultations with adolescent patients. *British Dental Journal, 177,* 94–98.

Wettergren, L., Bjorkholm, M., Axdorph, U., & Langius-Eklof, A. (2004). Determinants of health-related quality of life in long-term survivors of Hodgkin's Lymphoma. *Quality of Life Research, 13,* 1369–1379.

Wilson, I.B., & Cleary, P.D. (1995). Linking clinical variables with health-related quality of life. *Journal of the American Medical Association, 273,* 59–65.

World Health Organization. (1986). *The Ottawa Charter for Health Promotion.* Copenhagen: WHO.

Glossary

cleft lip and/or palate (CL/P): a congenital deformity caused by abnormal facial development during gestation.
dentistry: the branch of medicine that is involved in the evaluation, diagnosis, prevention and surgical or nonsurgical treatment of disease, disorders and conditions of the oral cavity, maxillofacial area and adjacent and associated structures and their impact on the human body (American Dental Association, 2011).

dental public health: the science and art of preventing and controlling dental diseases and promoting dental health through organized community efforts. It is that form of dental practice which serves the community as a patient rather than the individual. It is concerned with the dental health education of the public, with applied dental research and with the administration of group dental care programs as well as the prevention and control of dental diseases on a community basis (American Dental Association, 2011).

dental trauma: injury to the mouth, including the teeth, lips, gums, tongue and jawbones.

dentine sensitivity: the sensation felt when the nerves in the teeth are exposed to the environment.

oral and maxillofacial surgery: the diagnosis, surgical and adjunctive treatment of diseases, injuries and defects involving both the functional and aesthetic aspects of the hard and soft tissues of the oral and maxillofacial region (American Dental Association, 2011).

orthodontics: the branch of dentistry dealing with the prevention or correction of irregularities of the teeth.

orthognathic surgery: surgery to correct conditions of the jaw and face related to underlying skeletal discrepancies.

restorative dentistry: the study, diagnosis and management of diseases of the teeth and their supporting structures.

xerostomia: the medical term for the complaint of dry mouth due to a lack of saliva.

2

Promoting the Application of Health Psychology in Primary Health Care

Amy Baraniak

My health psychology career began perhaps even before embarking upon a psychology undergraduate degree. In 1998 the Meadowfields Practice opened in Derby. Meadowfields was the first nurse-led general practice in the United Kingdom and provided me with my first position in health care; as a receptionist and administrator. The purpose of this role was to fund my university fees; little was I to know that my planned career path into forensic psychology would take an about turn following an undergraduate health psychology module where the links between psychology and health became explicitly clear. I continued to provide administrative support to the practice throughout my university career (undergraduate and postgraduate) before taking on a full-time position when I started my Stage 2 training in Health Psychology at Staffordshire University. The innovative nature of Meadowfields enabled me to understand primary health care in a way that I perhaps wouldn't have been able to otherwise. The way in which the practice team strived to make the most appropriate use of the skills and expertise of each team member led very naturally to an interest in the way in which primary health care is structured, delivered and perceived by patients, health care professionals and the wider practice team working within it. My increasing knowledge and understanding of (health) psychology also enabled me to start questioning the way in which the psychological impact of ill health is addressed and managed within primary health care. Of most relevance here is the potential and realized value of health psychology within general practice, in terms of either a health psychologist within the health care team or the way in which the health care team can utilize health psychology theory, models and research to contribute to a holistic health care approach.

In order to be able to evaluate the potential and achieved contribution of health psychology to general practice, it is important to consider the role of general practice

Health Psychology in Action, First Edition. Edited by Mark Forshaw and David Sheffield.
© 2013 John Wiley & Sons, Ltd. Published 2013 by John Wiley & Sons, Ltd.

within the National Health Service (NHS). The following description is by no means exhaustive. General practice provides an interface between the patient and the health care service. Patients often perceive their practice as the gateway to additional services. Whilst some people may gain access to health care via services such as accident and emergency (A&E) and walk-in centres (WIC), in the case of acute and minor illness (such as tonsillitis, coughs and colds) people will generally seek help from their general practitioner (GP) in the first instance. It is well documented that there has been a shift in illness patterns; the greatest cause of death is no longer attributable to infectious disease but people are living longer with an increasing number of lifestyle-attributable chronic illnesses such as coronary heart disease, respiratory disorders and a range of cancers. General practice provides a hub for the provision of a range of screening programmes such as cervical and bowel cancer screening and, more recently, cardiovascular disease (CVD) risk screening. These programmes play a pivotal role in prevention and early detection of illness, providing an opportunity to treat the early onset of illness and improve longer term health outcomes. Another preventative intervention rolled out within general practice is the childhood immunization programme which aims to safeguard children from infectious diseases. Further to this public health role, primary care provides a base for the large number of patients living with long-term conditions to be treated and managed without intervention from secondary care services. Under the recent UK Labour Government the latter was conducted through the Quality and Outcomes Framework (QOF) which aimed to drive up quality of care and improve outcomes by addressing both clinical and organizational domains. It is yet to be seen how this will be driven forward in the future. As such a vast range of health behaviours occur in the context of this interaction between patient and general practice, many of which can be targeted by health psychologists to improve the delivery, uptake and effectiveness of services.

This brief description highlights a number of potentially 'problem' areas within a general practice setting that can be targeted with health psychology theory and intervention. Specifically we can look at the beliefs and perceptions of patients and health care professionals, consider why some people do and do not seek help when ill, address differences in access to health services across difficult ethnic populations and socioeconomic groups, increase uptake in screening and other preventative interventions, improve healthy lifestyle interventions for people at risk of illness (e.g. cardiovascular disease), improve uptake and adherence to treatment for acute (e.g. antibiotics) and longer-term illnesses (e.g. complex medication regimes and self-testing behaviours) as well as improve the quality of life and well-being for patients living with long-term illnesses.

In the period that I was employed by Meadowfields, it was not feasible to target so many areas; indeed, it would be improbable that an individual would be able to target each of these issues within a lifetime! It is important to note that my role was not specific to health psychology *per se* but focused on the QOF and ensuring maximum achievement in this contract. I also led on the implementation of additional (enhanced) services, including practice-based commissioning (PBC) which involved considering the development of new services that could be offered to tender in order to meet current government priorities such as improving access, bringing care closer to home, reducing hospital admissions and cost saving. A major challenge within this role was that not only did I need to meet the needs of the practice in terms of generating and maintaining their income, but also my health psychology training honed my focus on aspects of service delivery that could be developed and improved through the integration of health psychology to better meet the needs of the patients and professionals. One way in which this was achieved was through the utilization of lifestyle interventions predominantly, although I was also able to implement the delivery of practice-based computerized cognitive-behavioural therapy under the Improving Access to Psychological Therapies (IAPT) agenda. An alcohol screening questionnaire and intervention were commissioned as well as lifestyle interventions for people at risk of cardiovascular disease and a practice-based smoking cessation service. My work centred predominantly on the delivery of the smoking cessation intervention.

Brief Lifestyle Interventions in Primary Care

Proactive screening for risky behaviour and illness is intended to be a useful way of identifying people who can make changes to their lifestyle in order to reduce their future risk and treat illness as early as possible. If a screening tool is brief and simple to administer, then large-scale delivery of this can be implemented relatively easily. Additionally, brief interventions can be a cost-effective way of delivering a range of lifestyle interventions to a large population. With the time constraints that face clinicians within general practice, these are welcome methods of targeting health-impairing behaviours with minimal disruption to the intended content of consultation. Patients are usually seeking help for a particular problem, and the lifestyle issues are targeted secondary to this. A four-item alcohol screening tool was administered to all new patients aged 16 and over. The score on this questionnaire provided some indication of risky drinking behaviour and informed the health professional as to whether the patient would benefit from a brief or comprehensive written intervention. If scores indicated alcohol dependence or significant levels of abuse, the patient was offered referral to the local alcohol dependency service. The alcohol screening tool was integrated within the new patient questionnaire and clinical system to ensure data were collected and held accurately within the medical records. The intervention was delivered by a health care assistant or practice nurse during a new patient routine appointment. The screening tool and intervention were intended to be very easy and cost-effective to administer within this context. The use of the new patient medical to integrate this intervention was helpful as this is an appointment where patients can expect a discussion about a range of health issues. Whilst patients may raise more serious health complaints during these appointments, these problems are always referred on to another clinician, with the focus of the new patient medical being on broader health and lifestyle issues.

A second screening system and brief intervention was delivered to patients with high risk of CVD. Risk (high, medium or low) was assigned based upon existing data within the medical record. Patients in the highest risk categories were sent an invitation letter which informed them of their risk and offered an appointment with the practice nurse to discuss their risk and ways in which they could reduce this. This work was incentivized in that a target number of interventions had a payment attached. The benefits of this type of intervention include the early identification of patients at high risk of CVD which enables behaviour to be modified early to reduce risk and prevent illness in the longer term. This may go some way to addressing the increasing prevalence of CVD. Whilst raising awareness of the importance of addressing unhealthy lifestyles to patients who received the invitation letter, this type of intervention may also reinforce to professionals the need to take a multifaceted approach to health and illness, including the psychosocial determinants as well as the biomedical.

On reflection these types of intervention can be perceived to be easy to integrate into systems and processes, simple to administer and unproblematic to record. Written interventions can be rolled out on a large scale very quickly and with relatively low cost. Targeted interventions to high-risk groups will make headway in reducing high costs that may be associated with these patients if their risk is not reduced and they develop CVD. However, there are some dangers in relying on 'routine' data collection and 'easy' interventions. The patient can get lost in a string of data collection exercises and little attention can be paid to working with patients on the issues that are really crucial. This may be of particular importance in the context of a new patient appointment where such a large range of issues are covered that patients and professionals may misinterpret the salience of what is being discussed. In terms of identifying risk, there is a danger that patients perceive this as looking for illness where there is none and there has been anecdotal evidence of such complaints from patients. Achievement in the QOF relied not only on doing the work, but also on recording data in a particular way and at particular times of year within the medical record. In this context, incentivized routine intervention faces the possibility of perceptions from patients and professionals as being "just another measurement" rather than the importance of targeting risky behaviour being fully realized. Evidence for this emerges where screening tools are inaccurately or not completed, although this could also be accounted for by the confusion caused to patients and staff in the move from a traditional measure of alcohol use (units per week) to an alternative (such as number of drinks per drinking episode and number of episodes per week). This confusion highlights a lack of training in the use of the screening tools, which I perceived to be a barrier to the effective use of the alcohol screening tool and the delivery of interventions to address lifestyle issues. Furthermore, there is massive potential for interventions not being administered effectively (e.g. glossing over the importance of the written intervention, or not providing any context to the intervention). As the incentivization of interventions did not extend to follow up this was not done routinely, so ongoing support in lifestyle change was not provided as the norm.

The perceived ease with which these tools and interventions could be administered led to an attitude that *anybody* could deliver them. However, addressing sensitive issues such as alcohol abuse requires training in knowing how to deal with these issues and the potential multitude of accompanying issues. It is important also to consider the need for health professionals delivering interventions to be trained in behaviour change techniques and understand the theories underpinning behaviour change. Having this training will support them in being able to deliver interventions much more effectively. The lifestyle intervention for CVD risk was based on motivational interviewing techniques; interestingly practice nurses delivering this received only minimal training in these techniques. Similarly staff were not offered training in behaviour change or alcohol counselling. The investment in rolling out interventions of this nature will not pay off if there is no investment in suitable training for the professionals delivering them.

Whilst I was involved in the implementation of the alcohol and CVD risk interventions, my role predominantly focused on the provision of an in-house smoking cessation service. The Department of Health white paper *Smoking Kills* (1998) outlined targets to reduce smoking in under-16s from 13% to 9% or less, in adults (especially disadvantaged groups) from 28% to 24% or less and in pregnant women from 23% to 15% or less by 2010. NHS specialist Stop Smoking services were commissioned in 2001 and as a means of reaching these targets. Within Derby City and County there is an effective, comprehensive and widely utilized NHS smoking-cessation service. The Derby City service was expanded by enabling provision within primary care by practice teams in return for incentive payments depending on the number of successful quitters achieved within the financial year. There were numerous benefits identified in providing our own intervention as opposed to referring patients to the NHS service. As well as providing a source of income, the major benefits centred on access, such as extending the availability of the service and reducing waiting list times. In some cases I was able to offer immediate intervention which enabled patients to make progress with their quit attempt while they were highly motivated to engage in intervention. Where there was access to a prescribing clinician on site, access to prescription-only cessation aids was also improved as patients did not need to make subsequent appointments prior to making a quit attempt. Access to support was extended for clients as they were able to access the practice beyond the period of registration with the smoking service (8–12 weeks). I was able to be flexible in giving clients plenty of time to get ready to start a quit attempt where they wanted this. Furthermore, an in-house service enabled clinicians to address perceptions of smoking interventions as being group intervention which was a barrier to a number of potential quitters. Other benefits included the addition of a holistic approach to care. As smoking cessation appointments were recorded within the medical records, other team members could identify patients making a quit attempt and support them in this. Finally, as a trainee health psychologist I was able to utilize health psychology theory to target additional lifestyle changes that patients wanted to make. In many cases patients were concerned about gaining weight during their quit attempt and so wanted advice regarding this, but some patients also wanted concurrent weight loss and smoking cessation interventions. My expertise enabled me to do this without having to refer clients to additional services.

The work involved in establishing each of the outlined interventions was relatively straightforward. As mentioned previously, there was little question about the cost-effectiveness of them as they had been through commissioning processes. A combination of support from my employers and my expertise enabled the interventions to be rolled out relatively quickly and efficiently. However, there were a number of barriers to delivering these interventions as effectively as possible; a number of these have been outlined in this chapter. In addition to these, I felt that there continued to be a general lack of understanding amongst health professionals and the wider health care team as to what health psychology is and why there is a need for the integration of it within the work undertaken in primary care. With ever-increasing patient expectations and demand, behaviour change is often not considered a priority. Time limitations within individual appointments do not allow clinicians to broach lifestyle issues with patients unless it is something that relates explicitly to the problem they presented with in the first instance. The QOF requires a range of lifestyle data to be collected for all patients pertaining to smoking, weight, Body Mass Index (BMI) and offering smoking intervention but these are not necessarily asked by a clinician directly and if they are it might not be in a context where further discussion is possible. They can be collected on short questionnaires offered to all patients by reception staff. Furthermore, where an attempt is made, patients can disregard the line of questioning and advice as something that is 'required' (further exacerbated by the use of questionnaires and asking lifestyle questions out of any context!). The result of this can be patients who *are* eligible and motivated to change behaviour not being prompted, referred or supported in doing so. Incentivizing this kind of work seems to be helpful in starting to engage the health care team. It is frustrating that the work stops with the incentive and additional work that could further the effectiveness of behaviour change interventions is not followed up. This is further exacerbated where services may not even be considered for commissioning if they do not show a cost saving at the end of the financial year. The reduction in disease prevalence and hospital admissions and the increased contribution to society and the economy that will result from sustained positive behaviour change will not be realized by year end!

Health promotion and illness prevention are roles that have been held in primary health care traditionally. As the number of people living with chronic illnesses continues to increase with many people living with multiple conditions, it is essential that primary care can manage and intervene where needed and is appropriate for these patients. This will put increased strain on the health service but unless the multifaceted nature of health and illness is addressed in relation to both the onset and progression of illness, this problem will continue to exacerbate. It is evident that interventions need to be deliverable by the health care team. This work needs to be supported financially to enable staff to be trained appropriately to deliver behaviour change interventions as well as to support the time involved in delivering initial intervention and follow-up.

This leads to the question that if health care teams are delivering this work, where is the role for health psychologists? I do not foresee primary care providers employing a health psychologist or health psychology team to *deliver* interventions. I do foresee a number of opportunities for health psychologists to inform primary health care practices. Firstly, in terms of the interventions I have discussed here, is the potential role for health psychologists in training health care professionals in the effective delivery of behaviour change interventions. Having appropriately skilled staff who understand the intervention strategy they are using as well as alternative techniques to meet individual needs would be hugely useful. The one-size-fits-all method currently used is not conducive to effective behaviour change. The alcohol screening intervention, is perhaps, a prime example. I do not believe that a brief written intervention can be effective in addressing alcohol misuse in the UK population consisting of over 16 year olds! The determinants of alcohol use and misuse across the life span are so diverse that interventions will be more effective if they are targeted appropriately. Other issues that could be considered include the utilization of disease-specific smoking cessation interventions for patients suffering from chronic illnesses (are the needs of patients with chronic obstructive pulmonary disease (COPD) different to those of patients with coronary heart disease?). There is an additional role for health psychologists here in terms of evaluating the effectiveness of these interventions in terms of process and outcome evaluation and again training health care professionals to undertake their own useful evaluation of the interventions they are delivering to further inform their practice.

A range of patient and professional behaviours occur in the context of the patient–health service interaction which influence a range of outcomes. In addition to intervention design, delivery and evaluation in the context of lifestyle behaviour change, health psychologists need to demonstrate the value of health psychology practices and principles in the context of this interaction whilst pertaining to key primary care priorities (e.g. to reduce referrals to secondary care, reduce emergency and unplanned care, reduce prescribing costs and prescribing wastage and engage the public and patient interface and engagement of health care professionals in GP commissioning). This demonstration can be made only through the proactive work of health psychologists. The implementation of GP consortia may provide a gateway if health psychologists can promote the value of their work to meeting the needs of the consortia. This is a particularly valuable opportunity as consortia seek to address the health needs of their local population, rather than commissioning being undertaken at a higher level. The opportunity for developing local interventions and moving away from the one-size-fits-all approach is perhaps greater now than it has been previously. This initiative will also give rise to opportunities to work with health professionals to help them to make best use of the resources provided to them as well as provide expert input on effective service design and development in terms of the consideration of psychological aspects of health care. As services and patient pathways are redesigned, it would be sensible to apply psychological practices and principles to help make services as effective as they can be. It is in this work that the research, teaching and training, evaluation and consultancy skills of health psychologists could come in particular use.

Key Debates in Health Psychology

The Division of Health Psychology (DHP) surveyed its members in 2006 and reported concern at the lack of health psychology input within primary care particularly in light of targets that had been outlined in policy documents at that time. My own perception and understanding are that this situation has not altered in the intervening years. Working within primary care provided me with insight into some potential barriers that may exacerbate this situation.

We know that a wide range of behaviours play a part in the development and progression of illness (e.g. smoking, sedentary lifestyle and unhealthy diet) and that modifying these behaviours and helping people to adopt more healthy lifestyles can lead to an improvement in health. There is wide acknowledgement of the necessity of taking a multifaceted approach to health, including consideration of psychosocial determinants of health and illness. What I find particularly interesting in relation to this is that there seems very little effort to seek out the advice of experts in this area to consider ways of addressing these determinants of health. A key priority within the NHS is the reduction of health inequalities, something which health psychology can help to address by seeking to understand individual differences and group differences in their health needs and preferences and their utilization of health services. In addition, whilst there are national guidelines within the United Kingdom (National Institute for Clinical Excellence, or NICE) pertaining to behaviour change interventions, it is not always clear where these are being implemented in practice. In addition to factors contributing to health and illness, the government also recognizes the role of health and well-being in a general sense in increasing measure within policy. This is another area in which health psychologists would consider themselves experts. Whilst there may be psychologists informing government and policy makers at a national level, they are not being readily utilized to inform changes and implementation of policy at a local level. There is the opportunity to address this with the implementation of commissioning consortia.

An important feature of this debate is funding. I think funding in the context of health care is a particularly contentious issue as the idea that services are compromised because of inadequate funding does not sit well with most. However, money enables us to provide the health service we do and is vital in making decisions about what services will be and won't be delivered. We cannot deliver them all and indeed if there is no funding, the service ceases.

A huge barrier for health psychology is that whilst we may see a resulting short-term improvement in health after making healthy behaviour changes, the impact on morbidity, mortality and any cost savings will take many years to be realized. As such, investments in interventions to reduce longer-term risk are not financed readily when cost-saving targets need to be achieved by the close of the financial year.

A continued lack of understanding of what health psychology is and what it can offer within primary care adds to the dearth of health psychology input into this service. In light of this lack of understanding I firmly believe that it is the duty of health psychologists to take health psychology to primary care. Until health psychology is proactive in this way, the utility of health psychology and many potential improvements to patient care and professional practice will not be realized and the current position in which health psychology does not have maximum input might remain.

Reference

Department of Health, (1998). *Smoking kills: a white paper on tobacco use.* London: The Stationary Office.

Glossary

biomedical: the biological factors that play a role in the onset, progression and treatment of illness. Traditionally these were considered in isolation of other factors, such as psychosocial determinants.

Body Mass Index: a height–weight ratio giving a measure of whether someone is over, under or normal weight.

cardiovascular disease (CVD): an umbrella terms for a number of disease affecting the heart and/or circulatory system, for example coronary heart disease (CHD).

chronic illness: an enduring illness that can be treated and managed, but usually is not cured.

chronic obstructive pulmonary disease (COPD): an example of a chronic illness affecting the respiratory system. This illness is usually caused by exposure to tobacco smoke, although there are other causes.

computerized cognitive-behavioural therapy: a method of delivering the psychological intervention cognitive-behavioural therapy (CBT) for problems such as anxiety and depression.

coronary heart disease (CHD): an example of a chronic illness affecting the circulatory system and heart. There are other terms used interchangeably to describe the same or similar diseases.

diabetes: an example of a chronic illness where a person has unusually high levels of sugar in the blood due to the body failing to produce enough or any insulin, or having reduced sensitivity to insulin.

disease prevalence: a measure of the proportion of people with a particular disease or condition. This is usually measured as a percentage.

emergency and unplanned care: care provided unexpectedly (e.g. use of accident and emergency, emergency procedures and exacerbations of illnesses requiring emergency admission to hospital).

enhanced services: a range of services or policies that have been commissioned for delivery by general practices in addition to their core business. Some enhanced services are offered nationally, and some are specific to a locality. Examples include smoking cessation services and childhood immunization programmes.

general practice: the point at which a large number of people are registered with the health service. General practice provides one form of first contact for patients and is usually the gateway for them to additional services.

GP Commissioning: a new scheme introduced to further the work of practice-based commissioning in which the responsibility for commissioning of health services lies predominantly with GPs but also with wider teams of professionals within general practice.

GP consortia: a group of local general practice professionals responsible for the implementation of GP commissioning in their locality.

health behaviour: any behaviour that has a positive or negative impact on the health of the individual (e.g. smoking, eating healthily and seeking medical help).

health care professional: a person working within and providing health care services (e.g. doctor, nurse, midwife and health visitor).

Improving Access to Psychological Therapies (IAPT): an initiative aimed at improving the extent to which people could access therapies such as cognitive-behavioural therapy. This initiative included the training of therapists and the integration of services to ensure they were accessible to patients.

intervention: any process or act done to bring about a change in a targeted outcome, for example providing nicotine patches to reduce the withdrawal effects of stopping smoking.

long-term condition: an enduring illness that can be treated and managed, but usually is not cured. *See* chronic illness.

National Institute for Clinical Excellence (NICE): an organization which produces a range of guidance and policy documents pertaining to the management of illness and promotion of health.

practice-based commissioning (PBC): delivered as an enhanced service, practice-based commissioning was an initiative to encourage general practice to consider the health needs to their local population and current services with a view to proposing more relevant services that would meet the local needs.

prescribing costs: the cost associated with the use of prescription medications.

prescribing wastage: the amount of prescription medication collected and wasted due to incorrect use or non-usage.

primary health care: any health care service acting as a first contact point for people seeking help. Examples include general practice, walk-in centres and pharmacies.

psychosocial determinants: the range of psychological and social factors (and interplay between these) that play a role in the onset, progression and treatment of illness. Traditionally these are not considered within health care.

Quality and Outcomes Framework (QOF): the contract introduced to general practice under the UK Labour government for managing performance-based payment to general practice.

screening programmes: a programme involving people identified to be at risk of a particular illness being offered a test to identify whether they have early signs of developing or having the illness (e.g. cervical cancer screening and breast cancer screening).

secondary care: a health service that a patient does not usually have direct access to. Secondary care services are usually accessed through a referral process.

smoking cessation: the process of quitting smoking and maintaining this behaviour change.

Stage 2 training: the second (and final) stage of approved training for students who wish to achieve chartered and registered status as a health psychologist.

3

Health Psychology in the NHS: The Long and Winding Road . . .

Julian Bath

As a health psychologist working in the NHS in Gloucestershire for the past 12 years, the phrase 'never a dull moment' is one that springs to mind when reflecting on the past decade (and more) of my working life. Whether encountering what seemed the steepest of learning curves as a trainee health psychologist in the 1990s, or more latterly managing clinical staff across a variety of different services within Gloucestershire NHS Hospitals Foundation Trust, I have constantly been challenged, enthused and inspired by the unique environment that is the provision of health psychology services in the NHS. In this chapter I hope to relate some of these challenges and also describe some of the situations that have inspired me in the past and continue to do so in the present, amidst what are the increasingly shifting sands of the modern-day NHS. I hope primarily that this chapter will be useful to aspiring health psychologists who may want a taste of what it is like to work in the NHS as they embark on the 'long and winding road' that often constitutes a career in psychology.

The NHS is currently facing some of the biggest changes it has had to encounter in its relatively short history. With funding being effectively frozen over the next 3 years, NHS Trusts have to come to terms with the reality of providing the same quality of service on what is in real terms a reduced budget. Health psychology in the NHS is no different, and at the time of writing the Health Psychology Department (HPD) in Gloucestershire faces the same apparently bleak future as many other services up and down the country. Posts are disappearing as staff move on or come to the end of their contracts and are not replaced and with budget savings of up to 20% being asked for over the next 3 years, on top of a freeze on annual percentage rate pay increases, the future looks increasingly unsettled. This squeeze on resources has made developing services as a psychology manager difficult,

Health Psychology in Action, First Edition. Edited by Mark Forshaw and David Sheffield.
© 2013 John Wiley & Sons, Ltd. Published 2013 by John Wiley & Sons, Ltd.

and opportunities for assistant psychologists and trainee health psychologists have become rarer. Currently we have one full-time psychology assistant post in the HPD and two trainee health psychologist posts. These posts are fixed-term contracts with uncertainty as to whether they will be available when the current contracts come to an end. It is sad that training posts are disappearing and it feels important to me that in Gloucestershire and elsewhere, we fight to continue the tradition we have of providing training opportunities for health psychology trainees to complete the BPS Stage 2 qualification. This is particularly the case as I was the original Stage 2 trainee back in the 1990s helping to pilot the Stage 2 training route. Over the past decade we have seen a number of trainees come through the HPD and become qualified either through the grandparenting scheme or, more latterly, solely through the award of the Stage 2 qualification. Four of these trainees (including myself) currently work in the department as qualified members of staff. But what do health psychologists do in a large acute hospitals trust? I can probably best answer this question by describing the diverse services that I have worked within and some of the problems and successes that I have encountered along the way.

When I first came to the HPD at Gloucestershire Royal Hospital (GRH), it was as an MSc Health Psychology student from Bath University on placement for 5 months. Louise Earll, the Head of Department at the time, had come to Bath University to give a lecture to the MSc students about cardiac rehabilitation (CR) and the CR service in Gloucestershire. Louise provided a fascinating and colourful (the odd swear word!) account and I thought this would be the ideal place for me to go on placement, particularly as I was interested in alcohol issues and the links with coronary heart disease. I approached Louise after the talk and some months later ended up in Gloucester on placement. Several months later I was employed by Gloucestershire Hospitals Trust as a trainee health psychologist. This is of interest for two reasons. Firstly, it illustrates the importance of experience when applying for any position in psychology. My experience of being on a 5-month unpaid placement at HPD (along with a year-long NHS placement as part of my BSc at Bath University) was one of the crucial factors in securing the trainee position. In recent years this type of placement experience has become more important in helping individuals to get jobs in psychology in the NHS and will continue to be so as time progresses and potentially we lose more of the traditional assistant and training positions. Secondly, at the time there were not to my knowledge any other trainee HP posts around the country. Louise had advertised several times attempting to recruit a clinical psychologist to the available post in Renal Medicine and Rheumatology without success (things were very different in the mid-1990s with clinical psychologists outnumbering available posts!). Thinking latterly, along with other members of the DHP Committee who were developing the infant Stage 2 training route, Louise agreed to host a fixed-term (2-year) health psychology trainee post. Supervised by an experienced clinical psychologist, this post would enable the trainee to gain the competence to practice as a qualified health psychologist in the NHS, and would also solve Louise's inability to fill the clinical position. Training routes for the Stage 2 qualification were thus formed and when I eventually completed my 2 years in post I would discover that the focus on gaining knowledge and skills across teaching and training, research, consultancy and professional and ethical issues would justifiably shape my practice in health psychology to the current day.

My experience of being a trainee at HPD was what you might describe as a 'mixed bag'. I experienced an interesting learning curve in Renal Care, where with additional cognitive-behavioural therapy (CBT) training at Oxford Cognitive Therapy Centre, I was providing one-to-one support for patients with chronic renal failure and their families. Although closely supervised by an experienced clinical psychologist, this was possibly the most challenging of any work that I have done in my career to date. Renal medicine is a complex area, and one of the immediate issues for any trainee working in health (whether a health or a clinical psychology trainee) is to gain a good working understanding of the relevant medical condition as well as the psychological issues that a patient may present with. As an experienced clinician it is more straightforward as you have the years of patient experience to draw on that will enable you to manage most situations, whereas as a trainee, simply put, you do not. Developing relationships within a dynamic team across different sites (e.g. the dialysis unit and ward) was also a challenge as the culture of, for instance, the dialysis unit was very different from that of the renal ward, with a different day-to-day dynamic and different key staff to try to develop positive relationships with. Probably the most important issue learnt from this time was the dominance of the Medical Model within this kind of consultant-led team. Psychology was very much valued in its place, but more often than not it was seen by the consultants as an adjunct and a way of potentially 'fixing' a patient's anxiety or depression rather than helping them to adjust to a chronic condition. Health psychology was seen almost as a separate entity that could be called into the multidisciplinary team when necessary and could also be left to one side if it was deemed not. I learnt quite quickly that health psychology and health psychologists have little power in the NHS when faced with the might of medicine and its dominant model. On the other hand, I also learnt that you could be seen as invaluable to the team if through your work with a patient you could enable them to be discharged earlier or enable a patient to undergo a procedure that previously they had refused. Sitting in with an anxious renal patient who was having a fistula formed by a surgeon (she wouldn't have this crucial procedure done without me there) was a valued example of this.

The other area in which I worked as a trainee was a completely different type of experience. Over a number of years it had become apparent to the Senior Consultant Rheumatologist at GRH that some individuals were able to cope well with severe rheumatic disease whereas others struggled to cope with much milder disease. This led to consideration amongst the rheumatology team of the psychological and social factors involved in coping with rheumatic disease and in particular rheumatoid arthritis. As a result the rheumatologist approached Louise at the HPD to see if there was a potential solution. His aim was to answer the question of why some patients were able to cope better than others, regardless of the severity of their condition, and to put in place an intervention (to help patients cope better) that could be maintained by the nursing staff in the rheumatology team. This was my brief in rheumatology. The consultant understandably was thinking along the lines of having his own psychologist who would see patients one-to-one, as this was a model that he had seen in action in some of the other services within the acute Trust. However, as the funding was for only 2 years and may not have been recurrent (and being health psychologists!), we envisaged a different solution. We proposed a needs analysis of the service through interviewing patients and staff and then developing a questionnaire for staff and patients to complete. With the data from the needs analysis, we would train the senior nurses in psychological care skills (and the key areas that emerged from the needs analysis) and have these nurses 'cascade' this training down to the junior staff, with supervision, and keep this model rolling once the 2-year funding had ceased (see Nichols, 1995, for a good book on how to execute this type of approach). With a few tweaks along the way this latter model was the one that we followed, and over 2 years we implemented the needs analysis and trained the staff. At the end of the 2 years the consultant rheumatologist decided that although the rolling programme of training would work, he would also like to keep the psychology input which he saw as invaluable. A year from the end of the 2-year funding the rheumatology service was able to fund a part-time psychologist to deliver a small amount of one-to-one input, supervision of the senior nurses and input to group programmes. The service has continued to grow to the present time. This area of my training was varied and ticked a number of boxes of the key Stage 2 training competences of research, consultancy, teaching and training and professional and ethical issues.

Since becoming a qualified health psychologist, my main area of clinical work has been within cardiac rehabilitation. I have also managed the psychologists, both clinical and health, who have worked in the CR service over the past 5 years. Before I discuss this hugely rewarding work, I will briefly mention the other main responsibility that I have in the HPD which is as Clinical Governance (CG) lead for the department. My responsibilities here are primarily as the link between the HPD and our employer the Gloucestershire Hospitals NHS Foundation Trust for CG concerns and to channel national CG issues down to the HPD. Broadly speaking, Clinical Governance for the HPD involves having procedures in place to manage (and the documentation of) any pertinent issues that may impact on the provision of quality clinical care. In reality as a department we focus on a number of key areas such as health and safety, risk management, audit, research, health outcomes and staff issues. Quarterly hourly meetings are held which the whole of HPD attend, and prior to these meetings I meet with the Trust CG lead to discuss any issues that the Trust may have regarding CG that may need to be cascaded to the department. An example of a pertinent CG issue is the suicide risk assessment guidelines that we have produced and refined in the HPD over the past 10 years. These are a set of locally produced guidelines, originally based on national evidence, that are to be followed by clinical staff working with patients who present with a risk of suicide. These guidelines have been adjusted over the years to take into account changes in practice nationally as well as locally and are currently being adapted by the Trust for use in other clinical areas. I have been the department CG lead for the past 10 years, and although it has been a challenging role trying to engage an often underwhelmed department (plenty of tumbleweed moments in the HPD meetings!), it is an area of key importance and one where health psychologists, with our strong research and development background, can have a major role to play.

The Gloucestershire Cardiac Rehabilitation (CR) Service has been in existence since 1992 and I have worked in the CR Service since 2000, managing the psychologists in the Service since 2005 (there are currently two trainee health psychologists, two qualified health psychologists and a clinical psychologist). With a combination of group work, assessment, individual patient work, research and teaching and training opportunities it is in many respects the ideal service for a health psychologist to be working within in the NHS. The CR Service in Gloucestershire is offered to patients who have experienced a 'cardiac event' such as a heart attack or myocardial infarction (MI), acute coronary syndrome (ACS), a coronary artery bypass graft (CABG), an angioplasty and stents (PCI), newly diagnosed angina patients and patients with heart valve disease. The purpose of the service (which mirrors the National Service Framework for CHD aims for cardiac rehabilitation; Department of Health (DoH), 2000) is 'to help patients to return to as full and normal a life as possible, to regain their confidence, and to enable them to make any lifestyle changes that they wish to. This should enable them to enjoy the best physical, mental, and emotional health, and the best quality of life possible'. Clearly this mission statement is ripe for health psychology involvement with its emphasis on behaviour change, increasing confidence (or self-efficacy) and improving quality of life.

In considering my work as a health psychologist in CR it seems appropriate to look at the key areas of the CR service in turn, which loosely break down into the following five aspects: assessment, group work, one-to-one work, research and teaching and training.

Assessment

Although assessments of patients who have had a cardiac event can be and are carried out by any member of the CR MDT, including the health psychologists, it is the psychological factors that underpin this assessment. The assessment is a golden opportunity to widen patients' beliefs about what has caused their cardiac event and to begin to link the patients' understanding of their event to the concept of coronary heart disease as a chronic condition. All patients in Gloucestershire who are eligible for CR are offered a 45-minute assessment with a member of the CR team. In Gloucestershire, an assessment may start with questions relating to an individual's understanding of what caused their condition and then move through a description of CHD, its symptoms and its management followed by a detailed assessment of the individual's CHD risk factors. Initial misconceptions can then be carefully challenged.

As psychologists in CR, we have been instrumental in training other MDT members to become aware of patients' illness perceptions and the value to be gained in broadening their illness perceptions at assessment. The work of Petrie *et al.* (1996, 2002) has shown that patients' illness perceptions can positively influence their recovery in relation to both behaviours, such as returning to work, and also their physical recovery following a heart attack. Their intervention study at assessment with CR patients (and using the self-regulatory model as a framework; Petrie *et al.*, 2002) showed that patients' illness perceptions can change over time and that these changes can positively affect their physical recovery, as measured by a reduction in angina symptoms, following MI. The assessment that we use in Gloucestershire has this study very much at its heart, with the broad aim of widening patients' beliefs about their coronary heart disease as a major goal of the assessment.

Group Work

The CR Service in Gloucestershire offers up to ten 6-week group programmes to people with CHD following their cardiac event and these groups are in many ways the 'meat and drink' of cardiac rehabilitation. Patients attend one 2-hour session per week and then a follow-up session (at between 8 and 16 weeks after the end of the programme). A multidisciplinary team consisting of a cardiac nurse specialist, an exercise professional and a health psychologist (either qualified or trainee) currently deliver the programme. The content of the group programme focuses on changing lifestyles, including exercise, diet and stress management. The programme uses a cognitive-behavioural framework, emphasizing the links between thoughts, emotions, physical responses and behaviours. This is particularly to the fore in week 1 when the psychologist discusses the impact of a cardiac event using a cognitive-behavioural model, and in week 6 when discussing how anxiety and depression can get in the way of cardiac patients returning to their usual activities. The programme is also underpinned by a number of health psychology models, including the SRM, Lazarus' transactional model of stress (stress is discussed in detail in week 2 of the programme), the transtheoretical model and the theory of planned behaviour. A goal-setting and pacing approach that is presented in week 1 of the programme was initially developed for the management of individuals with chronic pain. Clearly the CR group programme is rich in health psychology theory and has provided excellent training opportunities for health psychology trainees when delivering the programme.

One-to-One Work

The National Service Framework for Coronary Heart Disease (DoH, 2000) stated that a small percentage of cardiac patients may benefit from 'more formal psychological interventions such as cognitive behavioural therapy'. In 2003 we created the Individual CR Psychology Service providing one-to-one sessions for CR patients, either as an alternative or as an adjunct to the CR group programme. The main aim of the service is to offer time-limited (usually 6–8 sessions), evidence-based psychological interventions with a qualified clinical or health psychologist, with the aim of promoting physical and emotional recovery. This is done by:

- Reducing distress and increasing understanding of CHD by correcting cardiac misconceptions or illness perceptions that could result in anxiety, depression, or poor post-cardiac event adjustment
- Providing the time and privacy to explore issues in greater depth, using a variety of psychological techniques, including cognitive-behavioural approaches, with the aim of increasing motivation and adherence to treatment
- Offering evidence-based psychological interventions for depression, anxiety and panic disorders
- Increasing patients' confidence in their ability to manage their CHD by reinforcing the positive self-management messages of the CR group programme

The one-to-one psychology service in CR has been successful in achieving its stated outcomes. Through health outcomes questionnaires we have shown a reduction in distress and improved quality of life and increased confidence for patients attending the service (85% of patients coming through the one-to-one service have an anxiety-related issue).

Research

The national research evidence suggests that psychological factors pre and post cardiac event are important in predicting health outcomes for cardiac patients. The impact of cardiac rehabilitation on these psychological factors and how this affects recovery after a cardiac event (such as an MI or CABG) are less clear. As stated earlier, the NSF chapter for cardiac rehabilitation links psychological support after a cardiac event to regaining self-confidence (DoH, 2000). This is certainly an important aim of cardiac rehabilitation, yet the process of psychological change after a cardiac event, such as how and why patients regain confidence, is less clear. The impact of a cardiac event on an individual is both physical and psychological in nature and because of this the cognitive, emotional, behavioural and physical changes that occur after a cardiac event, during CR and after CR, interact in a complex way. The self-regulatory model is key to much of the work that we do as health psychologists in CR (as mentioned in this chapter with regard to patient assessment). Research that we carried out, using data from the Gloucestershire group programme, with Susan Michie from University College London, studied the mechanisms of psychological change that occur following CR and how these changes might impact on recovery. Sixty-two patients were followed up 8 weeks after the end of their comprehensive CR programme and 29 of these patients were followed up again at 8 months post cardiac rehabilitation. Patients completed the Illness Perception Questionnaire before attending the CR programme and then again before attending both of the follow-ups. They also completed the Hospital Anxiety and Depression Scale (Zigmond & Snaith, 1983) and the SF-12 (Ware *et al.*, 1996), a 12-item, quality-of-life scale measuring physical and mental functioning, at all three of these time points. At 8 weeks and at 8 months post cardiac rehabilitation, patients showed increased perceived control over their condition, decreased anxiety and depression and more confidence in changing their eating habits (Michie *et al.*, 2005). The increase in perceived control predicted anxiety and depression at 8-week follow-up. The decrease in depression predicted lower anxiety at 8 weeks and lower anxiety, lower depression and better mental health at 8 months. Lowered anxiety predicted lower depression at 8 weeks but also lowered anxiety, lowered depression and a trend towards better physical health at 8 months (Michie *et al.*, 2005). The conclusion from this research is that the increased sense of perceived control over their condition that patients report following cardiac rehabilitation may impact on levels of distress (anxiety and depression) which may in turn have long-term benefits for both physical and mental health. The relatively small sample size and the absence of a control group meant that the findings cannot be attributed directly to the CR programme. However, the authors state that the changes taking place appear to be 'due to changes in illness perceptions, in particular perceptions of control and emotional changes rather than any alternative mechanism'. As a health psychologist working in CR this was an excellent example of how theory and practice can combine. A key outcome of this kind of local theory and practice research is that through feedback we psychologists can heighten the awareness of other health professionals in an MDT about key psychological concepts in a way that has understandable and tangible benefit. For example, cardiac nurse specialists in Gloucestershire have been particularly interested in the fact that patients' increased control over their condition may be linked to talks that they as nurses give to patients on the group programme. Topics such as 'Why it is important to take cardiac medication for life', for instance, may be vital to the process of increasing patients' perceived control over their condition. This helps to embed psychology into the CR programme.

Another area in which health psychologists have an important role to play in CR in Gloucestershire is the collection and analysis of the health outcome data. Questionnaire data from the CR group programme have been collected routinely at three time points (before CR, following CR and 6 months after completion of CR) since the inception of the programme in Gloucestershire in 1992 (one-to-one service outcome data have been collected since 2003). These data have shown year on year an improvement in overall quality of life and reduction in depression and anxiety, amongst other health outcomes. Gloucestershire now contributes to the national National Audit of Cardiac Rehabilitation (NACR) database for CR and we will shortly be able to compare outcome data with those of other CR centres around the country. The collection and analysis of outcome data have been areas that have been managed almost exclusively by the health psychology trainees in the HPD. It has presented a useful opportunity to manage a large database and utilize a number of analytical skills that are common to health psychologists.

Teaching and Training

Working in an established and well-known CR service has given myself and the other qualified staff and trainees excellent opportunities to teach at universities across the United Kingdom and to present research findings at local, national and international conferences. We have also published in peer-reviewed journals, as well as guest lecturing at a variety of health profession teaching events across the United Kingdom. More importantly we have provided numerous teaching sessions to other health care staff within the Hospitals Trust both within the MDT and with other cardiology staff. Spreading the word about CR and how it is underpinned by health psychology remains a crucial aspect of our HP roles!

In many respects cardiac rehabilitation has been the perfect service for a health psychologist such as me to work in for the past decade, as shown by the five key areas of input to the service described above. Many CR programmes around the United Kingdom are less overtly psychological than the Gloucestershire programme but all will have the core aim of helping (the majority of) patients back to normal functioning and this will necessarily have a psychological as well as a physical aspect. As health psychologists we are perfectly placed to influence the one through the other.

Whilst writing this chapter and reflecting on my work as a trainee and then a qualified psychologist, it strikes me that health psychologists need to be something of a 'jack of all trades' to be successful in the NHS. Some clinical psychologists who I have met and worked with along the way have shown an almost exclusive desire to work with patients individually, forgoing opportunities for group work and showing little interest in research. This can be totally appropriate depending on their individual situation, yet as health psychologists it seems that the diversity of our training pushes us towards involvement in research, group work, teaching and more. I see this as a positive thing although it can (and will!) lead to conversations around the high expectations that we set of ourselves to be that 'really great teacher', as well as 'that really great deliverer of group programmes' and so on. I hope that this chapter has captured something of the flavour of the work of a health psychologist in the NHS for both trainees and qualified psychologists. I have not spent a great deal of time describing my role as a manager of a psychology service in the NHS as I believe this requires a different platform. Suffice to say that this too has its challenges and often ones that we are not necessarily trained to deal with as health psychologists. Even so, these challenges are part of that 'long and winding road' that leads us to the door of the next funding opportunity or hopefully the next service development.

Key Debates in Health Psychology

One of the key issues that cuts across a number of areas of work for a health psychologist in the NHS is confidentiality. For me, as Clinical Governance Lead for the department, it has extra resonance as it is important that all of the psychologists who work in the HPD are aware of the pertinent issues regarding confidentiality, both locally and nationally. Working individually with patients brings up specific issues regarding confidentiality. Foe example it might be necessary for confidentiality to be breached in some cases (e.g. if a patient reveals an intent to harm) and it is important that patients are made aware of confidentiality issues at their first session with a psychologist. More problematic, though, tends to be issues surrounding confidentiality when working with the multidisciplinary team. Other health professionals will often have a looser interpretation of how confidentiality issues are operationalized. On many occasions I have been on a hospital ward to find a patient's notes lying open on a desk, where a doctor or nurse (or other health professional) has been reading them, only to become distracted and leave the notes unattended. Patients are often wandering around the ward and would have no problem in accessing information from these notes. The culture on the ward regarding confidentiality is thus different to that of HPD where the psychologists are very aware of the issues and would not find it acceptable to leave patients' notes open and unattended. Similarly, when working in cardiac rehabilitation I have found that nurses are often comfortable discussing clinical issues concerning individual patients when other patients have been present in a room. This appears to be a cultural issue whereby the cardiac nurses have years of experience of discussing patients on wards where other patients are close by or in hearing range. One positive change we have made in CR, driven by the psychologists, is to leave a room to discuss patients' clinical details as they should, of course, remain confidential.

References

Department of Health. (2000). *National Service Framework for coronary heart disease.* London: Department of Health Publications.

Michie, S., O'Connor, D., Bath, J., Giles, M., & Earll, L. (2005). Cardiac rehabilitation: the psychological changes that predict health outcome and healthy behaviour, *Psychology Health and Medicine, 10,* 88–95.

Nichols, K.A. (1995). *Psychological care in physical illness,* 2nd ed. Cheltenham: Nelson Thornes.

Petrie, K., Weinman, J., Sharpe, N., & Buckley, J. (1996). Role of patients' view of their illness in predicting return to work and functioning after myocardial infarction: longitudinal study. *British Medical Journal, 312,* 1191–1194.

Petrie, K., Cameron, L., Ellis, C., Buick, D., & Weinman, J. (2002). Changing illness perceptions after myocardial infarction: an early intervention randomized controlled trial. *Psychosomatic Medicine, 64,* 580–586

Ware, J.E., Kosinski, M., & Keller, S.D. (1996). SF12: an even shorter health survey. *Medical Outcomes Trust Bulletin, 4,* 2.

Zigmond, A.S., & Snaith, R.P. (1983) The Hospital Anxiety and Depression Scale. *Acta Psychiatrica Scandinavica, 67,* 361–370.

Further Reading

Bath, J., Bohin, G., Jones, C., & Scarle, E. (2009). *Cardiac rehabilitation: a workbook for use with group programmes.* Oxford: Wiley-Blackwell.

Glossary

acute coronary syndrome (ACS): a diagnostic term that covers the spectrum of clinical conditions ranging from unstable angina to (non-Q-wave) myocardial infarction.

angina: the symptom (chest pain, breathlessness or discomfort) that occurs when an area of the heart muscle does not get enough oxygen-rich blood.

angioplasty: coronary angioplasty is a procedure used to open blocked or narrowed coronary arteries using an inflated balloon-tipped catheter.

cardiac rehabilitation (CR): a programme of exercise, information and behaviour change sessions that helps individuals get back to everyday life as quickly as possible.

clinical governance (CG): the system for improving the standard of clinical practice.

coronary artery bypass graft (CABG): a type of surgery that improves blood flow to the heart by 'bypassing' a blocked coronary artery using a vein or artery from another part of the body.

coronary heart disease (CHD): the process by which cholesterol (or fatty plaque) is laid down in the coronary arteries that supply the heart muscle with its own blood supply.

fistula: an established connection (through a surgical procedure) between a vein and an artery to enable haemodialysis.

kidney dialysis: is the process by which an individual's blood is removed of toxins and fluid over a period of several hours.

myocardial infarction (MI): the medical term for 'heart attack', when a fatty deposit in a coronary artery ruptures, blocking the artery through a blood clot and causing damage to the heart muscle.

renal medicine: also known as 'nephrology', this involves the care of patients with all forms of renal (or kidney) disease.

rheumatology: a form of medicine devoted to the diagnosis and therapy of conditions and diseases affecting the joints, muscles, and bones.

stent: a tiny wire mesh tube that is inserted into a narrowed artery (usually following *angioplasty*) and is left there permanently, allowing a better blood supply.

4

A Journey into Health Psychology and Beyond

Sheila Bonas

Foundations

Like some of my colleagues who have written other chapters in this book, my journey into health psychology has been something of a serendipitous one. When I was doing my degree and later my PhD at the University of Warwick in the 1990s, the BPS Division of Health Psychology was still in the process of being formed, so initially there was no professional body to identify with. My first realization that what I was becoming was called a 'Health Psychologist' was when I went to the European Health Psychology Conference in Dublin in 1996 after having an abstract for a poster with two fellow postgraduate students accepted. The following year, the British Psychological Society (BPS) membership voted to redesignate the Special Group in Health Psychology as the Division of Health Psychology, and I joined as a student member. I am happy to have found this anchor for my professional development. I hope that DHP membership continues to grow in the wake of statutory regulation, as I think we need a professional body that is apart from the HPC, and can provide a forum for discussion of the development of the discipline.

My first degree was in psychology and philosophy, and I found the two topics highly suited to study together in a joint honours programme. Introductions to topics such as the philosophy of science, epistemology, logic and philosophy of mind have turned out to be of enormous benefit to my development as a researcher, and as a health psychologist. As an undergraduate, I sometimes found the philosophy very difficult to grasp (and often still do!), but it has provided a valuable foundation for building up my own approach to research and practice. I strongly recommend an investment in 'going back to basics' in looking at the theories of what knowledge

Health Psychology in Action, First Edition. Edited by Mark Forshaw and David Sheffield.

is, and how can we know anything; what is consciousness, and how are mind and body related? My own grounding in philosophy has been integral in how I engage with the biopsychosocial model that is at the core of health psychology.

Developing as a Researcher

My first postdoctoral post was as a research fellow on a project with a team of medics and medical sociologists who used qualitative as well as quantitative methods. This was something of a culture shock for me, as my otherwise excellent training in research methods had ignored any mention of qualitative approaches. This was a great pity, as with hindsight, my own PhD thesis would have benefited from some qualitative work in order to embrace the complexity of my research questions before trying to reduce them to a relatively small set of variables. I recall that after a visiting speaker seminar by an eminent qualitative researcher, one of our professors said that people who want to do 'that sort of thing (qualitative research) should just go off and write a novel'. Thankfully, such attitudes are becoming extinct as it is accepted that some research questions are better tackled by qualitative approaches. However, I feel that I was blinkered in the early stage of my research career by the culture of the psychology department that assumed that the only respectable way to conduct research is to do so from a positivist position, and to measure things quantitatively and seek the holy grail of statistical significance. It did not occur to me that reducing the often complex and fuzzy constructs that we use in health psychology like 'social support' or 'stress' to a number on a scale, and treating that score as interval data, was questionable until I came to work with colleagues who had different epistemological positions. I was then able to reflect on the use of a positivist approach to study socially constructed variables, and to question whether qualitative approaches might sometimes offer a method that was more consistent with my own epistemological position. My new colleagues helped me to realize that if one wanted to understand what something means to a person, or how they experience something such as illness, such meanings and 'sense making' of phenomena cannot be reduced to numbers. I would like to thank the sociologists and psychologists who had expertise in qualitative methods that I have worked with over subsequent years for their time and patience in supplementing my education in this area. As a broad discipline psychologists still seem to lag behind colleagues in other social and behavioural sciences in accepting that the diverse range of qualitative methods gives us additional tools in the toolbox for conducting research. However, amongst the family of psychologists, health psychologists have been among those most willing to take up qualitative methods and use them when they are the best fit for their research questions.

In my own research, experience has led me to a pragmatic position where I am content to use quantitative research methods, and apply experimental designs where that fits the research question. However, I am increasingly aware that designs that reduce data to mean scores can miss out on very interesting stories about the variability in scores within a particular population. Research that seeks to identify patterns in a population can contribute to development of theory, and can provide useful evidence upon which to base interventions at a population level. Such nomothetic research seeks to reduce the data to a simplified model or theory and is a useful enterprise. However, if one is working at a clinical level, one does not know where any individual patient is from in the distribution of scores. Therefore, research that is interested in the diversity within a population is useful for these purposes.

I have found that qualitative, idiographic approaches such as Interpretative Phenomenological Analysis (IPA) are useful for increasing awareness of how people may respond to a similar situation in very different ways. For example, in a recent National Institute for Health Research (NIHR)–funded study, I worked in a team that looked at sensitive consultations in an oncology department to see what contributed to high or low patient satisfaction with the consultation. The consultations were recorded and conversation analysis (CA) used to look at the language structures being used by both doctors and patients. We also interviewed the doctors and patients after the consultation and used IPA to explore how they experienced it, and how they evaluated it. The results indicated that one of the big difficulties for doctors in responding appropriately to patients' information needs was that they were diverse, and changed over time. In addition, the information needs of family members accompanying patients would sometimes differ from those of the patients themselves. The qualitative methods used were able to retain the complexity of the data, and we were able to use the evidence from this to inform development of a consultation aid for doctors and patients to use together in order to improve patient satisfaction.

Teaching Health Psychology

Teaching health psychology is something that I began as a postgraduate student, and have enjoyed a great deal. The idea that you only really understand something when you have taught it is something that rings true to me, so I think that the years of teaching have reinforced my own learning. In addition, much of my teaching has been with other health professionals. In my first lecturing job at Coventry University I taught nurses, midwives, physiotherapists and occupational therapists as well as psychology students. This taught me that the value of psychological research, theories and interventions are not at all obvious to people in other disciplines, and it has ensured that I remain motivated to keep teaching relevant for what students will need in practice. This was especially pertinent during the time I spent teaching health psychology to medical students in Leicester. Many of the medics were not at all shy in letting me know that they considered psychology to be 'the fluffy stuff' and not essential to becoming a good doctor. I should emphasize many medical students were very positive in their acceptance of a biopsychosocial approach; however, one was made aware that this was not a uniform view, and one had many sceptics in the audience.

Teaching medical students was challenging in many ways. The training in medicine is properly tough, and they face 'must-pass' examinations at frequent intervals, with the threat of failing and having their places on the course terminated. This often results in students being highly strategic in their approach to learning, and can lead to a desire to learn by rote 'the right answer' to every question they may face on an exam paper. Their previous learning has been focused on hard sciences such as biology and chemistry, where there is a 'right' answer. When they are faced with social and behavioural sciences, they enter an arena with a different sort of knowledge where outcomes are discussed in terms of probabilities. It can all sound rather 'fuzzy', and uncertain. Part of my job was to persuade students to tolerate some degree of uncertainty, and that despite this, learning about psychology is an essential component in modern medicine. Adherence to treatment was a good topic for persuading students that they needed to move on from a biomedical approach to medicine. Students were often shocked to find that high levels of non-adherence are the norm. Even people with a high risk of dying fail to follow treatment plans as advised. The conclusion I tried to guide them to was one that it is not enough to be merely a great diagnostician and clinician because if your patients do not take the medication or make the lifestyle changes that you advise, their health will not improve and you will achieve nothing apart from wasting NHS resources. It is essential to also have good communication skills, and to understand more about why patients think, feel and behave as they do. Wagging a finger at patients who are noncompliant, and telling them what to do in a paternalistic manner, simply does not work.

Student feedback on teaching from medical students has been frank, and not always complimentary. Having a fierce set of critics has led me to work harder than I might otherwise have done to make lectures and small-group sessions relevant and engaging, so I think that I have to thank them for keeping my on my toes. I have also learned to appreciate faint praise, for example one student wrote 'I thought this was going to be a bit of a bird's course, but it's actually been quite useful', and I took this as a triumph! One technique which seems to help motivate students is to start with the description of a problem they may face as a doctor (e.g. how to care for non-adherent patients, and how to help patients manage the pain that modern medicine is unable to take away with drugs or surgery). I found that the experience I had in working with doctors on health-related research, and practitioner work that I have done, was useful in informing teaching. For example, I was able to contextualize advice on practice within the real-world NHS resources. The time spent sitting in an oncology ward, taking consent from research participants and observing how a clinic runs taught me that implementing all of the 'good practice' tips would not be viable within the time available for consultations. If too many consultations overrun, very sick patients are kept waiting and the other members of the clinic team will be affected. Therefore, in role-play exercises we were able to ask students to think about how they would prioritize and manage to do as well as possible within that time. We also discussed how the patient experience is shaped by service policy and financial constraints as well as how the doctor performs. Experience from practice was also helpful in making the teaching more convincing and relevant. For example, being able to give examples of what happened with a particular patient can bring the theory to life, and may also lend the teacher some additional credibility as a practitioner.

Applied Practice

Working in a medical school brought contact with many doctors who recognized the useful research skills that psychologists are trained in. As a result, I was approached by medics who wanted me to work with them to research problems that they faced in practice. This sort of research was appealing to me in terms of the potential to actually make a difference to peoples' lives. In turn this awakened a desire to use the knowledge and skills that I had been building up as an academic health psychologist and apply them directly in a clinical context. Therefore I set about undertaking suitable courses to develop my intervention skills and prepare me to take up an applied role. Health psychologists who wish to work with patients in applied settings, supporting behaviour change or helping patients cope with chronic conditions, need to ensure that they have appropriate one-to-one intervention skills, and undertake appropriate continuing professional development (CPD), such as a British Association for Behavioural and Cognitive Psychotherapies (BABCP)–accredited Cognitive Behavioural Therapy (CBT) course.

At this time, I was also motivated to develop my counselling skills in response to my role as a personal tutor to students. I found that I was often in meetings where students would confide in me and seek support or advice concerning difficult personal problems. These included drug or alcohol dependence, eating disorders, experience of bullying or discrimination, concerns about their sexuality, general anxiety and depression, and, on thankfully more rare occasions, that they had been thinking of seriously harming themselves or of ending their lives. I would promptly refer the student to the appropriate health, counselling or support services, but was aware that it was important that I did this with sensitivity. That led me to take up some CPD to develop general counselling skills. This was not only to make me more skilled in communicating and supporting students, but also to help me to manage feelings of anxiety or responsibility that I could be left with after such a meeting.

After just a few weeks of the first counselling course, I was hooked on learning these new skills, and therefore started to think about continuing with training as a counsellor. There was a British Association for Counselling and Psychotherapy (BACP)–accredited postgraduate course in counselling at Leicester, and so I applied. The course happened to be on Psychodynamic Counselling, and it has a been an enriching experience to complete it, both in terms of developing my skills, and in terms of self-discovery and understanding.

I took the plunge of reducing my contract hours to half-time as a lecturer in the medical school in order to develop as a practitioner, and managed to complete the counselling training and gain supervised practice in the counselling service for Birmingham City Council staff. In addition, I took on a part-time post in an NHS pain management service. The NHS post was an ideal start to my applied work as a health psychologist as it had the excellent support and supervision that I felt I needed as a novice practitioner.

Working in pain management is being discussed in another chapter, so I will not dwell on that, other than to say that I found it highly rewarding to work with patients who were able to make significant improvements to their quality of life. The gate control theory of pain and the effectiveness of pain management programmes give good examples for health psychologists to use in order to support a biopsychosocial approach to health and illness.

The other area that I have worked in an applied setting was an adult Cystic Fibrosis (CF) centre. CF is a genetic condition that affects internal organs that produce secretions, causing sticky mucus to accumulate. The lungs are often the most seriously affected organ, resulting in impaired lung function and increased vulnerability to chest infections. The digestive tract can also be affected, making it difficult to maintain a healthy weight; some patients develop CF-related diabetes, and fertility can be impaired. Patients are advised to follow a complex and time-consuming treatment regimen including physiotherapy, routine use of oral and nebulised antibiotics, steroids and dietary supplements (e.g. taking liquid food supplements overnight through a naso-gastric feeding tube.) The improvements in treatment have extended the life expectancy of patients, however the median age CF patients are likely to live to is still just 38, with a large range either side of that median.

The psychosocial problems that arise from living with CF are many and varied, and this is recognized by including a psychologist on the team to provide support for patients in coping with their illness and the treatment. The multidisciplinary team included both junior doctors and experienced consultants in respiratory medicine, physiotherapists, dieticians, a social worker and clinical nurse specialists. I was covering maternity leave for the permanent psychologist, who was a clinical psychologist, but had also previously done a master's degree in health psychology. I met a senior clinical psychologist for supervision sessions, and felt well supported by a very able and 'psychologically minded' team. Some of the work with patients was familiar territory for health psychologists: managing stress, coping with chronic illness and managing behaviour change. However, unsurprisingly given the severity of the condition, this patient group had much more serious levels of anxiety, depression and other mental health issues than I had found in my work in pain management.

Living with CF sometimes caused many difficulties in the network of family relationships. While many families managed these difficulties with sensitivity and resilience, I also saw many who struggled to cope with the huge pressures placed on all of the family members. This is a challenge for the patient, when the people that they would most often call on for social support are struggling themselves. For example, people would often refuse to talk about their distress as they felt they should protect other family members who were also suffering. In cases where there is one sibling with CF and another without, the sibling without CF may feel neglected as more attention was given to the ill child; the child with CF may feel resentful of the one who is well. Sometimes parents felt guilt and responsibility for passing on a genetic condition. Some parents seemed to be keeping emotionally distant (perhaps unconsciously attempting to defend themselves from the terrible grief arising from the loss of a child that is likely to occur before their own death), and struggled to be with their son or daughter or talk about death as they were approaching the end. Other parents were sometimes over-protective, or over-indulgent in an attempt to keep a child safe or somehow to compensate for their illness. These observations must be placed in the context of how well most families coped with the challenges, and the great courage and compassion that I witnessed. However, among the patients referred to see me, I found that many had disordered or insecure attachment histories that may have been partly related to their illness. For example, there were exacerbated in some cases by frequent spells of hospitalization from early childhood, and by the parents' roles in treatment delivery. Because of the way in which CF had impacted on the whole family system, patients often found it helpful to have an opportunity to talk to me in confidence and offload difficult feelings that they did not want to burden their family members with. My counselling training was of great help with this.

Patients transitioned from children's services at around age 18. Moving to adult services was sometimes a cue for patients to challenge the treatment regimens, perhaps as an aspect of normal developmental processes where adolescents challenge authority and seek to assert their autonomy. I witnessed some cases where it appeared that years of repressed anger at feeling that they were made to comply with treatment as a child were finally acted out in relationships with health professionals. In addition, some patients arrived at a personal decision on where to compromise in terms of how much of their treatment to 'put up with' in balance with enjoying life to the full while they were young and still well enough to do things. The multidisciplinary team that I worked with were deeply concerned for patients who they saw as taking risks with non-adherence to treatment that could lead to them dying much earlier than they would if they did adhere. At the weekly multidisciplinary team meetings, each patient was discussed, and patients were often referred to me to discuss their (non-)adherence, and find out the full rationale for their behaviour. In doing this I was able to draw on the stages of change model, and use motivational interviewing to encourage patients to enter the 'contemplation stage'. I also shared some of the motivational interviewing techniques with other health professionals on the team who wanted to avoid getting into conflict with patients.

Deaths of patients were obviously tragic for their families and friends, but staff and other patients on the ward were also affected. Some of the patients who died during my time on the ward had been patients for many years, and had very good relationships with staff, and longstanding friendships with some fellow patients. Providing support and an opportunity for debriefing for staff, and also being ready for an increase in referrals from other patients who had been affected by the death, were important. It was also necessary to accept the need for self-care in this matter, and supervision meetings were helpful in this.

My perception was that doctors were generally more reluctant than other health professionals to take up opportunities to discuss the impact of the death of patients than other professionals, and that has informed my teaching with medical students on dying, death and loss. Some doctors feel it is important to always maintain a professional distance from patients, and I recall one doctor being very embarrassed by crying in front of the family of a deceased patient. Clearly, doctors do need to be able to manage their feelings and function in distressing circumstances, however in this case, the patient's family were greatly helped by the thought that their loved one had been looked after by people who really cared about them and did not think the doctor showing some emotion was in any way unprofessional. Death is not always a defeat, and it can be very rewarding to work with patients to help them live as well as possible through that last part of their lives. In order to work in an area of medicine where one faces the death of patients one has come to know well, it is important to find ways of processing feeling of loss if one is to avoid burnout in the long run. Some will find ways of doing that without talking to the team psychologist, but it is important to find some sustainable method of working through feelings, and I think that having one's own personal therapy can be very helpful.

One of the most difficult challenges that I faced was in managing the boundaries between what I felt able to do, and where the boundary was for referring patients to other clinical mental health services. Good supervision is crucial in this respect, and I was able to access advice from an experienced clinical psychologist with regards to this. In one case I had managed to establish a rapport with a very vulnerable patient who subsequently tried to harm herself. It was important that I had fully discussed the case with my supervisor, and had taken advice on how to proceed. My training as a counsellor had included working with suicidal clients, and if I had not had this experience I would have struggled with this case. I did refer the patient to liaison psychiatry services in the hospital, however it was important to have the skills to assess the patient, and gain sufficient trust for her to let me know about her suicidal thoughts.

I felt that I made a positive contribution as a health psychologist to the CF service in supporting patients and staff, and in contributing to teaching and research. However, with hindsight, I think that the profile of patients and their needs makes the post more suited to a clinical psychologist with specialist knowledge of health psychology. If I had not completed the postgraduate training in counselling, I think I would have found this job very difficult. In particular, I drew on the counselling training and experience of managing boundaries, containing difficult emotions, understanding attachment disorders, transference and counter-transference, patient assessment, working with patients with suicidal thoughts and using supervision effectively. Hence this is not an area that I would personally recommend a health psychologist to work in unless they have undertaken a considerable amount of relevant CPD, or were in a team that also includes a clinical or counselling psychologist for support, as referral of patients is not always a satisfactory solution in practice. For example, if a patient has taken some time to be able to trust you enough to disclose that they have symptoms appropriate for a clinical psychology or psychiatric intervention, even when done with sensitivity, prompt referral elsewhere has the potential to feel like rejection, and be damaging for the patient. If the patient is at immediate risk, liaison psychiatry can be called, but if the patient does not disclose the extent of their thoughts about self-harm when assessed by this new person, they may not receive any further treatment or follow-up. If you write to the patient's GP to suggest referral to mental health services, there can be a lengthy delay before they are seen. While I was well aware of the need to manage the boundaries of my competence, patients and other professionals were often not clear on the differences between a health psychologist and a clinical psychologist and expected me to be able to cope with any psychological difficulties, and so it can be a big challenge to maintain those boundaries. It is essential to have good supervision and line management back-up when dealing with this challenge.

Synergy

I have felt that my work in teaching, research and practice as a health psychologist has delivered synergy as each area has informed the others. The experience of working in health care settings has helped to give my research and teaching insights on what is useful and relevant in practice. I have found the diversity in my work very rewarding and enjoyable. Nevertheless, it can come at a cost as one may be seen as not having sufficient focus on any one area when it comes to seeking promotion in one's academic career.

The Future

At present I still enjoy having a toe in the academic world, and find supervising postgraduate research very satisfying as I work on projects that relate to clinical health psychology. This is a good partner to my private practice as a health psychologist and psychodynamic counsellor. I get referrals from Employee Assistance Programmes run by insurance companies for clients who need help with managing stress, coping with chronic pain and other illness, and more general problems that give rise to anxiety and depression. This tends to be short-term work using a CBT and/or mindfulness-based cognitive therapy frame. I also get self-referrals from the BPS and BACP registers, and from my own website that tend to be more for open-ended psychodynamic counselling work. I match the intervention to suit the individual client's needs and preferences, and have weekly supervision from an experienced supervisor who is a clinical psychologist and has also trained as a Jungian analytic psychotherapist, so she is able to provide supervision on psychodynamic work as well as CBT. In addition, I meet with three other health psychologists for peer supervision sessions where we discuss our practice and personal development. I hope to continue to work as a health psychologist within my practice, but am also drawn to continue my development and am considering training in Jungian analytical psychotherapy. This may seem an unusual combination of work, however psychodynamic approaches seem to suit work with some patients with physical health problems that may be real physical manifestations of unbearable emotional distress, or where the relationship between their psychological and biological processes are longstanding and not available to the patient through conscious reflection. I see the biopsychosocial model as an important foundation for psychodynamic approaches, and this is a unifying basis for the different therapeutic frames that I use. Another important motivation for doing the psychotherapy training is that it offers a voyage of personal discovery and development as it entails engagement in deep personal therapy as well as training, supervision and reflective writing.

In terms of the future of health psychology as a discipline, I hope that it continues to value close interaction between research, teaching and practice as they relate intimately to each other. It is important for the practitioner health psychologists, who now must be on the HPC register, to choose to maintain their involvement in the DHP, and keep the profession in step with the challenges and changes faced in UK health care.

Key Debates in Psychology

How should we manage the interface between health psychology and clinical psychology in NHS or other clinical settings?

In this chapter, some of the difficulties facing health psychologists managing the boundary between health and clinical psychology are described. Health psychologists have skills that are suited for many applied areas such as health promotion, rehabilitation and self-management programmes, or other behaviour change interventions. These skills allow them to fulfil useful roles in many applied settings. In the course of this work, they will inevitably encounter some patients who have pre-existing mental health problems, or have developed severe mental health problems arising from their physical health problems. It is therefore important to have appropriate assessment skills, and clear referral pathways to ensure that patients in need of clinical psychology or psychiatric interventions receive the care they need. Patients and health professionals alike often do not have a clear understanding of the differences in the roles of health and clinical psychologists, and expect any psychologist to be able to deal with any sort of psychological distress. In addition, it is not always the case that the referral pathways provide timely access to appropriate services.

The DHP has worked, and continues to work, to address these issues. Much work has been done in terms of educating others of what health psychologists can contribute, refining the training programme and providing routes to registration as a health psychologist. It is important that this work continues to keep pace with the radical changes that our health services face over the coming decades.

5

Health Psychology in Cyberspace

Neil Coulson

Where Did It All Begin?

I can trace my interest in health psychology right back to my undergraduate days at the University of St Andrews. Whilst it was over 20 years ago that I first encountered this new area, it also feels like it was just yesterday. Having decided to study in Scotland for my MA in Psychology I was lucky enough to be in the first group to be taught a new module on health psychology by a new member of staff in the department. That person turned out to be Professor Marie Johnston and being taught by her and learning about this new and emerging area comprised a defining moment in my development. I knew at that point that I wanted a career in the field of health psychology. How I was going to make that happen remained unclear, but for now I just enjoyed the experience and when the opportunity came up to undertake my final year empirical research project in the area I was delighted.

My first real experience of *doing* health psychology research took me to deepest, darkest Dundee and some of its finest car parks. To explain, my project was a worksite evaluation of a mobile heart disease–screening clinic, a converted double-decker bus to be precise. I loved every minute of it and together with my project partner, Linda Graham (now a clinical psychologist), we gathered our process and impact data and began to write up our dissertations. This was my first real taste of health psychology research, and I enjoyed being 'out in the field' and working with real people with real lives and not just collecting student data like some of my other classmates. Following on from this I was also able to secure some part-time, casual research assistant work exploring men's beliefs and attributions about heart disease. Yet again this involved work in the Dundee area and my part of the project was to collect data from 'dustbin

Health Psychology in Action, First Edition. Edited by Mark Forshaw and David Sheffield.
© 2013 John Wiley & Sons, Ltd. Published 2013 by John Wiley & Sons, Ltd.

men' during their coffee and lunch breaks. If nothing else it helped develop my skills of negotiation and persuasion in the context of study recruitment.

Following graduation the road towards my desired career in health psychology was a little bumpy. My next goal was to get a PhD in a relevant topic and whilst getting a place to study was relatively straightforward it was the financial aspect that proved to be a deal breaker. It was time for a plan B! I then moved to the University of Edinburgh and decided that I would undertake an MSc in Health Promotion & Health Education and then afterwards try again for a PhD place, hopefully with funding! I figured that with a relevant MSc degree under my belt I would be in a stronger position in an increasingly competitive field.

Success

After completing my MSc degree I saw an advert for a research assistant position with attached opportunities to do PhD research funded by the Ministry of Agriculture, Fisheries and Food (as it was then called). The only problem was that it was at the other end of the country, Devon to be precise, and I was in Edinburgh. However, needs must when the Devil drives, and I applied for and was offered the post. I then made my way down to the University of Exeter and began my part-time PhD whilst working full-time with Professor Dick Eiser and Professor Christine Eiser. I think this experience taught me a valuable lesson in that one shouldn't give up at the first disappointment, and in fact this is something that has helped me throughout my academic career since then. Whilst I would have preferred, in some ways, to do a PhD full-time I think on reflection it was the right move for me as I developed many more skills doing the research assistant job alongside than I might have done if I were focussing solely on my PhD.

My PhD examined children and young people's perceptions of food-related risks. This involved a mixed-methods series of studies including interviews with young children and questionnaires completed by adolescents. It was also during this time that the bovine spongiform encephalopathy (BSE) or 'mad cow disease' crisis struck, and doing a PhD on perceived food risks my thesis inevitably changed. Again, this experience proved to be 'character building' in that often one can't plan for everything when it comes to research and the unexpected may happen. How was I to guess that the most serious food scare to hit the United Kingdom was about to unfold? However, in this case it allowed me to take advantage of the situation and learn from it.

After three years the post came to an end and in order to support myself financially whilst writing up I applied for and obtained my first lectureship at the University of Plymouth. This was a joint post which involved teaching both undergraduate students in psychology but also health professionals and trainee nurses. Whilst it was an absolutely exhausting role, it was nevertheless an excellent way to gain valuable experience of teaching health psychology to different groups. The needs of undergraduate psychology students are very different to those of other groups (e.g. midwives or community nurses) and during my 3 years in this post I learned a considerable amount.

After I completed my PhD I continued to do some research in the area of food risk, particularly factors that underpin trust in sources of food-related risk information. This was OK, but to be honest I really wasn't that enthusiastic about the topic. My interests were elsewhere, but the only problem was I didn't know where at that point in time. It wasn't until my next lectureship at the University of Derby that I can say that I truly found my research calling and it was all such a surprise how it happened.

Life Happens

Life indeed happens and sometimes in a good way and sometimes not so good – well, this was a case of sometimes not so good! Facing a family bereavement and a lot of stress I soon began to feel ill, I lost a horrendous amount of weight and for a while I thought my number was up. Thankfully it wasn't, but during that time I spent many hours alone surfing the internet trying to find out what was wrong. It was my first journey into cyberspace and that proved to be a true turning point in my academic and research career. As I surfed the net I was struck by the sheer number of websites that offered users the opportunity to chat to others facing similar problems. So, being the nosey person that I am, I decided to look further and found dozens of websites which hosted online bulletin boards (i.e. discussion forums) on all sorts of health-related topics. As I read through some of the conversations or 'threads' I couldn't believe just how much information people were willing to share about their illness and also the extent to which virtual strangers were offering emotional support and advice. As I read more I became increasingly aware that I hadn't really seen much in the health psychology literature about this growing phenomenon. At last, my calling!

Health Psychology in Cyberspace

From this initial exploration my programme of research was born and I started to develop a number of studies which examined the role of online communities (also known as 'online support groups') for those individuals affected by long-term illness. At this point I didn't have any particular illness in mind, and indeed this has persisted since then. However, I had to start somewhere and so I began with a study looking at the types of social support offered within an online community for individuals living with irritable bowel syndrome. This first study, published in *CyberPsychology & Behaviour* (now known as *CyberPsychology, Behaviour & Social Networking*), was an exploratory paper looking at the types of social support which were offered through such bulletin boards. I reviewed 572 messages that had been posted to the IBS website board and used a deductive thematic analysis using five main categories of social support. As I undertook this analysis it was evident that there was potentially a lot to examine with regards to patients' use of discussion boards, their reasons for doing so and what difference it actually made in terms of relevant clinical and psychosocial outcomes.

Soon after I published this study I took a post at the University of Nottingham as an Associate Professor of Health Psychology in the Institute of Work, Health & Organisations. This proved to be a very positive move not least for the opportunities to develop one's research ideas in a thriving research-led institution. With IWHO being a purely postgraduate institute, I was then able to develop some new ideas in the area of online communities which might be suitable for MSc and PhD projects. This has led to a significant expansion of my interests not only in the specific areas outlined previously but also in the range of illnesses and conditions. Indeed, since then I have undertaken or supervised studies exploring breast cancer, prostate cancer, heart disease, infertility, HIV/AIDS, muscular dystrophy, eating disorders, diabetes, Huntington's disease, Parkinson's disease and others. Indeed, as I write this book chapter the first two of my PhD students who chose to explore topics in this new and highly original area have been awarded their degrees following their successful *viva voce* examinations.

Of particular interest as I was developing this programme of research was the issue of ethics. In particular, since I started my studies with an analysis of bulletin board messages I had to consider the ethical issues surrounding such research almost immediately. As I looked further into the (limited) literature on the ethics of reading and analysing online discourse, I was struck by the disagreements between different researchers. On the one hand I identified a very pessimistic position which appeared to suggest that under no circumstances should it or could it ever be ethical to read and analyse messages posted to bulletin boards. In stark contrast I found other authors who argued that it should and could be permissible but a number of ethical issues had to be considered thoroughly. My first reaction was to turn to our professional body, the British Psychological Society (BPS), and look to see what they say with regards to research conducted using the internet. However, I was disappointed in that I could not identify any published guidelines and the existing documentation related specifically to research using human subjects in a very traditional manner. Faced with an absence of clear guidance I was forced to try to consider all the ethical issues in depth myself and hopefully arrive at a position where I felt happy that I was acting in an ethically responsible fashion. Indeed, the issue of ethics has been the single most common query which has come back from journal editors and peer review commentaries. Sometimes they are asking out of genuine interest, sometimes clearly misunderstanding what it is that's actually been done in the study and/or analyses. Nevertheless, a clear position needs to be articulated and thankfully a couple of years later the BPS did in fact publish some guidelines (BPS, 2007) though many in the field agree that they have not been as helpful as one might have hoped. However, they have provided some useful guidance, though some areas are less well articulated (e.g. informed consent, the distinction between public and private space and quoting from online narratives publicly available online).

A related area that struck me early on was the absence of any clear guidance on methodology surrounding the analysis of bulletin board messages. Whilst there is an abundance of articles, chapters and textbooks covering a range of qualitative research issues, I found little about this specific source of online data and how best to study it. Whilst I have attempted to develop some methodological guidelines of my own, this is still a work in progress, I feel, as the development of the internet and Web 2.0 has led to a rapidly changing context in which researchers like me operate. For me, developing new tools to research and analyse in the virtual world is one of the most significant challenges for researchers in this area.

As we move forward, I am especially interested in how we as health psychologists respond to the fast-moving innovations in technology and the World Wide Web. For me I see great potential in how we apply our psychological theory to emerging areas in the health care arena. As a consequence I see great challenges but also great opportunities to develop, test, refine and extend our theories in health psychology as well as the tools that we use to do so. The question is: will health psychology be able to keep up with new innovations in technology? Only time will tell. . . .

What Else Do I Do?

The other main strand to my work is my engagement with our professional body, the British Psychological Society. A few years ago I replied to an advertisement for individuals to join the Division of Health Psychology Training Committee. Of all the committees that I have joined in recent years, this is probably one of the most interesting and rewarding as it provides the opportunity to help promote and enhance the quality of health psychology training delivered through HE providers. As a member of this committee, one is invited to become part of a visiting team to go out to HE providers who are seeking accreditation (or re-accreditation) and consider the quality of their course and how it meets the needs of its students and associated professional training requirements. In almost every case this is an exceptionally positive and illuminating experience and is an ideal way to network and connect with other health psychologists (and teams) up and down the country. Indeed, many personal friendships and professional relationships I have today with colleagues in the health psychology field began through visits. Setting aside the personal gains from working on this committee (of which I am now the current Chair) one thing that has struck me over the years is the increasing quality of our training programmes. There are many highly dedicated individuals across a range of institutions that are doing a splendid job when it comes to supporting the development of the next generation of health psychologists. In particular, I have been struck by the innovative teaching practices which are evident in our institutions and the variety of ways in which health psychology is being taught to our trainees and assessed.

A related role which I retired from in 2009 was that of the Chief Assessor for the Board of Assessors in Health Psychology. This was the first-ever appointment to this position and was created to help develop and oversee the assessment of our Stage 2 trainees. Whilst it was initially for 3 years, I agreed to two further 1-year extensions giving me a wealth of experience and insight into the challenges of undertaking the Stage 2 Qualification in health psychology. I particularly enjoyed this role as it become clear quite quickly that with such a new qualification there was still much uncertainty and probably a lack of clarity concerning what exactly was expected of trainees. This was interesting because over the years I, along with the Chief Supervisor and Registrar Dr Mark Forshaw, have had to think on our feet as it were on several occasions and try and formulate answers to often complex questions given the potential for such diverse training experiences.

More recently, however, the Stage 2 curriculum has been revised and I (as Chair of the DHPTC and also as the Chief Assessor) was invited to join the small working group to consider how best to revise it (and the associated assessment load). What was apparent from the outset was that there was a clear need to update, revise and streamline our curriculum. In particular, we acknowledged the need to make interventions a much more explicit part of our training and saw it as a core competence rather than an optional one which was the case in the old curriculum. This I believe was warmly welcomed by trainees, supervisors and employers alike and I think will stand health psychology in a strong position for future growth and development.

This year I have returned to the Board of Assessors (now known as the Health Psychology Qualification Board) as their first-ever external examiner for the Stage 2 qualification in Health Psychology (also unofficially known as the 'independent' or 'BPS route'). This is a role I am particularly looking forward to and it will allow me to continue with my quality assurance and professional development agenda.

I have also recently been elected to the role of Chair Elect for the BPS Division of Health Psychology (DHP). This is a great honour and a challenge which I am very much looking forward to, although it will be hard work. There is still much to be done in advancing the health psychology agenda and we are currently in a very uncertain time with many significant changes being implemented with regards to how our health care system functions and is funded. We often struggle to find our own voice and be understood by not only the public but also other health professionals. We must constantly strive to promote our own discipline and what health psychology can bring to the table. Whilst colleagues may debate whether ultimately health psychology will make its mark through professional practice and/or its contribution to research and evidence-based health care, there is no doubt in my mind that both are valuable and as we move forward we must promote and advance the contribution made by both areas of health psychology. There are also many challenges for us as we learn and digest the implications of the Health Professions Council (HPC) becoming the statutory regulator of practitioner psychologists. Whilst at first glance all appears to have been relatively smooth in terms of transition and many of the fears and anxieties articulated before this time have not materialized, we should not be complacent but rather keep a watchful eye on HPC developments and ensure we are doing the best for our profession as we can (e.g. moving to make the threshold for entry to the HPC register for health psychologists explicit in its doctoral level).

Key Debates in Health Psychology

As health psychology has grown as a discipline over the past 25 years or so we find ourselves fitting broadly into one of two camps. There are those who primarily wish to be an academic health psychologist with a focus solely on research and those who wish to make their contribution in practice. Nevertheless, regardless of which particular orientation one holds, to be a health psychologist in the eyes of the Health Professions Council or a Chartered Psychologist with full membership of the Division of Health Psychology, one needs to achieve the required standards for entry to the HPC register or Stages 1–2 of the BPS curriculum. As it currently stands this is a master's degree for health psychologists (with the award of the British Psychological Society qualification in health psychology, or equivalent). Thus far, the vast majority of education providers have interpreted this (correctly in my view) as meaning an accredited Stage 1 course (i.e. MSc Health Psychology) followed afterwards by Stage 2 such as a Professional Doctorate in Health Psychology or a PhD with the BPS Stage 2 Qualification in Health Psychology. What is important, and should not be overlooked, is that the threshold for entry implies a doctoral threshold but without actually making this explicit. The BPS qualification in health psychology is doctoral in nature, and therefore anything equivalent should be just that – but it remains to be seen whether the HPC will consider the doctoral level important. Rather, it may be less about the actual level of the award but more about evidence that the Standards of Education & Training and Standards of Proficiency have been achieved. Therefore, one potential problem we may see in the future is a proliferation in the types (and levels) of courses which are aimed at the future health psychologists of tomorrow. The extent to which this will happen or the seriousness of it is hard to quantify but, if asked, I am confident most credible health psychologists would argue for a doctoral-level entry to the HPC register and membership of the BPS Division of Health Psychology as the most sensible position in order to protect both public safety and our own professional identity and development.

Reference

British Psychological Society. (2007). *Report of the Working Party on Conducting Research on the Internet: guidelines for ethical practice in psychological research online.* Leicester: BPS.

Glossary

bovine spongiform encephalopathy (BSE): also commonly known as 'mad cow disease', a fatal neurodegenerative disease in cattle.

online bulletin board: an online discussion site where people can hold conversations in the form of posted messages.

social networking site: an online service, platform or site that focuses on building connections between people (e.g. Facebook and Twitter).

Web 2.0: Web applications that facilitate interaction online such as social networking sites or virtual communities.

6

Working in Academia: A Different Kind of Practice, but Practice Nonetheless

Lorna Dodd

How It All Began . . .

While studying my undergraduate degree, a BA in Physical Education & Social Applied Psychology, I developed an interest in the field of public health and lifestyle with a particular passion for the application of psychological promotion, maintenance, prevention and improvement. Studying aspects of ways to measure, monitor and intervene strengthened my enthusiasm for this area of psychology and has formed the foundation and direction setting for my professional journey of scholarly, research and employment activity to date. Studying the physical education element of my degree complemented my interest in psychology, specifically with regard to health behaviours and the promotion and maintenance of health. At this stage I was not aware that my area of interest fell under the discipline of health psychology. I was familiar with psychology disciplines such as clinical, forensic and educational, and these professions were publicized widely throughout my degree, but health did not get the same kind of exposure. Since then I can reflect and see how much the discipline of health psychology has grown and developed, though in my professional role as a senior lecturer of psychology at a university college, it is still evident that students are unclear of what this profession entails (some think it is another name for clinical psychology) and in particular what health psychologists do and where they can work.

After graduating with an undergraduate degree, I was offered a role (and an opportunity to begin paying off my student loan) as a full-time Graduate Assistant in Psychology and Physical Education at a higher education (HE) college. My time was divided between working within the psychology and the physical education departments. Thus, at this stage such a role complemented my knowledge gained

Health Psychology in Action, First Edition. Edited by Mark Forshaw and David Sheffield.
© 2013 John Wiley & Sons, Ltd. Published 2013 by John Wiley & Sons, Ltd.

to date, obtained through my degree. My role was to assist each department in their undergraduate programmes providing both technical assistance and student support across a range of modules, as well as assisting and undertaking research activity. During this time I developed competencies in the use of psychological equipment and gained experience in delivering workshops and seminars (e.g. on research methods – SPSS) and laboratory sessions. This role also provided me with an opportunity to get involved in real-world research and work collaboratively with other psychologists. During this time I was encouraged to attend conferences, present work and write up research for publication (Al-Nakeeb *et al.*, 2004; Duncan, Dodd *et al.*, 2005; Duncan, Woodfield *et al.*, 2005; Myers *et al.*, 2004). Within 12 months of this post, I really began to get a feel of what it would be like to become an academic, embark upon research and practice within your field of interest. It became clearer that my interest was centred on health behaviours and the impact of adherence and non-adherence to a healthy lifestyle. My work environment was with young adults (e.g. students), thus their health-related lifestyles were of importance to me, as adherence to a number of risky behaviours would impact upon a number of factors in their lives. Furthermore, as future policy makers, teachers and professionals, the students' health and well-being became of particular interest. It became evident that my area fell within health psychology. Thus, by the end of my first year as a graduate assistant, I moved full-time into the psychology department to enable me to focus my career path towards health psychology.

I was fortunate that both the university college and the psychology department were keen to support my professional development, thus during this time I completed numerous postgraduate qualifications including a Diploma in Psychology (Conversion for Postgraduates) conferring graduate basis for registry (GBR – which is now GBC) with the British Psychological Society (BPS), a Postgraduate Certificate in Education, a Postgraduate Diploma in the Social Sciences and a MSc in Psychological Research Methods. Enhancing my research methods knowledge beyond the undergraduate level developed my understanding and knowledge of appraising and synthesizing literature, enunciating research questions and utilizing different methodologies, ways to analyse data, and manuscript preparation. Having a good understanding of research methods is advantageous as researching and practicing health psychology go hand in hand; thus all of this contributed to my development towards becoming a health psychologist.

In recognition of these accomplishments, in September 2005 I applied for a 12-month fixed-term psychology lecturing position at a university and was successful. This role enabled me to continue with research and scholarly activity, as well as my journey towards chartered health psychology status. My main teaching responsibilities were in delivering research methods lectures. During this year I felt ready to embark upon health psychology training and also began an MSc in Health Psychology at Coventry University – Stage 1. This enabled me to not only extend my knowledge base, but also develop valuable research links (e.g. Coventry Health Services Research Centre), with whom I conducted a process and outcome evaluation of a piloted parent–child communication programme about relationships and sex – a funded project (Bayley *et al.*, 2006). This was my first experience of a miniature consultancy project and working collaboratively with an established health research centre with other health psychologists. In 2006 I was then appointed as a Psychology Lecturer at Newman University College, in Birmingham.

In 2007 I commenced the Doctorate in Health Psychology at Staffordshire University. Prior to this I spent just under 12 months deciding on the best route to take towards becoming a health psychologist in academia. I spent time discussing with academics who had completed a doctorate route or a PhD, and those who were teaching on doctorate programmes. Traditionally, a PhD was the desired route for academia. However, I selected the doctorate route, as opposed to that of a PhD, as I felt that it focused on developing both applied skills and research skills equally. This split was congruent with and beneficial to an academic setting, which encourages teaching, research, consultancy and professional practice, in this particular current climate. I felt that the doctorate programme would enhance my professional and research skills, for example would enhance my knowledge further to design, implement and evaluate specific research on promoting and improving health in a variety of populations, but specifically the student population.

Once chartered it was my ambition to continue employment in academia; teaching health psychology, conducting research and providing consultancy. Thus, I felt that the doctorate qualification would further demonstrate to both myself and future employers and clients that I have the necessary competences in the core aspects of health psychology and professional practice.

I felt also that an academic setting was a suitable placement for supervised practice of health psychology–related work. Such a placement setting can be viewed as a multidisciplinary environment (as highlighted previously), and I was encouraged to conduct research and consultancy, as well as being active within a variety of committees. This is in line with health psychology work (Michie, 2004). My placement setting enabled me to demonstrate many of the required health psychology doctorate competencies. However, to fully meet the criteria of others, I sourced external opportunities where I had the added advantage of access to other universities and agencies to fulfil all competencies.

Furthermore, I chose Staffordshire University to study the doctorate not only because of the quality of academic staff who underpinned the programme, but also because the University has a thriving health research centre culture with an excellent national and international reputation. Balancing the demands of working and studying at times was exhausting. However, it has trained me to be proactive and now I feel that I have the skills to manage teaching, research, consultancy and family life, and I enjoy every aspect of my professional work.

Day-to-Day Life in Academia

Promoting health psychology work in academia occurs through my role as a Senior Lecturer in Psychology at Newman University College. I am also Programme Leader for our blended-learning MSc in Clinical Applications of Psychology. I am predominately responsible for teaching research methods modules, a third-year Health Psychology module, and for both undergraduate and postgraduate research projects.

Teaching the Health Psychology module is definitely the area I thrive on. This is a perfect opportunity for me to promote health psychology as an exciting field within psychology that has important contributions to make to our understanding of the causes, progression and treatment of illnesses. The module explores the theoretical models which attempt to explain and predict health behaviour and examines the practical application of these models in health promotion campaigns. It focuses upon the relationship between stress, health and illness, and the factors that mediate this relationship (e.g. individual differences). It considers the impact of living with a disability and/or a chronic illness from the biopsychosocial perspective, and considers the impact of illness cognitions on behaviour. The module further considers the impact of being hospitalized on a patient's health and well-being from a psychosocial perspective. Thus, the focus of this module is concerned with the promotion and maintenance of health, the prevention and management of illness and the identification of biopsychosocial factors contributing to health and illness. The module allows me to continually draw upon my own health psychology–related research and demonstrate how theory can and is implemented into practice. Therefore, I am able provide students with examples of where health psychologists work and where their skills and knowledge are required. This module truly inspires students, for example,

> I had never thought of becoming a Health Psychologist. If I am honest I was not sure of what it was. But studying this module has made me realise that the area I was interested in is Health Psychology and not Clinical. It would have helped if an introductory module at the beginning of my degree was available to introduce me to the different disciplines. (Final-year student, end-of-module evaluation feedback)

This quotation is representative of many students' views, and taking on board students' feedback, last year as a department we have now developed an introductory module introducing students to a range of Applied Areas of Psychology, which includes a number of sessions on health psychology.

Student feedback from the Health Psychology module yearly was very positive, and it was evident that students enjoyed the 'learning by doing' activities and the interactive lecture style where they could take part and engage with the material. In 2008 I was awarded a Fellowship in Academic Practice at my University, with a bursary. I integrated online-delivered problem-based learning (PBL) scenarios into the Health Psychology module, which was evaluated and presented at the International Blended Learning Conference, at the University of Hertfordshire (Dodd & Holloway, 2009). Developing PBL tasks online (e.g. using the functions of our institution's Virtual Learning Environment, or VLE) engaged the students and encouraged a deeper and more independent learning approach. Furthermore, providing students with PBL health psychology scenarios that mirrored health psychology work enabled the students to have a hands-on experience of what health psychologists actually do, for example, "The pod cast and video made the PBL task more real, as if I was a real Health Psychologist doing the task and getting info from my line manager" (final-year undergraduate student).

Whenever possible it is also important to promote the psychological principles, practices, services and benefits of health psychology to different health professionals. Knowledge of health psychology principles and practices provides health practitioners with an understanding of how psychological factors can impact on behaviour, the role of behaviour in the aetiology of illness and the interaction between psychology and physiology and vice versa (Kaptein & Weinman, 2004; Ogden, 2007). Furthermore, many health professionals are now faced with a greater prevalence of lifestyle problems from their clients that are either a cause or consequence of their illness or disability. For example, there is an inverse association between inactivity and mental health (Galper, Trivedi, Barlow, Dunn, & Kampert, 2006). Therefore, health professionals treating clients with such issues would benefit from integrating health psychology knowledge and its applications to address the individual and contextual aspects of the client. Human beings are complex, and it is unlikely that a single theoretical and discipline approach can provide a direct panacea for a client's problems (Chwalisz, 2008).

Thus, whilst studying for the doctorate I had the opportunity to promote health psychology to different groups of health professionals (and postdoctorally I am still engaging in such an activity), for example to nurses on health promotion within mental health, to counsellors on the benefits of integrating health psychology principles into the counselling profession, to MSc Health Psychology students on my experience of studying for the doctorate and the Stage 2 process, and to Professional Doctorate in Health Psychology students on my experience of undertaking a consultancy tender. Conveying information to different health professionals who hold different philosophical, epistemological and ontological views, and attempting to demonstrate how health psychology practices may be useful in their own professions, can be quite a challenge, and at times I was not prepared for the barriers that other health professionals put forward towards health psychology, for example, psychodynamic counsellors focus heavily on a person's unconscious needs to change a person's behaviour. Thus, though rewarding, promoting health psychology is also a challenge, but a necessity.

Alongside the teaching element of my profession are administrative duties, of which I am responsible for several. For example, I am an active member of a number of committees and boards, both within the institution and outside. It is also my responsibility to deal with queries and applications for the MSc in Clinical Applications Programme, and I am currently the ethics link for the psychology department, which is a very enjoyable role. All students embarking upon research, for example, for their dissertation are required to apply for ethical approval. In the first instance their application will come to me as ethics link, prior to the Universities Ethics Committee. This is a very interesting role as I get to see all the different types of research that students would like to undertake. It is also a very challenging role because of the number of ethical issues that some of the research raises.

Seeing students, health professionals and even colleagues engage with health psychology is extremely rewarding. It is difficult to put the feelings into words when you can see students excited about the area as they begin to debate, discuss and ask questions. It is even more rewarding when you are asked to write references as they seek further postgraduate study to embark upon their future development towards becoming a health psychologist (e.g. MSc in Health Psychology). It is then that you really know that you have delivered and promoted your subject and that it has really touched the students and made a difference, and that you are part of shaping the future of health psychology.

Research Activity – Health Psychology in Practice

Embarking upon research is not only part of my role as a Senior Lecturer, but also an opportunity to specialize in my area of health psychology and collaborate with other interested parties. Completing my doctorate really pushed me to engage in research at a higher level, focus on my research area and develop my confidence in conference presentations and manuscript publications. I began the doctorate in 2007 and submitted my thesis in January 2010, the *viva voce* followed in April of that year and I graduated in July.

Since 2007, I have conducted a number of research studies, and been involved in several collaborative projects and consultancy requests. As mentioned previously I am interested in the health behaviours and health-related lifestyles of young adults, students in particular. One of the main reasons for this is that it is well documented that unhealthy lifestyle behaviours are primary causes of premature morbidity and mortality. Inactivity, smoking, immoderate alcohol use and poor diet are the four major behavioural contributors to chronic illnesses such as cancer, diabetes and cardiovascular disease (Mokdad *et al.*, 2004; World Health Organization (WHO), 2002, 2003). Such modifiable behaviours are usually established during youth or young adulthood (Steptoe *et al.*, 2002). Despite the widely documented consequences associated with unhealthy lifestyle behaviours, globally a substantial proportion of young adults, notably HE students, engage in such unhealthy lifestyle practices (Steptoe & Wardle, 2001; Steptoe *et al.*, 2002). A more comprehensive picture of the health lifestyles of HE students is required. Many of these illnesses are attributable to unhealthy lifestyle choices.

Thus, one of my doctorate papers focused on investigating the prevalence and clustering of five lifestyle risk factors (psychological stress, physical activity, fruit and vegetable intake, binge drinking and smoking) within a UK HE institution with the aim to describe the characteristics of the differing student health lifestyles in relation to demographic characteristics. The premise was that such findings will aid health professionals to understand how behaviours cluster together and design more effective intervention strategies within HE establishments (Dodd *et al.*, 2010).

This research involved a number of tasks including a review of related literature and prevalidated health-related questionnaires, identification of a suitable item pool of questions, design of the questionnaire in terms of format, layout and structure, piloting of the questionnaire, assessing the reliability of the subscales, producing a question protocol, creating a database for the analysis of data, and further supplementary activities, such as writing a research grant proposal and completing the ethics submission for the research. Once this was completed, data collection and analysis occurred, before writing it up for conference and journal manuscript submission.

This assisted me in developing a number of key research skills, but was not without its challenges. One would think that working in a setting where the sample is easily accessible would overcome the issues of low response rate. However, this sample is no different to any other sample with regard to this; yes, I could access them easily, but I still had to think about how to overcome low participant uptake and issues around the representativeness of the sample.

By means of studying the doctorate I also had the opportunity to undertake a systematic review, which focused on the topic of tanning. To date, the incidence and prevalence of nonmelanoma and malignant melanoma types of skin cancer are increasing globally each year, with 2–3 million and 132 000 cases reported yearly respectively (WHO, 2009). Within the United States, skin cancer accounts for more than 50% of all new cancers diagnosed each year (American Cancer Society, 2006). In comparison, in the United Kingdom, latest figures show skin cancer accounts for more than 30% of new cancer diagnoses each year (Cancer Research UK, 2009). The latter figure is extremely concerning as the UK climate is considerably different from that of the United States, with UV levels and hours of sunshine significantly lower. In addition, within the United Kingdom malignant melanoma is the second most common cancer in adults aged 15–34 years and incidence rates have quadrupled since the 1970s (Cancer Research UK, 2009). Despite the adverse health effects associated with tanning, ultraviolet (UV) radiation exposure from the sun and/or artificial tanning devices seems to be gaining considerable popularity and having a tan is perceived as desirable. Consequently, UV protection represents a major global health concern. My interest in this topic has developed not only from these alarming statistics, but also from a wider interest in the health behaviours and health lifestyles that young adults partake in. Thus, the systematic review assessed the effectiveness of appearance-focused interventions aimed at preventing skin cancer (Dodd & Forshaw, 2010). The findings from this systematic review paper led me onto conducting an empirical research project on the factors influencing tanning practices using an extended theory of planned behaviour (TPB) model within students.

These experiences have most notably developed my personal and professional conduct. For example, it has made me more aware of professional boundaries (e.g. power differentials) within teams and of subtleties of working relationships. Quality control was also central to these experiences. Throughout this period, I ensured that data remained secure and confidential and that I was compliant with ethical and legal standards. This included the following requirements: informed consent in any application was always sought, all participants were briefed about their involvement, participants were regularly informed throughout the process of their right to withdraw at any time without explanation or withdrawal of any incentive provided, and confidentiality was assured (British Psychological Society, 2006; Michie, 2004). To ensure these requirements were met, systems were put in place, for example storing personal identifiable information separate from data, replacing personal identifiable information with an alphanumeric participant code, storing paper data in locked filing cabinets, and storing electronic data on a network which was password protected with access restricted to designated researchers. Thus, data storing was in compliance with the Data Protection Act (Office of Public Sector Information, 1998). Ensuring and maintaining confidentiality were vital within my research as I was asking questions on topic areas that were personal and sensitive (i.e. students' health behaviour).

Conducting research gives me the opportunity to really engage in the discipline of health psychology. There is a real enjoyment and sense of satisfaction that what you are researching and finding out will make a difference. By appraising and synthesizing empirical evidence, it becomes clearly apparent where future research is required, and you know that what you are doing will add and extend what is already out there. This will then (one would hope) impact upon practice.

Therefore, as a health psychologist in academia my role is very much an interdisciplinary one, fostering interest in health psychology through my teaching, conducting research within health psychology to contribute new knowledge and inform practice, providing expert knowledge and skills in health psychology in a consultancy role, and promoting health psychology to different types of health professionals to encourage collaboration of knowledge.

The Doctorate in Health Psychology

Undoubtedly, studying the Doctorate in Health Psychology has provided me with a large variety of skills that most definitely benefit a career in academia; for example, it has developed my teaching, research, consultancy, professional and reflection skills – all are integral parts of a successful academic career as a health psychologist. In particular, 'reflection' was an integral part of my professional development towards becoming a health psychologist. Through reflection, practitioners are able to look retrospectively on their experience, evaluate their performance, formulate changes and take action to improve practice (Fry & Ketteridge, 2007). The reflection process involved identifying aspects that worked well and those areas where future improvements could be made (Hounsell, 2007). To assist me in executing this process, Gibbs's (1988) stages of reflexive practice cycle was utilized, which involved the documentation of 'what had happened', 'how I felt', 'good and bad aspects of the experience', 'what can be learnt from the experience' and 'what could be done in similar situations'.

There are a number of methods and tools to assist with self-reflection of practice. Documentation of my experiences took the form of a weekly reflective log or journal that was summarized monthly. The very act of writing down these aspects enabled me to reflect on my practice further, in a 360-degree manner.

Publishing research was also extremely important to me, for the reasons stated in this chapter, and the doctorate qualification helped me to develop my knowledge and skills further. In addition, during the programme, both my supervisor and the programme team encouraged and fully supported me in writing up my research for conferences and journal publication. Thus, during the course of the doctorate, I presented my research findings at seven different conferences and published three papers in highly respected journals. From my perspective, I feel that this is an excellent route to take in considering a career as a health psychologist.

Where Next for Health Psychology?

I mentioned at the very beginning that during my degree I was unaware of the discipline of health psychology even though my research interests mirrored what health psychologists do. Many years have passed since then, and now as a practising health psychologist I can see how health psychology has grown and developed. However, it is still important to raise awareness of what health psychology is and what health psychologists do, and that it is a discipline in its own right. Students always ask me the pertinent question – 'Why is clinical training funded and not health?' Health psychology trainees are disadvantaged because they have to fund themselves (and, as I well know, this is not cheap), whereas clinical trainees are funded by the NHS. Thus, if this gap between the training provisions for clinical and health in the future were to be reduced, interest and awareness of this discipline would greatly increase.

Key Debates in Health Psychology

Raising Awareness of the Benefits of Health Psychology

From the very beginning of my health psychology journey, I felt that I have had to explain and justify what health psychology is and what health psychologists do. Through time this is now beginning to change, and health professionals and organizations are beginning to realize the importance of health psychology principles, practices and services. Raising awareness, then, becomes an important issue. Within academia I am able to raise awareness of this profession to the upcoming generation of psychologists. Regardless of whether they go into health psychology, they will graduate with an understanding and hopefully a realization of what health psychologists can offer and how the principles and practices can be implemented into their chosen psychology profession, whether that is clinical, forensic or even counselling.

Within health psychology training we develop and extend a number of key skills such as research, consultancy, teaching, professional and reflection skills, thus we need to promote these and be active in demonstrating how they can be applied. Importantly, we need to promote awareness to other health professionals; as Chwalisz (2008) states, human beings are complex and it is unlikely that a single theoretical or discipline approach can provide a direct panacea for a client's problems. Many health professionals are now faced with a greater prevalence of lifestyle problems from their clients that are either a cause or consequence of their illness or disability. This is where our specialist knowledge can complement other disciplines and demonstrate the need for health psychologists!

References

Al-Nakeeb, Y., Lyons, M., Duncan, M., Myers, T., Woodfield, L., Dodd, L., *et al.* (2004). Lifestyle, adiposity and cardiovascular disease risk factors of a higher education college community. Paper presented at the European College of Sport Science Conference, Clermont-Ferrand, France, 3–6 July.

American Cancer Society. (2006). Cancer facts & figures. Retrieved from http://www.cancer .org/downloads/STT/CAFF2006PWSecured.pdf

Bayley, J., Dodd. L., Newby, K., Wallace, L., & Brown, K. (2006). What shall we tell the children . . . about relationship and sex? Pilot evaluation of a theory-and-evidence based programme. Paper presented at the Division of Health Psychology Conference, University of Essex, 13–15 September.

British Psychological Society (BPS). (2006). Code of ethics. Retrieved from http://www.bps .org.uk/the-society/code-of-conduct/

Cancer Research UK. (2009). CancerStats key facts on skin cancer. Retrieved from http://info.cancerresearchuk.org/cancerstats/types/skin/

Chwalisz, K. (2008). The future of counseling psychology: improving quality of life for persons with chronic health issues. *The Counseling Psychologist, 36*, 98–106.

Dodd, L., Al-Nakeeb, Y., Nevill, A., & Forshaw, M. (2010). Lifestyle risk factors of students: a cluster analytical approach. *Preventive Medicine, 51*, 73–77.

Dodd, L., & Forshaw, M. (2010). Assessing the efficacy of appearance-focused interventions to prevent skin cancer: a systematic review of the literature. *Health Psychology Review, 4*, 93–111.

Dodd, L., & Holloway, A.M. (2009). Integrating online-delivered problem-based learning scenarios into a health psychology module: students' perceptions to online collaborating and learning. Paper presented at the the Higher Education Academy – Fourth International Blended Learning Conference, University of Hertfordshire, 17–18 June.

Duncan, M., Woodfield, L., Lyons, M., Dodd, L., & Al-Nakeeb, Y. (2005). Prevalence of overweight and obesity in British children from different ethnic groups. *Journal of Sports Sciences, 23*, February 1.

Duncan, M.J., Dodd, L., & AI-Nakeeb, Y. (2005). The impact of silhouette randomisation on the results of figure rating scales. *Measurement in Physical Education and Exercise Science, 9,* 61–66.

Fry, H., & Ketteridge, S. (2007). Teaching portfolios. In H. Fry, S. Ketteridge, & S. Marshall (Eds.), *A handbook for teaching & learning in higher education: enhancing academic practice.* London: RoutledgeFalmer.

Galper, D.I., Trivedi, M.H., Barlow, C.E., Dunn, A.L., & Kampert, J.B. (2006). Inverse associations between physical inactivity and mental health in men and women. *Medicine & Science in Sports & Exercise, 38,* 173–178.

Gibbs, G. (1988). *Learning by doing: a guide to teaching and learning methods.* Oxford: Oxford Further Education Unit, Oxford Polytechnic.

Hounsell, D. (2007). The evaluation of teaching. In H. Fry, S. Ketteridge, & S. Marshall (Eds.), *A handbook for teaching & learning in higher education: enhancing academic practice.* London: RoutledgeFalmer.

Kaptein, A., & Weinman, J. (2004). *Health psychology.* Oxford: Blackwell Publishing.

Michie, S. (2004). A framework for professional practice. In S. Michie & C. Abraham (Eds.), *Health psychology in practice.* Oxford: BPS Blackwell.

Mokdad, A.H., Marks, J.S., Stroup, D.F., & Gerberding, J.L. (2004). Actual causes of death in the United States, 2000. *Journal of the American Medical Association, 291,* 1238–1245.

Myers, T., Griggs, G., Al-Nakeeb, Y., Lyons, M., Duncan, M., Woodfield, L., *et al.* (2004). Lifestyle and health habits of a HE community. Paper presented at the European College of Sport Science Conference, Clermont-Ferrand, France, 3–6 July.

Office of Public Sector Information. (1998). Data protection 1998. Retrieved from http://www.opsi.gov.uk/acts/acts1998/ukpga_19980029_en_1

Ogden, J. (2007). *Health psychology: a textbook.* Buckingham: Open University Press.

Steptoe, A., & Wardle, J. (2001). Health behaviour, risk awareness and emotional well-being in students from Eastern Europe and Western Europe. *Social Science & Medicine, 53,* 1621–1630.

Steptoe, A., Wardle, J., Cui, W., Bellisle, F., Zotti, A., Baranyai, R., *et al.* (2002). Trends in smoking, diet, physical exercise, and attitudes towards health in European university students from 13 countries, 1990–2000. *Preventive Medicine, 35,* 97–104.

World Health Organization (WHO). (2002). *The World Health Report: reducing risks, promoting healthy life.* Geneva: WHO.

World Health Organization (WHO). (2003). *Diet, nutrition and the prevention of chronic diseases.* Geneva: WHO.

World Health Organization (WHO). (2009). How common is skin cancer. Retrieved from http://www.who.int/uv/faq/skincancer/en/index1.html

Glossary

nonmelanoma and malignant melanoma: types of skin cancer.

ultraviolet (UV) radiation exposure: nonvisible radiation emitted from the sun and other sources (e.g. artificial tanning devices).

7

Shared Decision Making

Darren Flynn

Introduction

My interest in the field of shared decision making (SDM) was ignited in 2003 when I, with colleagues, published a book (Flynn, van Schaik, van Wersch, Douglass & Cann, 2003) that reviewed the literature on the impact of non-medical factors on medical decision making. We identified a wealth of studies that reported evidence of statistically significant variability in medical and surgical decision making as a function of nonmedical factors such as characteristics of patients (e.g. gender and presentational style), clinicians (e.g. age and extent of clinical experience) and the health care context (e.g. access to specialist services). In the final chapter we extolled the potential of SDM for reducing unwarranted variation in rates of medical and surgical procedures. SDM incorporates multiple domains such as patient education, risk communication, clinician–patient communication and behaviour change. This multidisciplinary character of SDM captured my imagination, and was instrumental in my decision to join a leading academic decision centre in the United Kingdom – Newcastle University's Decision Making and Organisation of Care Group led by Professor Richard Thomson. My current role has provided unique and exciting opportunities to amalgamate my interests in multiple areas (patient education, behaviour change and medical decision making) covering the entire sphere of influence in health psychology (i.e. application of psychological theory and methods to management of health problems, health promotion, psychological factors associated with illness and quality improvement in both health care practice and policy; Division of Health Psychology, 2011).

It is hoped that this chapter will stimulate further interest and research from both academic and practitioner health psychologists, including trainees in this

Health Psychology in Action, First Edition. Edited by Mark Forshaw and David Sheffield.
© 2013 John Wiley & Sons, Ltd. Published 2013 by John Wiley & Sons, Ltd.

increasingly important concept in health care. The chapter will begin with a description of SDM, followed by an overview of the key concepts and processes (a
comprehensive review is beyond the scope of this chapter). It will conclude with a
discussion of areas that have been neglected in the literature on SDM, which in my
view would be fruitful avenues of research for health psychology.

What Is Shared Decision Making?

SDM is located at the intersection of paternalistic decision making (clinicians using
their expertise to make decisions for patients without considering their preferences
or values) and informed decision making, whereby clinicians convey relevant information to patients who then take responsibility for decision making based on
their preferences and values (Say *et al.*, 2006). There is a lack of consensus on an
all-encompassing definition of this increasingly important component of health
care – referred to variously as informed (shared) decision making, concordance and
evidence-based patient choice (Coulter & Ellins, 2006). Notwithstanding the importance of this debate, a commonly used definition of SDM is 'decisions that are shared
by doctor and patient and informed by best evidence, about not only risks and benefits but also patient-specific characteristics and values' (Towle & Godolphin, 1999,
p. 766). In this regard, SDM is congruent with principles of patient-centred care and
requires two kinds of expertise: (1) clinicians' knowledge of efficacy and outcomes
of treatment options, and (2) patients' expertise on their values and preferences with
regard to the available treatment options (Coulter, 2009).

   SDM has potential to deliver more equitable use of health care interventions with
demonstrable benefit, as well as reducing superfluous variation in health care (Légaré
et al., 2010; Mulley, 2009). It is increasingly recognized by policy makers that patients
should be both informed and actively involved in decision making about their care
(Coulter & Ellins, 2006). SDM is part of The Health Reform Bill (HR 3590) in the
United States, and the recent White Paper published by the UK Coalition Government 'Equity and Excellence: Liberating the NHS' states that SDM should become
standard practice with 'no decision about me without me' (Department of Health,
2010, p. 13). Combined with concomitant initiatives in the United Kingdom (e.g.
NHS Choices), SDM is poised to be at the nucleus of health care for the foreseeable
future. However, without guidance from research to support the implementation of
SDM in routine clinical practice, the transition to this model of health care will be
seriously compromised. In my view the 'core business areas' of health psychology
should be recognized as a valued resource to fill the void in our understanding and
expedite progress in this field. Hopefully, the following sections of this chapter will
serve to convince the reader that this is indeed the case.

When Is SDM Appropriate?

SDM is a well-researched field in medicine for preference-sensitive health care decisions, in other words, when there is more than one reasonable treatment option

and where the optimal 'treatment choice' is a function of a patient's preferences and values with regard to the likely balance of benefits and risks associated with the options (Charles *et al.*, 1997; Sepucha *et al.*, 2004).

A quintessential preference-sensitive decision is the treatment of prostate cancer. Treatment options for this condition include surgery, hormone therapy, radiotherapy, chemotherapy and surveillance (or watchful waiting). All of these options involve 'trade-offs' between benefits and risks in the short and long term. For example, radical prostatectomy is irrevocable and outcome probabilities for benefits and adverse effects (risks) associated with this (and other) treatments are not clear with large differences in frequency, duration and severity reported in the literature (Flynn, van Schaik, van Wersch, Ahmed & Chadwick, 2004). Importantly, there is still no unequivocal evidence to support one treatment option over another (Holmberg *et al.*, 2002). Therefore, according to the SDM model the optimal choice of treatment (including doing nothing) is guided by the patient's preferences and values.

Patient Preferences for Involvement in Decision Making

Research evidence indicates that patients desire (to some extent) involvement in decisions about their care, although clinicians frequently make incorrect assumptions about their patients' preferences for involvement in decision making (Strull *et al.*, 1984; Towle & Godolphin, 1999).

Tools are available to assess the preferred treatment decision-making role of patients such as the Control Preference Scale (CPS) developed by Degner and Sloan (1992). This scale can be used to categorize preferences as autonomous, collaborative or passive. With colleagues, I conducted a formative evaluation of a computerized patient education programme for men recently diagnosed with prostate cancer using the CPS, and found that at the pre- and post-trial study conditions, 68% and 71% respectively of participants (mean age = 67 years) preferred an active or collaborative role in treatment decisions (Flynn *et al.*, 2004). Similarly, in a cross-sectional survey of 73 adults with idiopathic scoliosis (86% female, mean age 42 years) we identified that a majority reported a preference for a collaborative (42%) or autonomous (38%) role in treatment decision making (Flynn *et al.*, 2006).

Patients' preferences for involvement in treatment decision making is influenced by a variety of patient characteristics (e.g. demographics, experience of illness and medical care, attitude towards involvement, and the interactions and relationships they experience with health care professionals) that are likely to develop over time and alter across the illness trajectory (Deber *et al.*, 2007; Say *et al.*, 2006). We also found evidence of the influence of patient characteristics on preferred treatment decision-making role in our studies of men with prostate cancer and people with idiopathic scoliosis. The former were more likely to report an active role in decision making if they were married, whereas for the latter group, higher perceived condition-specific knowledge was associated with preferences for an active role in decision making.

It is also important to note that patient 'preferences' in the context of SDM also refers to preferences for information, as even in cases where people do not wish to be involved in decision making they may still desire information in order to understand why a specific decision was made (Strull *et al.*, 1984). Information exchange plays an integral role in SDM as it enables patients and family members to understand their condition and likely prognosis; understand the process and potential outcomes of treatment options; provides a sense of control and reduces anxiety – all of which can facilitate participation in decision making (Coulter *et al.*, 1999; Flynn *et al.*, 2004).

Eliciting a person's preferences for information and engagement in decision making is a crucial process in SDM model of health care. However, we should be mindful that patients can still decide to take a passive role in decision making. Otherwise, ironically we are impeding choice, and this could potentially lead to labelling patients who do wish to engage in SDM as 'resistant to engagement' resulting in negative consequences congruent with those reported in the behaviour change literature.

Risk Communication

Risk communication involves conveying probabilistic information on the possible outcome states of treatment options for a health condition in terms of the positive (benefits) and adverse (risks) effects. SDM will be seriously compromised without effective methods of presenting probabilistic information on the benefits and risks of diagnostic tests and medical and surgical treatments (often referred to as 'outcome probabilities') that augments interpretation and understanding by patients and clinicians.

Methods for conveying information on outcome probabilities are variable and can have a differential impact on perceptions of risk and decision making in both clinicians and patients (e.g. Carling *et al.*, 2009; Covey, 2007; Hoffrage *et al.*, 2000). As an illustrative example, let us imagine that a new drug has been developed and the following event rates for mortality from a randomized controlled trial are reported:

- Control group = 0.15/15%
- Experimental group = 0.10/10%

Three commonly used measures of treatment effect are:

1. Absolute risk reduction (ARR) = event rate in the control/comparison group minus event rate in the experimental group = 0.15 − 0.10 = 0.05 (5%). The absolute benefit of the new drug is a 5% reduction in mortality.
2. Relative risk reduction (RRR) = Absolute risk reduction divided by the event rate in the control group = 0.05 / 0.15 = 0.33 (33%). The relative benefit of the new drug is a 33% reduction in mortality.
3. Number needed to treat (NNT, the number of patients who would have to receive the treatment for 1 to benefit) = 1 divided by the ARR = 1 / 0.05 (or 100 / 5) = 20. For every 20 people treated with the new drug, one death will be prevented.

At this point we must consider the methods available to communicate the outcome probabilities for mortality. Broadly speaking we could use textual (verbal descriptors such as 'very low risk', 'low risk', 'medium risk' or 'high risk'), numerical (e.g. percentages for RRR and ARR or NNT), graphical (e.g. bar graphs, pictograms or pictographs) or a combination of numerical, textual and graphical methods.

Verbal descriptors such as 'very low risk' or 'rare' could be used, but this type of 'elastic language' has been heavily criticized as it can be used 'variably and inconsistently depending upon the context of the risk being described' (Thomson *et al.*, 2005, p. 466).

In terms of numerical methods we should use ARR, as RRR leads to misunderstanding and overestimation of the treatment effect and increased likelihood of selecting an intervention (e.g. Moxey *et al.*, 2003). Nevertheless, presenting ARR using percentages (as well as RRR and NNT) does not make the baseline risk explicit that could lead to misunderstanding (O'Connor *et al.*, 2005). Gigerenzer (2002) proposes that understanding is maximized when event rates for outcomes are presented as 'natural frequencies' (that include base rate information). For example, *out of 100 people who take the new drug, 5 of them are likely to die.*

In addition, it is considered good practice (O'Connor *et al.*, 2005) to refer to a specific group of people (reference class; e.g. 'patients with condition X' who are treated with our drug) and time frames for the outcome probabilities (for both treatment with and without our new drug) using consistent dominators (e.g. out of 100, as opposed to a mixture of out of 100 and out of 20); for example:

- Out of 100 people with condition X treated with the new drug, 10 out of 100 are likely to be dead after 1 year
- Out of 100 people with condition X who do not receive the new drug, 15 out of 100 people are likely to be dead after 1 year

It is also important to communicate uncertainty by preceding the above statements with phrases such as 'our best guess is that . . .' as well as addressing 'stochastic' uncertainty (O'Connor *et al.*, 2005) – 'Out of 100 people with condition X treated with the new drug, 10 out 100 are likely to be dead after 1 year; *but we do* not *know which out of these 10 who receive the new drug will die*'.

We also need to be mindful of 'framing effects' (Tversky & Kahneman, 1981) where people make different choices in logically equivalent choice situations that are presented in different ways such as relative versus absolute risk (Wilson *et al.*, 1988), including probability of survival, or benefits (positive framing), versus death, or adverse effects (negative framing). Using our new drug as an example, the outcome probabilities could be framed negatively (out of 100 people with condition X treated with the new drug, 10 out of 100 are likely to be dead after 1 year) or positively (out of 100 people with condition X treated with the new drug, 90 out of 100 are likely to be alive after 1 year). However, to eliminate this type of framing effect it is considered good practice to present both positively and negatively framed information (O'Connor *et al.*, 2005).

Graphical methods (e.g. bar graphs, pictograms and flowchart diagrams) can be particularly useful for (1) enhancing comprehension of complex probabilistic information by activating peoples' automatic visual perceptual capabilities, and (2) facilitating the communication of uncertainty, clarifying personal values with regard to outcomes states and minimizing framing effects (Gadhia *et al.*, 2010; O'Connor *et al.*, 2005).

Good risk communication as described here is easier said than done! Medical science is often viewed through a lens of certainty, and Gigerenzer (2002) in his excellent book *Reckoning with Risk* reminds us of Franklin's Law – 'there is nothing certain, but death and taxes' as a mind tool for dispelling the 'illusion of certainty' in health care contexts. Furthermore, Gigerenzer and colleagues (Gigerenzer *et al.*, 2008) highlight how framing manipulations are used both intentionally (as a marketing tool) and unintentionally (due to poor statistical literacy), and asserts this has serious health consequences. Gigerenzer's view (and I agree) is that we should teach statistical thinking and transparent representations of outcome probabilities to school children (and to clinicians in universities). Personally, the rationale for these interventions is clear. The question is how best can we address this overlooked, but important 'health protective mechanism'? Health psychology could make a valuable contribution to influencing policy and the development and testing of theory-based interventions targeting statistical literacy and communication of probabilistic information to the public.

Competencies of Health Care Professionals and Patients for Shared Decision Making

Frameworks have been published that describe the range of clinical competencies (knowledge and skills) to facilitate engagement of patients in SDM. For example, Towle and Godolphin (1999) describe the following competencies for clinicians for SDM: developing partnerships with patients, ascertaining patients' preferences for information and engagement in decision making, risk communication, negotiating decisions in collaboration with patients and agreeing on a plan of action.

Towle and Godolphin (1999) also recognize that specific competencies are required of patients (that invariably would also apply to family members) for SDM such as developing and engaging in partnerships with clinicians; coherently communicating their health problems, beliefs, feelings and expectations to clinicians during consultations; identifying and critically evaluating health information and negotiating decisions in collaboration with clinicians.

The breadth of knowledge and skills (and confidence) required for SDM from clinicians and patients always strikes me as quite remarkable. Absence of these competencies in clinicians and/or patients will invariably incapacitate SDM, which is reflected in findings that 'good' SDM takes place only 10% of the time (Godolphin, 2009). Consequently, SDM interventions have been developed to support key processes such as information exchange, eliciting patients' preferences and values, and risk communication (Coulter & Ellins, 2006).

SDM Interventions

Interventions have been designed to support engagement of patients in decision making with health care professionals (variously referred to as patient decision aids, decision support technologies or interventions). 'Decision aids differ from usual health education materials because of their detailed, specific, and personalised focus on options and outcomes for the purpose of preparing people for decision making' (O'Connor *et al.*, 2009, p. 3).

The number of paper-based, DVD and electronic (online) decision support interventions (DSIs) is growing and a regularly updated repository is available on the Ottawa Hospital Research Institute website (http://decisionaid.ohri.ca/AZlist.html). DSIs have been reported to impact positively on a range of outcomes such as patients' knowledge, perception of risk, decisional conflict (psychological uncertainty related to feeling uninformed) and clarity about their personal preferences (O'Connor *et al.*, 2009). Several authors propose that the most important outcome of SDM is 'decision quality' expressed as a function of condition-specific knowledge and the extent that treatment choice is congruent with patients' preferences and values (Sepucha *et al.*, 2004, 2007).

However, given the lack of promotional activity many people are likely to be unaware of the rationale for, and potential benefits of, engaging in SDM. There are a multitude of important health messages in our society such as avoidance and cessation of tobacco, engagement in physical activity, wearing sunscreen and minimizing intake of high-fat food to name but a few. In my view a mass media campaign involving TV advertisements, radio and printed media extolling the merits of SDM as mechanism for improving quality of health care decisions (and other outcomes) is warranted – without a wide and sustained proliferation of this message, SDM could be a benefit enjoyed by the few instead of the many.

How Can Health Psychology Contribute to the Agenda for Patient Choice and SDM?

If the vision of the United Kingdom's recent White Paper *No Decision about Me without Me* is to become a reality, investment in research and development is vital. What follows are four areas that I would particularly like to draw to the attention of health psychologists. They have been neglected in the literature on SDM, and in my view they would be fruitful areas of research enquiry, as well as teaching and consultancy activity for health psychologists.

Interventions for Enhancing the Willingness and Capacity of Clinicians, Patients and Family Members to Engage in SDM

The three most commonly reported barriers to SDM are time constraints, lack of applicability connected with patient characteristics and the clinical situation;

conversely, the most commonly reported facilitators are motivation of service providers, and beliefs that SDM can have a positive impact on the clinical process and patient outcomes (Gravel *et al.*, 2006). Therefore, as these authors conclude, interventions to facilitate SDM in practice need to be multifaceted and target a range of factors. Developing quality decision aids is important, but this is not enough for 'effective SDM'.

It is my considered view that clinicians as well as 'buying in' to the process of SDM also need to develop and refine competencies for SDM. Indeed 'can a well-designed decision aid, knowledge of a patient's numeracy, or presentation of data in a suitable format really make a difference if the clinician does not listen or does not make the patient feel comfortable asking questions or expressing reservations?' (Helfand, 2007, p. 516). I would go further – 'Can a decision aid be a useful adjunct to the clinical process if patients lack awareness of the value of SDM; and perhaps crucially do not have the experience, knowledge, skills and/or confidence to engage meaningfully in discussions with clinicians about their health care?'

A paucity of attention has been devoted to developing and testing theory-based interventions for 'enhancing' the capacity (development of competencies for SDM) and/or willingness (motivation and intentions) of clinicians and patients who report preferences for *paternalistic approaches* and a *passive role* in decision making, respectively. With regard to patients and family members they may lack the range of competencies required to engage in the process of SDM and/or may also *not* consider engagement in decision making as beneficial for health. These conditions may also be true for many clinicians, and with respect to both groups it could be argued that a change in behaviour is required to engage in the process of SDM and augment the effectiveness of DSIs.

Conceptualizing competencies for SDM as 'behaviour' opens the door to health psychology, as it permits the development and evaluation of interventions that target potentially modifiable variables that are antecedents of behavioural intentions and actual behaviour such as knowledge, beliefs, attitudes and self-efficacy.

The Development, Implementation and Evaluation of Theory-Based DSIs

Frameworks are available to guide the development and evaluation of DSIs such as criteria developed by the International Patient Decision Aids Standards (IPDAS) Collaboration (Elwyn *et al.*, 2006) and more recently IPDASi (Elwyn *et al.*, 2009). However, a review of DSIs identified that the majority are developed without theoretical foundations (Durand *et al.*, 2008). This has important implications as 'advancing behavioural science requires a good understanding of how interventions are informed by, and test, theory' (Michie & Prestwich, 2010, p. 1). In this regard, the wealth of health psychology theory relevant to SDM, in particular behavioural change theory, has untapped potential for informing the design, evaluation and implementation of DSIs in routine health care practice. Health psychologists take note!

SDM in Mental Health Settings

Despite policy recommendations and recognition that involvement of patients with mental health conditions is consistent with building therapeutic alliances (Deegan & Drake, 2006), research has found that SDM in mental health contexts is largely restricted to information exchange (e.g. Goosensen *et al.*, 2007; Loh *et al.*, 2006; Patel *et al.*, 2008). Consequently, opportunities to support empowerment and autonomy of patients are being overlooked, and the development of effective SDM interventions could have tangible benefits in terms of assisting a patient's journey towards recovery (Deegan & Drake, 2006; Patel *et al.*, 2008).

Patients diagnosed with mental health disorders, including those with severe mental illness, desire information on their condition and are both *capable* and *willing* to be involved in decision making (e.g. Adams *et al.*, 2007). However, research on SDM interventions in mental health contexts is sparse (Duncan *et al.*, 2010). Elucidating a framework of clinical competencies and development of theory-based DSIs to support engagement of mental health populations in SDM have been neglected in the literature, including the development of reliable and valid process and outcome measures (Simon *et al.*, 2009; Wills & Holmes-Rovner, 2006).

I found this lack of attention in the literature on SDM surprising. In the great majority of mental health disorders there are real choices between alternative therapies that are sensitive to patients' preferences and values in many ways (Deegan & Drake, 2006; Hamann *et al.*, 2006). There are different balances of risks and benefits of psychotropic medication (e.g. Benzodiazepines can help reduce anxiety, but there is a trade-off with the risk of side effects such as drowsiness and memory problems) and varying individual preferences for different medical or psychological interventions (e.g. Lang, 2005). Also, let's not forget Franklin's Law – the outcome of none of these management options is certain!

SDM in Emergency Contexts: The Example of Treatment in Acute Stroke

This section is based on my current research post at Newcastle University. Acute ischaemic stroke (AIS) is caused by a sudden blockage in an artery that supplies blood to the brain (Wolfe & Rudd, 2007). Thrombolysis with intravenously administered recombinant tissue plasminogen activator (rt-PA) has improved the prognosis for AIS (reduced disability after a stroke), but this treatment must be given within 4.5 hours from the onset of stroke symptoms (Hacke *et al.*, 2008). Therefore, protracted discussions about treatment options are not appropriate in acute stroke care, because for every 1 minute that treatment is delayed approximately 2 million more brain cells die (Gadhia *et al.*, 2010; Saver, 2006) – hence the aphorism 'Time is brain'.

It could be argued that due to the extreme time-limited 'emergency context' of acute stroke (and that many patients lack capacity due to their stroke), communicating information on outcome probabilities and engaging patients (and family members) in thrombolytic treatment decision-making discussions is not feasible or appropriate. However, informed consent must be sought when patients are deemed to have capacity, and engaging patients (where appropriate, such as those with 'mild strokes') and family members in treatment decisions is ethically and morally justi-fiable as (1) the evidence for rt-PA is contentious, (2) treatment decision making involves trade-offs between disability and death, (3) there is risk of intracranial haemorrhage (bleeding in the brain that can cause death or severe disability) asso-ciated with rt-PA and (4) outcome probabilities are likely to differ as function of patient characteristics (Ciccone, 2003; Lees *et al.*, 2008; Lou *et al.*, 2008; Flynn *et al.*, 2011; Wardlaw *et al.*, 2009).

A dearth of work has investigated optimal methods of presenting information on outcome probabilities and appropriate engagement of patients and family mem-bers in decision making in emergency care settings. Given this context 'traditional' SDM interventions and approaches that have developed and tested for use in non-emergency settings (described earlier in this chapter) are inappropriate.

With colleagues at Newcastle University, I am currently involved in the develop-ment of a DSI for thrombolytic treatment in acute stroke care, which is part of a larger programme of research – DASH (Developing and Assessing Services for Hyperacute stroke: http://www.ncl.ac.uk/ihs/research/project/2565). We conducted a review of DSIs in thrombolytic treatment for acute stroke to establish current knowledge in this area (Flynn *et al.*, 2010). This review (along with other development work such as exploratory interviews) was used to inform the design of prototype tools to support eligibility decision making on rt-PA and risk communication. We presented these prototypes to clinicians, patients and family members within interactive workshops to explore their preferences on their form and content (and perceived utility during the hyper-acute period of stroke). My experience of working on DASH has further demonstrated the value of meaningfully involving patients and family members (as well as clinicians) in the iterative design and testing of health care interventions. The rewards of user-centred design are great, although be prepared to invest considerable time, resources and planning to this important endeavour. Also, strive to keep an open mind, and perhaps above all respond with enthusiasm if the direction of the research takes you down unanticipated and unexplored avenues!

Conclusion

Uncertainty is ubiquitous in health care, and for many health conditions the optimal choice of treatment is a function of patients' preferences and values. In the context of SDM, a 'good decision' is one where a patient is well-informed about their condition and with support from a clinician(s) makes a decision and receives treatment that is consistent with their preferences and values (Sepucha *et al.*, 2004, 2007).

SDM requires a range of competencies from both clinicians and patients. DSIs are available for a variety of conditions to support key processes of SDM in health care consultations. Nevertheless, barriers to SDM in routine clinical practice remain, and in my view key facilitators would be the development of (1) theory-based inter-ventions targeting the capacity and willingness of patients and clinicians to engage in SDM, and (2) development and testing of DSIs informed by health psychology theory and research. Furthermore, our understanding of SDM in mental health and emergency settings is still in its infancy, and more research is urgently needed in these contexts.

SDM is poised to be a prominent tile in the mosaic of contemporary health care, and in my view health psychology is well-positioned to support the agenda for patient choice. I hope this chapter has served as a 'call to arms' for researchers, practitioners, teachers of health psychology and trainee health psychologists to become actively involved in this increasingly important multidisciplinary field in health care.

Key Debates in Health Psychology

Graphical risk presentations (alongside verbal explanations by clinicians) are purported to be particularly useful for conveying information on outcome probabilities for treatment options. Nevertheless, there is no definitive evidence to guide the optimal choice of graphical method for a specific index decision. Below are a series of research questions informed by literature reviews (e.g. Ancker *et al.*, 2006; Lipkus, 2007; O'Connor *et al.*, 2005) and primary research articles (e.g. Dolan & Iadarola, 2008; Hawley *et al.*, 2008; Schapira *et al.*, 2006) that I would like to encourage health psychologists to explore:

- What are the optimal form and content of graphical risk presentations for specific index conditions? In particular, are the magnitudes of outcome probabilities important? For example, risks $\leq$ 1 in 1000 associated with many medical and surgical procedures, which in many cases may have irreversible effects and impact severely on quality of life (or even lead to death).
- What patient characteristics are associated with understanding of different graphical risk presentations?
- How do different graphical risk presentations impact on perceived favourability of treatment options for specific health care conditions?
- Does the 'personalization' of outcome probabilities using techniques such as statistical modelling lead to more 'effective' SDM than 'aggregate-level' risk and benefit information?

References

Adams, J.R., Drake, R.E., & Wolford, G.L. (2007). Shared decision-making preferences of people with severe mental illness. *Psychiatric Services, 58*, 1219–1221.

Ancker, J.S., Senathirajah, Y., Kukafka, R., & Starren, J.B. (2006). Design features of graphs in health risk communication: a systematic review. *Journal of the American Medical Informatics Association, 13*, 608–618.

Carling, C.L.L., Kristoffersen, D.T., Montori, V.M., Herrin, J., Schunemann, H.J., Treweek, S., Akl, A.E., & Oxman, A.D. (2009). The effect of alternative summary statistics for communicating risk reduction on decisions about taking statins: a randomized trial. *PLoS Med*, 6(8), e1000134.

Charles, C., Gafni, A., & Whelan, T. (1997). Shared decision-making in the medical encounter: what does it mean? (Or it takes at least two to tango). *Social Science and Medicine*, 44(5), 681–692.

Ciccone, A. (2003). Consent to thrombolysis in acute ischaemic stroke: from trial to practice. *The Lancet Neurology*, 2(6), 375–378.

Coulter, A. (2009). *Implementing shared decision making in the UK: a report for the Health Foundation.* London: Health Foundation.

Coulter, A., & Ellins, J. (2006). *Patient-focussed interventions: a review of the evidence.* London: Health Foundation.

Coulter, A., Entwistle, V., & Gilbert, D. (1999). Sharing decisions with patients: is the information good enough? *British Medical Journal*, 318, 318–322.

Covey, J. (2007). A meta-analysis of the effects of presenting treatment benefits in different formats. *Medical Decision Making*, 27, 638–654.

Deber, R., Kraetschmer, N., Urowitz, S., & Sharpe, N. (2007). Do people want to be autonomous patients? Preferred roles in treatment decision-making in several patient populations. *Health Expectations*, 10, 248–258.

Deegan, P.E., & Drake, R.E. (2006). Shared decision making and medication management in the recovery process. *Psychiatric Services*, 57, 1636–1639.

Degner, L.F., & Sloan, J.A. (1992). Decision-making during serious illness: what role do patients really want to play? *Journal of Clinical Epidemiology*, 45, 941–950.

Department of Health. (2010). *Equity and excellence: liberating the NHS.* London: The Stationery Office.

Division of Health Psychology, British Psychological Society. (2011). What is health psychology? Retrieved from http://www.health-psychology.org.uk/dhp_home.cfm

Dolan, J.G., & Iadarola, S. (2008). Risk communication formats for low probability events: an exploratory study of patient preferences *BMC Medical Informatics and Decision Making*, 8, 14.

Duncan, E., Best, C., & Hagen, S. (2010). Shared decision making interventions for people with mental health conditions. *Cochrane Database of Systematic Reviews*, Issue 1, Art. No. CD007297. doi:10.1002/14651858.CD007297.pub2

Durand, M.A., Stiel, M., Boivin, J., & Elwyn, G. (2008). Where is the theory? Evaluating the theoretical frameworks described in decision support technologies. *Patient Education and Counselling*, 71, 125–135.

Elwyn, G., O'Connor, A., Stacey, D., Volk, R., Edwards, A., & Coulter, A. (2006). Developing a quality criteria framework for patient decision aids: online international Delphi consensus process. *British Medical Journal*, 333, 417–419.

Elwyn, G., O'Connor, A.M., Bennett, C., Newcombe, R.G., Politi, M., Durand, M., Drake, E., Joseph-Williams, N., Khangura, S., Saarimaki, A., Sivell, S., Stiel, M., Bernstein, S.J., Col, N., Coulter, A., Eden, K., Härter, M., Holmes Rovner, M., Moumjid, N., Stacey, D., Thomson, R., Whelan, T., van der Weijden, T., & Edwards, A. (2009). *Assessing the quality of decision support technologies using the International Patient Decision Aid Standards instrument (IPDASi).* PLoS ONE, 4(3), e4705. doi:10.1371/journal.pone.0004705

Flynn, D., van Schaik, P., van Wersch, A., Douglass, A., & Cann, P. (2003). *Non-medical influences upon medical decision-making and referral behaviour.* Westport, CT: Praeger.

Flynn, D., van Schaik, P., van Wersch, A., Ahmed, T., & Chadwick, D. (2004). The utility of a multimedia education program for prostate cancer patients: a formative evaluation. *The British Journal of Cancer, 91*(5), 855–860.

Flynn, D., van Wersch, A., van Schaik, P., Ferguson, V., & Papastefanou, S. (2006). The design of information material for people with scoliosis. *Journal of Bone and Joint Surgery, 88-B,* 225.

Flynn, D., Murtagh, M., Stobbart, L., Ford, G.A., & Thomson, R.G. (2010). *A review of decision support and risk communication in thrombolytic treatment for acute stroke.* EACH 2010 conference, 5–8 September, Verona, Italy.

Flynn, D., McMeekin, P., Ford, G.A., Rodgers, H., & Thomson, R.G. (2011). Development of a decision analytic model (DAM) to support decision-making and risk communication for thrombolytic treatment in acute stroke care. *Cerebrovascular Diseases, 31*(2), 34.

Gadhia, J., Starkman, S., Ovbiagele, B., Ali, L., Liebeskind, D., & Saver, J.L. (2010). Assessment and improvement of figures to visually convey benefit and risk of stroke thrombolysis. *Stroke, 41*, 300–306.

Gigerenzer, G. (2002). *Reckoning with risk.* London: Penguin.

Gigerenzer, G., Gaissmaier, W., Kurz-Milcke, E., Schwartz, L.M., & Woloshin, S. (2008). Helping doctors and patients make sense of health statistics. *Psychological Science in the Public Interest, 8*(2), 53–96.

Godolphin, W. (2009). Shared decision making. *Healthcare Quality, 12*, e186–e190.

Goosensen, A., Zijlstra, P., & Koopmanschap, M. (2007). Measuring shared decision making processes in psychiatry: skills versus patient satisfaction. *Patient Education and Counselling, 67*, 50–56.

Gravel, K., Legare, F., & Graham, I. (2006). Barriers and facilitators to implementing shared decision-making in clinical practice: a systematic review of health professionals' perceptions. *Implementation Science, 1*, 16. Retrieved from http://www.implementationscience.com/content/1/1/16

Hacke, W., Kaste, M., Bluhmki, E., Brozman, M., Davalos, A. Guidetti, D., Larrue, V., Lees, K.R., Medeghri, Z., Machnig, T., Schneider, D., von Kummer, R., Wahlgren, N., & Toni, D. (2008). Thrombolysis with alteplase 3 to 4.5 hours after acute ischemic stroke. *New England Journal of Medicine, 359*, 1317–1329.

Hamann, J., Langer, B., Winkler, V., Busch, R., Cohen, R., Leucht, S., & Kissling, W. (2006). Shared decision-making for in-patients with schizophrenia. *Acta Psychiatrica Scandinavica, 11*, 265–273.

Hawley, S.T., Zikmund-Fisher, B., Ubel, P., Jancovic, A., Lucas, T., & Fagerlin, A. (2008). The impact of the format of graphical presentation on health-related knowledge and treatment choices. *Patient Education and Counseling, 73*, 448–455.

Helfand, M. (2007). Shared decision making, decision aids, and risk communication. *Medical Decision Making, 27*, 516.

Hoffrage, U., Lindsey, S., Hertwig, R., & Gigerenzer, G. (2000). Medicine: communicating statistical information. *Science, 290*, 2261–2262.

Holmberg, L., Bill-Axelson, A., Helgesen, F., Salo, J.O., Folmerz, P., Haggman, M., Andersson, S.O., Spangberg, A., Busch, C., Nordling, S., Palmgren, J., Adami, H.O., Johansson, J.E., & Norlen, B.J. (2002). A randomized trial comparing radical prostatectomy with watchful waiting in early prostate cancer. *New England Journal of Medicine, 347*, 781–789.

Lang, A.J. (2005). Mental health treatment preferences of primary care patients. *Journal of Behavioral Medicine, 28*(6), 581–586.

Lees, K.R., Ford, G.A, Muir, K.W., Ahmed, N., Dyker, A.G., Atula, S., Kalra, L., Warburton, E.A., Baron, J-C., Jenkinson, D.F., Wahlgren, N.G., & Walters, M.R. (2008). Thrombolytic therapy for acute stroke in the United Kingdom: experience from the safe implementation of thrombolysis in stroke (SITS) register. *Quarterly Journal of Medicine*, *101*, 863–869.

Légaré, F., Ratté, S., Stacey, D., Kryworuchko, J., Gravel, K., Graham, I.D., & Turcotte, S. (2010). Interventions for improving the adoption of shared decision making by healthcare professionals. *Cochrane Database of Systematic Reviews*, Issue 5, Art. No. CD006732.

Lipkus, I.M. (2007). Numeric, verbal, and visual formats of conveying health risks: suggested best practices and future recommendations. *Medical Decision Making*, *27*(5), 696–713.

Loh, A., Simon, D., Henning, K., Hennig, B., Harter, M., & Elwyn, G. (2006). The assessment of depressive patients' involvement in decision making in audio-taped primary care consultations. *Patient Education and Counselling*, *63*, 314–318.

Lou, M., Safdar, A., Mehdiratta, M., Kumar, S., Schlaug, G., Caplan, L., Searls, D., & Selim, M. (2008). The HAT Score: a simple grading scale for predicting hemorrhage after thrombolysis. *Neurology*, *71*, 1417–1423.

Michie, S., & Prestwich, A. (2010). Are interventions theory-based? Development of a theory coding scheme. *Health Psychology*, *29*(1), 1–8.

Moxey, A., Dip, G., O'Connell, D., & McGettigan, P. (2003). Describing treatment effects to patients: how they are expressed makes a difference. *Journal of General Internal Medicine*, *18*, 948–995.

Mulley, A.G. (2009). The need to confront variation in practice. *British Medical Journal*, *339*, 1007–1009.

O'Connor, A., Llewellyn-Thomas, H., & Stacey, D. (2005). *IPDAS Collaboration Background Document*. Retrieved from http://ipdas.ohri.ca/resources.html

O'Connor, A.M., Bennett, C.L., Stacey, D., Barry, M., Col, N.F., Eden, K.B., Entwistle, V.A., Fiset, V., Holmes-Rovner, M., Khangura, S., Llewellyn-Thomas, H., & Rovner, D. (2009). Decision aids for people facing health treatment or screening decisions. *Cochrane Database of Systematic Reviews*, Issue 2, Art. No. CD001431.

Patel, S.R., Bakken, S., & Ruland, C. (2008). Recent advances in shared decision making for mental health. *Current Opinion in Psychiatry*, *21*(6), 606–612.

Say, S., Murtagh, M., & Thomson, R. (2006). Patients' preference for involvement in medical decision making: a narrative review. *Patient Education and Counseling*, *60*, 102–114.

Saver, J.L. (2006). Time is brain – quantified. *Stroke*, *37*, 263–266.

Schapira, M.M., Nattinger, A.B., & MCauliffe, T.L. (2006). The influence of graphic format on breast cancer risk communication. *Journal of Health Communication*, *11*, 569–582.

Sepucha, K.R., Fowler, F.J., & Mulley, A.G. (2004). Policy support for patient-centered care: the need for measurable improvements in decision quality. *Health Affairs* (Suppl.), VAR 54–62.

Sepucha, K.R., Ozanne, E., Silvia, K., Partridgem, A., & Mulley, A.G. (2007). An approach to measuring the quality of breast cancer decisions. *Patient Education and Counseling*, *65*, 261–269.

Simon, D., Wills, C.E., & Harter, M. (2009). Shared decision-making in mental health. In A. Edwards & G. Elwyn (Eds.), *Shared decision-making in healthcare* (2nd ed., pp. 269–276). Oxford: Oxford University Press.

Strull, W., Bernard, L., & Charles, G. (1984). Do patients want to participate in medical decision making? *Journal of the American Medical Association*, *252*, 2990–2994.

Thomson, R., Edwards, A., & Grey, J. (2005). Risk communication in the clinical consultation. *Clinical Medicine*, *5*(5), 465–469.

Towle, A., & Godolphin, W. (1999). Framework for teaching and learning informed shared decision making. *British Medical Journal*, *319*, 766–771.

Tversky, A., & Kahneman, D. (1981). The framing of decisions and the psychology of choice. *Science*, *211*, 453–458.

Wardlaw, J.M., Murray, V., Berge, E., & del Zoppo, G.J. (2009). Thrombolysis for acute ischaemic stroke. *Cochrane Database of Systematic Reviews*, Issue 4, Art. No. CD000213.

Wills, C.E., & Holmes-Rovner, M. (2006). Integrating decision making and mental health interventions research: Research directions. *Clinical Psychology*, *13*(1), 9–25.

Wilson, D.K., Purdon, S.E., & Wallston, K.A. (1988). Compliance to health recommendations: a theoretical overview of message framing. *Health Education Research: Theory and Practice*, *3*, 161–171.

Wolfe, C.D., & Rudd, A.G. (2007). The burden of stroke White Paper: raising awareness of the global toll of stroke-related disability and death. Retrieved from http://www .safestroke.org/Portals/10/FINAL%20Burden%20of%20Stroke.pdf

Glossary

decision quality: cited by several authors as the desired (optimal) outcome of shared decision making – defined as patients' levels of condition-specific knowledge and extent that treatment choice is congruent with their preferences and values (Sepucha *et al.*, 2004, 2007).

decision support intervention: a type of complex intervention that aims to facilitate the process of shared decision making (also referred to as 'decision aids' or 'decision support technologies').

framing effect: the influence on individuals' choices as a result of presenting information on outcome probabilities in different ways (Tversky & Kahneman, 1981); for example, using relative risk reduction (as opposed to absolute risk reduction) to convey information on the size of a treatment effect.

outcome probability: probability of an event (health outcome).

preference-sensitive health care decisions: health conditions that have more than one 'reasonable' management option and where the optimal choice is guided by patient-specific preferences and values.

risk communication: techniques used to convey probabilistic information on outcomes (i.e. outcome probabilities for beneficial and adverse effects) of the available treatment options for a health condition.

shared decision making: health care decisions shared by patients and clinicians informed by best evidence, and patients' preferences and values.

surveillance: no active treatment is administered to a patient – instead regular monitoring of the signs and symptoms of a health condition is undertaken (also referred to as watchful waiting or active monitoring).

thrombolysis: the breaking down of blood clots with thrombolytic drugs such as biogenetically engineered 'Recombinant Tissue Plasminogen Activator' (rt-PA).

8

Writing, Training, Teaching, Researching, Consulting, Quality Assurance and the Kitchen Sink

Mark Forshaw

What I Do

Discovering the true provenance of a quotation is often difficult, partly because there is sometimes deliberate obfuscation. However, what I do know is that Aaron Sorkin is attributed with most recently putting to paper the following: 'Decisions are made by those who show up'. Whether it originally came from Woody Allen, Harry S. Truman or someone else entirely, I at least know where I first heard it. It's in *The West Wing*. I can summarize what I do very simply. I show up. By so doing, I help make decisions.

I used to be one of those people who complained at decisions made, actions taken, policies effected. I felt that I was on the receiving end of other people's decisions, and often didn't agree with those decisions. In fact, I still do, quite often, disagree with them, some of which I have actually helped make myself. However, now I accept, much more readily, the *process* by which those decisions have been made, and that in itself is the spoonful of sugar that helps the medicine go down. What changed was that I got involved, and stayed involved for long enough to really understand what happens in the background to make things happen. In short, a large part of my work is now in the politics of psychology.

My earliest work was actually in cognitive psychology, and indeed my PhD involved assessing the nature of crossword puzzle–solving expertise in older people. Back then, there was no 'health psychology' in the United Kingdom to speak of, or at least not a formal, recognized training route. It simply wasn't possible to be a health psychologist except in the largely informal way that many of the founders of UK health psychology were; a committed and tirelessly researching band of people,

Health Psychology in Action, First Edition. Edited by Mark Forshaw and David Sheffield.
© 2013 John Wiley & Sons, Ltd. Published 2013 by John Wiley & Sons, Ltd.

often clinical psychologists by training, who churned out important work within behavioural medicine, and health-related aspects of applied psychology. Although there was a gerontological aspect to my doctoral work, it was firmly grounded in cognitive psychology. I am, therefore, something of an imposter. It was whilst writing up that I got involved in a large, international project looking at postoperative cognitive deficits in older people. Basically, we had anecdotal evidence of memory loss and so on in older people who had undergone surgery, and therefore anaesthesia, which we believed might have been due to hypoxia, the starvation of the brain of oxygen which is to a great extent unavoidable when you render someone unconscious. Thus, the International Study of Post-Operative Cognitive Deficits (ISPOCD) project was born, and I spent many hours testing a control group of older people on a battery of tests, and training research nurses, anaesthesiologists and the like, around Europe, in administering our test battery. It began simply as a job, because I needed a job. It wasn't a passion driving me, I have to admit. However, this was a turning point for me, because I started to apply my cognitive psychology training to a practical, health-related issue. I had started to become a health psychologist, without even knowing what one was. My next post was also at the University of Manchester, and I spent 18 months or so involved in a project investigating the feasibility of neonatal screening for hearing impairment. I was based in the Centre for Audiology, Education of the Deaf and Speech Pathology, but also worked regularly with colleagues at the MRC Institute of Hearing Research at the University of Nottingham. By the end of this work, in the mid-1990s, I felt that my career was based much more in health than anything else, and this was a position from which I have never looked back. By the time that I started my first lectureship at Coventry University in 1996, I was much more oriented towards health psychology, and was starting to realize it was a growing phenomenon in the United Kingdom, and shortly thereafter the Division of Health Psychology was born. I joined, through the 'grandparenting' route, as did the entire first few hundred members of the Division of course, and since then have had a professional identity which was previously eluding me. I have a lot to thank the founding members of the Division for, including handing me a framework for my interests. With hindsight, I regard those early years of turning away from cognitive psychology into the emerging world of health psychology as a critical time for me, although I didn't actually see it as such when it was happening.

Since then I have been treading the boards as a lecturer, learning the trade, as it were, with my teaching split between health psychology and research methods, and of late I have now been able to almost entirely devote myself to health psychology at various levels and forms, but largely postgraduate. Along the way I have been something of an all-rounder when it comes to research, in that I have never been the kind of person who could devote themselves to a specific research thread, as such. Either that, or I simply haven't found the thread yet. I admire those people who can spend a career tearing something apart and studying every aspect of it inside and out. Part of me wishes I could have done that, because it is a great way to carve out a career and be respected in the more traditional academic sense. However, I would simply get bored. After some years trying to come to terms with the lack of focus to my work,

I have mostly accepted that the focus will either land in my lap, or it won't. I tend to think that it won't. What is good is to have a sense of worth derived from being someone who does a bit of everything. I am a jack of all trades. Perhaps that means I am a master of none, as the figure of speech goes. If so, then so be it. I won't be known as the world expert on something or other, but I might be useful at times. Knowing a bit about everything has its moments. What people often don't know is the full version of the phrase: 'Jack of all trades, master of none, though ofttimes better than master of one'. In Dutch, I would be a *manusje van alles*, and that's more often than not a very positive phrase. I labour this point for one reason only; someone reading this might be struggling with similar career issues, and it helps to know what others have made of themselves in the same boat. So far in my career I have researched and published in issues around hearing impairment, the social model of disability, low back pain, hand–arm vibration syndrome, menopause, homeopathy, the philosophy of qualitative methods, tanning behaviour, giving and receiving feedback, headaches and migraines, ageing and memory and self-care interventions. If there is a theme there, I cannot see it, except that everything in the list is psychological and somehow health-related. I am drawn to work on things that interest me, regardless of what they actually are. That doesn't make me a focused 'career researcher', but rather the opposite. In a sense, I am demand-driven, and rarely does theory matter to me. Perhaps, in a way, I am a practitioner working in a mostly academic environment. A 'pracademitioner', if you like.

Outside of the research arena, I have two distinct strands to my expertise, if I can lay claim to any. The first is in writing. My first book appeared in 2002, and since then there have been a handful published. I am contracted to write or edit more, so there will be around 12 within a couple more years. There are various myths that I can dispel here. Contrary to what my students often imagine, it is not a money-making exercise, because sales of niche books are rather low, and royalty payments only a small proportion of the net profits. In fact, books often cost money to produce, because one often needs to buy books as background reading, and so on. Furthermore, one doesn't have to forgo sleep or holidays to write. To some extent, I have streamlined the process, writing short books and avoiding dense texts packed with references. Other people write those much better than I ever could. I also actually like writing, and it is surprising how the words stack up when in the right mood. In terms of content, writing is a way of expanding one's audience for the things one normally says in lectures or supervision meetings. If you feel something is worth pointing out to 50 students in a room, it is probably worth considering putting it into print for more people whom you can never hope to meet. Writing of textbooks and the like is certainly not something that everyone ought to try, and many academics feel that they have better things to spend their time on, and of those who would like to write a book, some do not always have a market for their work. There is a financial bottom line to consider, and the expertise of some academics does not lend itself to high-volume sales. This isn't a slur on that expertise, since some small areas are very important, but if a book is unlikely to sell a certain number of copies, it will lose money, which publishers are not terribly keen on, for understandable reasons. For me, understanding the market for books is part of being a writer, and links in very well with my departmental role as a lead for consultancy and third-stream activity. I am expected to understand the commercial world, and to 'sell' our talents as psychologists to people in that world.

The second clear strand to my work is in the realm of psychology politics and quality assurance, which are inextricable, in my opinion. Quality assurance is political, whether we like it or not. Today's standards are tomorrow's bad ideas, very often. Similarly, some of today's good ideas are tomorrow's standards. The more one becomes involved in quality assurance, the more one appreciates that judgements of quality do not exist in a vacuum, but rather are made in social and economic contexts.

Some years ago now, I responded to an advertisement to join the British Psychological Society (BPS) Division of Health Psychology Training Committee (DHPTC), the Committee then solely responsible for the accreditation of postgraduate health psychology training courses in the United Kingdom. This included both Stage 1 (MSc) and Stage 2 (doctoral) training courses run by universities up and down the country. Subsets of members of the committee visit institutions and report back on standards, making suggestions to the committee which then at the time were verified by the Membership and Professional Training Board of the BPS. To universities, this has been seen as a stamp of quality, but also until recently, with the Health Professions Council taking over these regulatory functions from the BPS, these accreditations were the most common way in which trainees acquired their qualifications in order to become practising health psychologists. Quite why at the time I decided to join this committee, I don't recall, other than curiosity, and a desire to be involved. I did so with some trepidation, because prior to this the functioning of the BPS and its Boards and Committees was something of a mystery to me, and I must confess that I did not have a positive view, mainly fuelled by my own ignorance. At the time, I felt that the Society was not necessarily serving my interests, and not necessarily something easy to fathom or penetrate. In fact, I was utterly wrong. My first meeting of DHPTC was interesting, and although I barely said a word or understood much of what was going on, I was made welcome, and soon settled in. I cast aside my unfounded prejudices, and got on with being a contributing member of the committee. One year later, I was surprised to find myself being asked to become Chair, a post which with some anxiety I took up, and went on to hold, for one reason or another, for 5 years. I then slipped away to the much less onerous post of Deputy Chair, and my involvement now, after 9 years or so, is simply as a visitor on accreditations from time to time. In that time, I have conducted accreditation visits to almost every university running health psychology training, sometimes more than once, and learned so much, not only about health psychology itself but also about people, management, processes and the power of words to support or discourage. Visiting quality assurance teams do not always have the answers, but they are expected to solve problems, interpret regulations and avoid, in thankfully rare situations, squabbles and spats. It is a skill we have to learn, to be able to convey the fact that in order to help, one might have to temporarily hinder, and one sometimes has to be cruel to be kind. Constructive support is very, very close to demoralizing criticism, and a lot hinges on the words used. That, indeed, is why so much is political.

During my time as Chair of DHPTC, I became also a member of the BPS Board of Examiners in Health Psychology, which then became the Board of Assessors (BoAHP), but is now called the Health Psychology Qualifications Board (HPQB), for necessary technical reasons which I will not explain here. The Board has responsibility for the BPS Qualifications in Health Psychology, the non-university equivalents to the MSc courses and professional doctorates and the like. After a while, I took up the post of Registrar for that Board, which is also combined with Chief Supervisor. The Chief Supervisor is another quality assurance role, involving overseeing training of candidates, approving and training their supervisors, approving plans of training and generally looking after the qualifications, until such time that assessment is to take place, when the Chief Assessor has a key role. Furthermore, after serving my time in this role I have also become Chair of HPQB, something I see as entirely compatible with all the other roles. This all might seem a trifle greedy, but actually these roles are so demanding that one does not have hundreds of suitably experienced people desperate to take over. In time, I hope that will change, and as health psychology grows, I feel confident that it will.

I also currently chair the BPS Qualifications Standards Committee (QSC). This committee has a responsibility for overseeing the work of all the Qualifications Boards, across the various professional divisions within psychology, which means that we can set policies and procedures across all qualifications, share good practice and create a parity of quality and justice through all Society qualifications, which have just finished being 'visited' by the Health Professions Council as part of their approvals process. No longer does the BPS itself assess its own qualifications; an external regulator has that function, which necessitates a lot of hard work by very dedicated people, within the BPS and the members of the Boards. Before I got involved, 10 years or so ago, I had no idea just how much work goes into everything behind the scenes. I also would never have got to meet such pleasant and collegiate people, nor have developed my own skills in quality assurance. Decisions, it is true, are made by those who show up, but by showing up you also meet the other people making the decisions. As psychologists, it is a sorry state of affairs if we don't relish meeting people.

There are a cluster of activities around quality assurance which are concatenated in such a way that one can easily become very busy, very quickly: external examining, for example, and serving as quality assurers in other contexts. I am now serving as a lay member of the Quality Assurance Committee of the College of Podiatrists, which is another way to share good practice in both directions, and see how another professional body functions, just as my time on the Registration Authority of the Science Council also did. I also sit on the Council of the Institute of Health Promotion and Education. It is always interesting to see how much we have in common with other professions, but we also, as psychologists, can be quite unique in other ways. Psychologists, for instance, are rather diverse. Unlike any other profession I know, except perhaps medicine, we have a whole host of professional psychologists doing entirely different things all of which are based on a core training. What the average occupational psychologist gets up to bears little resemblance to the work of the average sports and exercise psychologist, and so on. Each area overlaps with each other in some ways (health psychology and occupational psychology meet each other around measurement of stress and work-related well-being, for example), but there are times when they look like distinct professions. This has been a source of some difficulty in the preparations leading up to the single, unified registration of psychologists by the Health Professions Council. I would imagine that all parties involved struggled at times with finding a way to conceptualize the practitioner psychologist in an inclusive way.

Of course, researching, writing and professional body activities are not all I do. A large portion of my contractual work is focused around a further two strands, which are supervision and enterprise. The bulk of my teaching work isn't really teaching at all, and I am committed to making that particular point. Whilst I have served my time as a lecturer, having spent many thousands of hours telling students about the theory of planned behaviour, or how ANOVA works, I do very little of that today. Most of my contact with students or trainees is with my professional doctorate trainees (from both clinical and health doctorates) and with research project students of all levels. I find this a highly rewarding process and something that enables me to develop as I coach and support others. *Coaching* is the operative word here. Good supervision is all about incremental encouragement, the step-by-step travel from novice to qualified professional with an experienced person directing and commenting along the way. As health psychologists, we often fail to see that supervising our trainees is a form of intervention, albeit not a health intervention directly. We can and do make a difference to the lives and careers of tomorrow's health psychologists, and I am always acutely aware of the responsibilities this entails. Their career choices, well-being, confidence, self-esteem and so on are partly in our hands. We have the power to make health psychology engaging and exciting, and equally we can turn it into an outright chore. Not only is this a challenge, but it is one which I feel enriches me also. I owe a lot to my trainees over the years; it is not a one-way process. The conversations about their work have given rise to reflections on my own, and my research has been closely linked with theirs. Rather than expecting them to simply fit in with my own research programme, they have had the freedom to explore their own interests, partly because, as I have already said, my own research is not narrowly focused. Therefore, again this has proved to be a boon rather than a problem to me.

A good proportion of my work centres on enterprise and third-stream activities (the first and second streams are teaching and research). I have a departmental role in liaising with the outside world, and not only convincing private companies and councils or the National Health Service to commission us to carry out work, but also convincing my academic colleagues that they possess the skills necessary to do this, and in project management. Naturally, when we attract funding for health-related projects, I tend to manage those myself, leaving the other psychology work to those better suited. In recent months we have run evaluations and other projects for a range of clients, in the areas of smoking cessation, empathy assessment in care workers, training for nurses and social marketing, amongst others. Working with external clients is much less predictable than standard academic work, although one always has the satisfaction of knowing that, although one's efforts rarely result in formal publications, they are addressing real-world issues, since no client hands over funds to support blue-skies research. They ask us to consult for them because they have a specific, tightly defined issue to investigate, and that is precisely what we must do. Since taking up this mantle I have come to understand so much about the functioning of not only smaller companies but also giants such as the National Health Service. Again and again, the work is carried out in a context that is as much political as it is about health care or health psychology. No government invests billions in health care without having a say in what happens, and how and when.

Ups and Downs

The benefits and challenges of my work can be summarized quite neatly, in that in some ways they are the same. If one enjoys hard work that changes from day to day, and that involves working in 15-minute chunks of time before the next telephone call or appointment or email directs you to something different, then all of these things are a constant struggle, and a source of pleasure. I am exceedingly busy, as anyone who knows me will attest, but I would rather that than the opposite. Health psychology has given me a home, and kept me busy with housework. I get to meet the neighbours regularly, and I am never bored.

What Next?

Health psychology is certainly developing and changing, and is a dynamic and exciting area of work to be involved in as a result. The most exciting aspect of that change, for me, is where it is coming from. For most big things in life, change tends to be top-down. Governments or managers or heads of groups tell us what to do, and we do it. Although my own roles mean that I am expected to listen to trainees and act upon their suggestions and ideas, I am pleased that this means that, of late, some of the change in the United Kingdom has been driven by trainees and early-career health psychologists as much as, if not more than, by those of us in midcareer or the founders who constitute the bedrock of our discipline. In November 2009, we launched the revised Stage 2 curriculum and regulations, the result of a long process (3 years or so) of debate and consultation. The working party that set this revision going was mixed, consisting of all the stakeholders, from those in high esteem to those just putting their foot on the ladder, and the result was a well-thought-out and workable revised qualification. The documents we at the Society produced are clearer, the qualification is streamlined and the overall process of completing the Stage 2 Qualification in Health Psychology is less ambiguous, more efficient and altogether a more pleasant experience for trainees. This is the early feedback I have received directly from those who have enrolled or transferred over from the previous qualification framework.

The revised qualification is notable in particular for placing an increased emphasis on health psychology interventions. No longer do we regard this as an optional area of competence. All health psychologists are now expected to have intervention work as a string to their bow. This doesn't mean that everyone must train in cognitive-behavioural therapy, or motivational interviewing, for example, but it does mean that we recognize that a lot of the work we do is interventional in its nature, even when we haven't previously categorized it as such. Health promotion activity and public health work are examples of interventions on a different scale from one-to-one 'therapies', and those of us engaged in action research in a health environment are also interventionists, even if we don't always see it at first. The intention is not to directly compete with our colleagues in clinical or counselling psychology, although the common ground between us is clearly there. The intention is to complement. Together, psychologists of all persuasions can make their individual contributions to moving us all forward, in health care, in knowledge building and research and, as a direct result, as a society.

Key Debates in Health Psychology

One of the most interesting and controversial issues facing UK health psychology in recent years has actually been the issue of statutory regulation, which is not by any means a topic confined to our domain. All psychologists have had to engage with this to some extent, and all practising psychologists, whether clinical, occupational, forensic and so on, are affected by the political, legal and social changes that have befallen us since July 2009, when the Health Professions Council became the statutory regulator of practitioner psychologists.

For many years it was clear to psychologists that we needed some way of regulating the profession outwith the professional body itself. As a voluntary regulator the British Psychological Society ran the risk of criticism, however well it did the job. When the Health Professions Council was established, it soon became clear that they were the front-runner in taking over this function. Of course, the Health Professions Council is not simply a regulator of professions, and in fact a large part of its work is involved in assuring the quality standards of training courses that churn out those professionals. Again, the BPS had a well-established set of accreditation processes which effectively were to become redundant, theoretically, when the HPC took over that function. Not only would the HPC decide who could call themselves a health psychologist, but also they would decide, essentially, which courses were suitable for training them.

I could write volumes on the various debates around these topics, but instead I shall focus on one consequence of statutory regulation; the protection of titles. After much discussion spanning literally years, the HPC now protects titles which include 'Registered Psychologist', 'Practitioner Psychologist', and 'X Psychologist', where X denotes a specific professional entity. Therefore, 'Health Psychologist' and 'Counselling Psychologist', for example, are protected, and only those appropriately qualified and signed up to the HPC-maintained register can use them.

However, the HPC has, as one of its purposes, the protection of the public against 'rogue traders' as it were. And indeed, should a health psychologist misbehave, they could lose their licence to practice in that profession, effectively, as could a forensic psychologist and so on. However, one could argue that the biggest single threat to the public is the number of unqualified and unregulated people who lay claim to the title 'psychologist'. In the United Kingdom, after all the legal changes and statutory regulation that have occurred, it is *still* the case that *anyone*, absolutely anyone, can call themselves a psychologist, and cannot be prosecuted directly for doing so. If they mislead the public, then secondary legislation would be applicable, but that would be secondary legislation, as I say. A law forbidding the use of the term 'psychologist' by unqualified people has to be better than one saying that you can sue someone for implying that they were qualified, but only if you can demonstrate that they have caused you harm or loss in some way. Right now, the public might well assume that a psychologist is a qualified individual, whereas few of them will truly understand the implications of the differences between a health psychologist, a clinical psychologist and the like. Some are arguing that what we have protected prevents the public from being hurt by the individuals least likely to ever have done so. I welcome the legal protection of my title, as a health psychologist. However, I would also welcome a greater protection still, to remove the many thousands of unqualified people selling untried, untested and potentially harmful tools and techniques to an unsuspecting, vulnerable public in the name of a generic 'psychology'.

9

What Are the Roles of a Health Psychologist in Clinical Practice? Defining Knowledge, Skills and Competencies

Claire Hallas

As a chartered health psychologist since 1998 and now as a HPC-registered health psychologist, I have worked in a variety of roles both within academia and in clinical practice. However, the two contexts are not distinct within health psychology practice. In this chapter I want to explore the competences, skills and knowledge that academic and applied health psychologists have and those which are generic, specific and transferable within differing contexts. The future of our developing applied health psychologist workforce depends on the progression of postgraduate training programmes and access to national funding so that we can integrate our qualified professionals into applied health care contexts to work alongside our applied psychology colleagues and other health care professionals.

Early-Career Health Psychology Competences

I started my working career after my postgraduate training as a lecturer in health psychology in a university academic department. The psychology department I worked in was engaging, forward thinking and innovative in teaching health psychology and determined to lead the field in the training and accreditation of the Stage 1 and Stage 2 health psychology programmes. I became part of the newly created Centre for Health Psychology team which was the first in the United Kingdom to be recognized and accredited by the British Psychological Society (BPS) Division of Health Psychology Training Committee (DHPTC). My responsibilities were to lead the undergraduate Health Psychology degree module and the accredited MSc in Health Psychology optional module in Chronic Illness Management. It was a dynamic start to my early

Health Psychology in Action, First Edition. Edited by Mark Forshaw and David Sheffield.
© 2013 John Wiley & Sons, Ltd. Published 2013 by John Wiley & Sons, Ltd.

career which gave me valuable skills in teaching health psychology using a wide range of teaching methods such as large-group lecturing, interactive small-group tutorials, patient case study clinical skills training, role playing and personal supervision of student research and coursework. In the department I worked collaboratively with other members of the Centre staff to supervise and develop research project work with the research assistants and to supervise PhD, MSc and undergraduate health psychology projects. This was an exciting time as it widened my general knowledge of health psychology, and the expanding theoretical and applied intervention literature, and allowed me the privilege of focussing on new topics of research interest which were not specifically associated with my PhD specialism (anxiety, depression and coronary heart disease). During my time in my initial first work role I learned a variety of skills which could also be applied to clinical settings and various populations. Individual patient-interviewing techniques, psychometric questionnaire assessment, neuropsychological testing and clinical-interviewing skills were gained through training, supervision and practice. Clinical data management, advanced research methods and ethical practice applied to health and medicine were developed through working with a variety of hospital, community and academic departments and with multidisciplinary professionals (e.g. health and clinical psychologists, neuropsychologists, medical and surgical professionals, nurses, clinical physiologists, technicians, clinical research and audit officers, and ethics departments). These early career skills are ultimately the foundation of progression of a career in applied health psychology.

Expanding and Developing Our Health Psychology Roles

Teaching and research supervision were only *components* of my academic role as widening opportunities developed internally within the department and externally within BPS and DHP. The external opportunities to expand my role as a health psychologist also came at this time from a much respected senior colleague who discussed the possibilities of me taking on the Co-ordinating Editor role of the DHP publication *Health Psychology Update*. My colleague gave me an insight into how this role could help me develop new psychology skills, meet new health psychology colleagues and broaden my academic experiences whilst also really making a difference to the focus of the national publication. I jumped at this exciting offer and so after my role was agreed with the DHP I began my 3-year term as Editor (little did I know at the time where this would take me!). This was a really interesting role involving working with the BPS communications committee, becoming a member of the DHP Executive committee to report on publication issues, commissioning high-quality articles and features from UK and overseas health psychologists, making editorial decisions about content and style, managing subeditor roles and work and producing three paper copies of the publication per year. This role confirmed the necessity of excellent organizational and time-keeping skills, with a need for strategic vision in future planning. It also enhanced communication skills within different networks and learning strategies to facilitate motivation amongst colleagues and the wider health psychology community to engage in writing and debating.

My work within the BPS broadened my workplace horizons, allowing me to meet new colleagues and friends and get to experience the national focus of our profession. However, it was also challenging at times and it did lead to frustrations about deadlines and insufficient article submissions from a newly emerging and sometimes quiet health psychology community. However, ultimately at the end of my editorial term, together with the publication team we had produced a substantial contribution to the development of the publication in terms of style and content. Professional issues within health psychology were debated and discussed and attention had become focused on the area of applied health psychology – an issue close to my working heart. Focusing on the competences and training that health psychologists needed to be able to apply their skills as professional practitioners working in health care consultancy, medical and health patient environments and community-based public health roles had become important. Our discussions developed awareness of the ability of health psychologists to work outside of academic environments. These skills and competences were apparent to me early on in my training and that the application of generic psychological skills (teaching, training, consultancy, research and clinical interventions) applied to health contexts was the future of the mainly academic health psychology profession – to apply the research outcomes into actual health care and patient outcomes. But, it naïvely (at the time!) shocked me when this view was not always shared by other psychologists or even those within the health psychology community – although this did not deter me!

Subsequently, a 10-year career evolved within the DHP Executive Committee as a result of my editorial work and my interest in continuing with national issues related to applied health psychology training and the Government's interest in our role within health care services. A variety of national work[1] followed which promoted health psychology within the BPS and more widely in the Department of Health (DoH), National Institute for Clinical Excellence (NICE) and Public Health Executive. These roles led me to improve written and oral communication skills that targeted national government policy needs (i.e. rapid communications highlighting evidence-based outcomes) and professional and managerial competencies to work on the Government's Agenda for Change applied (health) psychology job profiles. With my DHP colleagues, we worked on many DoH projects including intervention resources needed to meet new health care targets, White Paper recommendations on a variety of public health issues and often spontaneous proposals from new Government Ministers' ideas! Health psychology skills that were particularly valued by the Government were focused on community public health interventions, as they placed less focus on the individual approach to understanding behavioural aspects of health behaviour and modification and, instead, focused on general attitudes and behaviour. One of our greatest strengths as health psychologists was to convey the impact of theoretically based evidence in behaviour change to address public health targets in obesity management, long-term conditions (e.g. respiratory and cardiac disease, and diabetes) and promoting health lifestyles with exercise and the management of binge drinking. Our evidence-based psychological interventions were designed to produce changes in populations but had the individual's un-healthy behaviours and health-related attitudes at the heart of the evidence base which gave great strength to the government's health policy and practices (e.g. particularly the community health trainer projects) and showed the govern-ment clearly that psychologists (particularly health psychologists) were valuable in the wider physical health care sector rather than focussing on purely mental health care.

Health Psychology in the National Health Service – Key Competences

Whilst working on the national executive health psychology projects, I also had my day job! During training and throughout my working career I had always been in-volved with the clinical application of research and sought to combine both within clinical practice to maximize excellence in clinical care and outcomes which were un-derpinned by high quality research data. Working in a variety of clinical services (e.g. community mental health teams, inpatient secure care, medical and surgical teams, and chronic illness rehabilitation programmes), and on research trials (neuropsy-chology studies), enabled me to experience valuable supervision and postgraduate training in psychotherapeutic skills which provided me with sound clinical skills and the research evidence base to develop the clinical application of health psychology interventions with individuals and families.

Working for 17 years within UK NHS community and university hospital ser-vices (general hospital and cardiothoracic) and for 2 years as a Consultant Health Psychologist in a university general hospital within the Middle East has highlighted the key psychological competences that are required to survive and thrive in the health care workplace. Firstly on a clinical knowledge level it is important to under-stand, research and immerse yourself in the daily working practices of your chosen clinical specialism (e.g. oncology, chronic illness management). Understanding the terminology, basic medical knowledge and treatments, colleagues' roles and respon-sibilities, clinical team dynamics and characteristics is crucial for functioning and flourishing as a psychologist. Being involved in the medical and allied professional teams academic and clinical activities, developing personal relationships with indi-vidual staff and supporting their work from a professional psychological perspective will enhance interpersonal communication, patient outcomes and efficient thera-peutic services. Competences to manage effective health psychology services should be focused around understanding the pragmatics of working within a multi-outcome health care system, delivering effective referral processes and screening, awareness of the limitations of the scope of the service and managing psychological care in the context of the physical health milieu (environmental setting, treatment priorities, symptoms and time available). These competences appear generic across different health care and cultural contexts. More so, since my career has taken me overseas to work in a developing Arabic Islamic country (the Sultanate of Oman) the need to employ skills to enhance personal working relationships and to reflect upon the differences in the cultural expression of health communications, treatment and service delivery are even more important.

Secondly, from a psychology service manager perspective, different skills are required to control financial and human resources, lead, motivate and support staff in CPD and training, plan and prioritize services strategically and balance implementing an evidence-based patient-centred service whilst meeting Trust, regional and national targets. Keeping up to date with Government health care policy and political drivers is crucial for maintaining a forward-thinking and responsive service that is able to meet targets and budgets and within available resources. Training in supervision skills, mentoring, team management and budget control is essential when psychology roles involve more than just clinical work.

During my career I have been responsible for delivering and managing psychology services, but also providing a consultative role within the wider NHS trust regarding national policy and framework delivery, integrated care pathways development and NICE guidelines implementation plans. These wider roles required key psychological competences such as consultancy skills (i.e. feasibility assessments, project design and management), teaching and training skills (i.e. workshops and presentations, evaluating training outcomes and designing e-learning forums) and research management (i.e. study evaluation, audit and postgraduate research supervision). There were two hospitals within the Royal Brompton & Harefield NHS Trust where I worked, and during my time I progressed from a junior specialist to a consultant health psychologist managing a small department of psychologists and a psychiatrist across the two hospitals, and within my base hospital as the site manager for the Rehabilitation & Therapies overall team deputizing for the NHS Trust Director at many Trust and regional committees. This involved knowledge about health care–commissioning priorities, strategic planning of services and human resource development.

As a Health Psychologist I worked in a variety of roles within specialist heart and lung medical teams providing individual therapy and family interventions, ward-based teaching programmes and professional advice and consultation services regarding patients and health care policy. Psychology Services worked collaboratively with medical and nursing professionals and other allied health professionals within the rehabilitation and therapies services (i.e. social workers, dieticians, occupational therapists, physiotherapists and chaplains). Often these professionals told stories of their experiences of working with psychologists. The phrase 'Living in their ivory tower' was used quite a lot! My goal, however, was to develop a user-friendly, accessible and accountable outcomes-based service for patients (clients) and professionals so that psychology was meaningful with respect to medical and health care outcomes and from a patient quality-of-life perspective. Interactive services to join service, staff and patients together were developed such as a patient user satisfaction-with-service questionnaire, support information leaflets and a patient FAQ website. Skills acquired in research design and analysis, questionnaire and survey development and IT (databases, e-learning and web design) were invaluable in managing these clinical governance systems.

In addition, a goal was to build a department that crossed the boundaries and divisions of the psychology profession and represented the varied needs of the patients, rather than reflecting prejudices of recruitment processes and individual service managers' preferences for particular psychology roles within services. We were proud to have health and clinical psychologists, a neuropsychologist and counsellors working together within the service and to supervise a variety of postgraduate psychologists in training so that they would gain exposure to different training models, develop a broad range of competences in theoretical and applied clinical skills and feel equipped to develop and provide therapy and intervention services within a variety of clinical settings from intensive care and inpatient medical wards to outpatient rehabilitation group programmes, and to communicate effectively with a varied group of interdisciplinary professionals.

Reflections on the Variety of Health Psychology Skills

A career that has involved working within the DHP, a university academic system, UK NHS and overseas health care systems has highlighted real challenges of managing and organizing personal and professional time to meet and manage diverse work commitments. Working with multidisciplinary and cultural professionals is a real joy and benefit of being in the health care system, as it provides an opportunity to learn to work with practitioners and patients in varied ways, allowing us to become more open and flexible in our professional attitudes and beliefs about others' motivations for their professional behaviour. This facilitates personal confidence as an independent practitioner, but also a commitment to the value of working as a multidisciplinary team member in health care services. However, it is also a real challenge at times to manage these varied relationships, especially when health care decisions or ethical choices in patient care are conflicting between judgements of psychologists and other health care staff. At these times you need to draw upon the benefits of supervision, peer support and professional training to reflect on and formulate these interpersonal dynamics.

More recently, my role as a Consultant Psychologist in the Department of Behavioural Medicine, Sultan Qaboos University in Oman has both clinical and academic components, and has refocused my teaching skills within medical education; the task is to train undergraduate medical students and postgraduate Resident Physicians in communication skills as the university has recently revised its medical degree programme (which is only 15 years old) to include greater exposure to clinical communication skills training, health psychology knowledge and models applied to medicine and behavioural change techniques to enhance adherence, patient safety and the quality of life of their chronically ill populations. It was initially debated within the university medical departments as to which professional role or medical specialism should be responsible for this training. All physicians agreed that every medical specialism should be able to teach clinical communication skills, however the consensus that was agreed upon was that (health) psychologists have unique competences and skills in understanding human health care behaviour and we have the core skills to deliver communication knowledge and skills about patient–physician emotional and behavioural interactions within the health system. This role has enabled me to disseminate a wide base of health psychology knowledge and its health care application through developing a 16-week clinical skills training programme, which means that the evidence is clinically focused within different medical specialities and has meaningful patient-orientated and medical outcomes associated it.

For example, health psychologists can help medical students to understand about the process of communication through our knowledge of the psychological processes impacting on health care communication in differing health care areas; sensitive patient groups (e.g. HIV patients), challenging populations (e.g. psychiatric patients or with respect to the breaking of difficult news) and across medical contexts (e.g. gynaecology and paediatrics). Our knowledge of social cognitive theories, behaviour change interventions associated with preventative health and chronic illness management and the psychological experience of illness, disability and health is intrinsic to communication about motivation to change healthy behaviours, adherence maintenance and rehabilitation outcomes.

So now I find that have returned once again to my health psychology roots; to educate and disseminate the role of applied health psychology and its value to medicine, health care systems and public and community health work! In 1998 as a newly qualified health psychologist I began my quest to combine academic and clinical practice and to develop applied health psychology as a profession intrinsically associated with advancing health care interventions based on our social-cognitive models underpinning health behaviour. However, now as consultant psychologist I still find that there is the basic need to be competent in the 'bread and butter' of health psychology knowledge which can be taught through interactive, skills-based teaching methods. Health psychologists develop these skills early on in their training but they will be needed and valued throughout their career; these are the fundamental skills that must be kept up to date as they have direct outcomes on patient care and health care practices.

New Horizons

Working as a health psychologist in a developing country such as Oman with a limited social care infrastructure and a rapidly advancing health care system has been really challenging. Firstly the profession of health psychology is unheard of, as is also the wider discipline of psychology as an academic science. The practice of psychotherapy and intervention services within hospital-based general medicine and psychiatry services has been very limited until one year ago. There are no

undergraduate or postgraduate training programmes in psychology in Oman and so
those individuals who are working in 'counselling', 'IQ testing' or 'social work' roles
in hospitals often have a basic bachelor's degree in psychology or sociology from the
United States, Canada or Australia (educationally easier to be accepted into from the
Omani educational system) or have a bachelor's degree from an Omani educational
institution that has combined subjects of sociology, anthropology, business science
and cultural psychology. Recently, a US-trained postgraduate-qualified clinical psychologist (of Arab origin) has been employed within the Psychology Team, however
this position is unrecognized in status, training expertise or experience. This does
lead to misunderstandings about the competences of psychologists and their level
of skills compared with physicians and with more general social care professionals.
This can be demoralizing, demotivating and difficult for psychologists trying to develop new services. As a UK health psychologist I have the luxury of being respected
for having a highly regarded educational qualification and psychology training that
is recognized worldwide and for having valuable experience in an established and
revered health care system. However I still have the same difficulty as working as an
applied health psychologist in the United Kingdom, as I am often asked to clarify and
explain the competences, differences and similarities between the applied psychologists and my psychiatry colleagues. However, in general, reactions from professionals
within the multidisciplinary team are based upon your ability to work with their
particular problems, not your job title. My work in Oman does have a feel of the early
days of the NHS when psychology services were scarce, although more interestingly
it does not feel too dissimilar to the way in which psychology and therapy services
are now being reconfigured to include CBT therapists who can be from a variety of
professional backgrounds and training.

   Health psychology is a profession that has investigated the impact of cross-
cultural, multifaith, social and environmental issues on health, disability and well-
being, showing variations in health systems, disease patterns and patient outcomes. In
a collectivist society such as Oman, where there are strong cultural beliefs associated
with bodily possession by a spirit (expressed in Arabic as Jinn or Djinn), the Evil Eye
and significant stigma regarding the acknowledgement of emotional problems and
illness, the treatment of physical symptoms and mental illness varies between both
traditional practices (e.g. through a Sheikh with religious and spiritual guidance)
and modern medicine. As a Health Psychologist, the challenge is to understand
how these ancient rituals and modern treatments impact on patients' illness beliefs
and treatment expectations and ultimately their combined effects upon adherence,
prognosis and medical decision making. Furthermore, understanding how treatment
decision making and care are prioritized by the collectivist (familial) view of a
patient rather than their individual needs and wishes can be frustrating from a
Western perspective. For example, a recent referral to the Psychology Team was for
a young male testicular cancer patient with anxiety and depression. The treating
physician believed that he could be treated successfully with a good prognosis after
chemotherapy. However, his parents' culturally traditional (and religious) views
(about his body being possessed by a Jinn and how his body was a gift from God that

could not be altered) prevented them from agreeing for their son to have surgery or chemotherapy before trying traditional healing methods. The patient himself, however, did not associate with these traditional beliefs about his illness or body and therefore disagreed with his family which, within Arab culture, is considered disrespectful – as a consequence he had become depressed and anxious about his future. Although the treating (Arab) physician agreed that it was the patient's choice to have treatment, and not the family's, he did not want to intervene in 'family business' as he himself held strong beliefs in the family's right to be involved in the decision. This brief example shows the challenges of working as a Health Psychologist in an Eastern culture from a Western perspective and the frustrations or difficulties that may come from managing these differences. However, there are real advantages from these experiences, such as learning about new cultures, religions and faith practices and new perspectives on illness, body and personal health belief systems. The ability to research and investigate the applicability of our interventions within new environments and to deliver new health psychology services to a system that has been desperate for support gives you a real sense of professional worthiness and value.

And So to the Future!

Looking to the future, there has been considerable advances in the application of health psychology within the health care sector and the opportunities for health psychologists to work in non-academic roles having positively developed. In particular the skills of health psychologist are now becoming attractive within commercial and private health care sectors. This brings me now to a new challenge in my career! By the time that this book is published, I will have returned to the United Kingdom to take up a UK Clinical Team Lead post within a global commercial health care organization that employs health psychologists to design, develop and implement community-based medication and self-management interventions on behalf of their clients (e.g. pharmaceutical industry, insurance, NHS and Government agencies). This will require me to again adapt and enhance my skills within a new health care context and to find creativity to design and develop evidence-based health care interventions for both public health and business commercial outcomes.

There is a need for all applied psychologists to work together to enhance physical health care services and to develop public health and community programmes further. Health psychologists must be reflective of their abilities to work ethically with individuals, groups and communities; however this is the case for all trainee and qualified psychologists, not specifically for health psychologists alone. Individual relationships with clients, patients and users do require therapeutic training and supervision at all levels of experience and care. However, the needs of the service should also determine the type of training, supervision and support that is required for each psychologist. Working with individuals requires professional awareness of the process of the interpersonal treatment–intervention (therapeutic) relationship, the delivery and design of interventions to be effective and personal insight and reflection to maintain boundaries regarding professional behaviour. However, this is not the exclusive responsibility of health psychology as a subspeciality; rather, it is the focus for all practising health care professionals.

The varied roles of Health Psychologists already within the wider health service are clear evidence that multidisciplinary professionals value our skills and contribution to health care outcomes, patient-focused care, public health and community well-being, research and audit and medical and health care training. These roles, nevertheless, would benefit from being highlighted specifically as health psychologist posts rather than generic service-led titles (e.g. cardiac rehabilitation co-ordinator, or smoking cessation specialist) as the competences of health psychologists are those that meet the needs of the service. However, this is slowly starting to change as more health psychologists are defining their skills and competences within the workplace and redeveloping their job descriptions and specifications required specifically for their role. It is hoped that health psychology roles can also be extended within traditional psychology services within the NHS (hospital and community services) so that the skill mix and knowledge base of psychology services can be widened to meet a variety of patient needs and across the spectrum of physical and mental health problems (they rarely exist in isolation).

Commitments within the United Kingdom, through the BPS, to extend and enhance intervention and clinical skills within health psychology training over the next few years will no doubt consolidate on the unique application of health psychology skills within health care and particularly within applied clinical practice. That said, more needs to be achieved in the long term to include wider generic health care training within postgraduate courses that allows health psychologists to stand on a perceived equal footing with our medical and nursing colleagues and other applied psychologists and allied health professionals. Competences are needed in areas that are wider than health psychology knowledge, particularly in relation to clinical assessment and formulation skills, the structure and delivery of clinical services and the National Health Service and public health systems, understanding clinical and research governance and working with multidisciplinary teams. The list could go on, but these few are fundamental to being able to practice as a competent applied health psychologist within the health care sector.

The future of applied health psychology is currently dependent on the readers of this book, on those individuals who are motivated, interested and dedicated to expanding this much needed area of health psychology. Academic health psychologists cannot surely have a future without the application of their valuable outcomes into the 'real' health world, and consequently we cannot survive without their commitment to high-quality, large-scale research to drive our practice forward. We also need the confidence as individuals and as professionals to develop our skills to work across the spectrum of health care contexts. We must work together as a profession and as health care professionals to secure our future and most importantly for the health of our nation.

Key Debates in Health Psychology

Can a Health Psychologist Work with Individual Clients or Patients? Yes, Provided That They Have the Appropriate Training, Supervision and Practice within Professional Boundaries in the Work Context

Health psychologists have generic knowledge and skills that they are able to apply with individual clients across a range of common health contexts and problems. In particular health psychologists are best placed to deliver interventions with individual clients that have difficulties with changing behaviour that increases health risks (e.g. smoking, alcohol and diet) and supporting an individual's adaptation to health events, illness or treatment. Specific skills that are beneficial for individual client work are health goal setting, activity pacing and health behaviour implementation plans to motivate, change and maintain adaptation to chronic illness and treatment recovery and to increase adherence to patient self-management of their health problem. Health psychologists are able to utilize their knowledge regarding theoretical modelling of beliefs and attitudes towards health and treatment behaviours, their psychometric assessment and motivational interviewing skills to assess clients' beliefs about their health, treatment and care and their motivation, attitudes and intentions towards changing their health behaviours. Health psychologists have a wide knowledge of psychological processes that underpin a variety of health behaviours in various health contexts and are trained in communication models that can enhance health outcomes for individual clients/patients. Interviewing skills, discourse analysis of psychological processes and constructs related to health and communication skills are common to health psychologists and enable individual client work. Formulation of the context of an individual's health problem and their goals and the client's individual intervention plan should be designed through a strong evidence base, and therefore the implementation of this plan regardless of whether it is applied to an individual client or a research study with a large population (all individuals within it!) is similar. Intervention implementation plans such as message reframing, cognitive restructuring, planning and resource management are usually adapted for individuals, however they remain grounded in the health psychology evidence base. Where debate ensues about the competence of health psychologists to work with individual clients is regarding the issue of clients who have both mental health and physical health problems. Health psychologists must have basic knowledge and assessment in screening mental health problems and being able to refer individual clients to the wider multidisciplinary team when appropriate and then together with their applied psychology and psychiatry colleagues work to maximize patient care and intervention effectiveness. We should also ask the question regarding the boundaries of other applied psychologists – and whether they would refer an individual client with mental health and physical health problems to see a health psychologist for specialist behaviour change management!?

Health psychologists, as all applied psychologists, must work within their professional training boundaries and under supervision appropriate to their needs. This code of conduct is for all practising, independent, professional psychologists within the United Kingdom and does not discriminate between applied psychologists of health, clinical and counselling specialisms and does not stipulate in which work context and with which types of patient/client populations each individual applied psychologist can work. It is up to the individual psychologist to decide on their fitness to practice within a work context and it is their responsibility to seek supervision and support to ensure professional reflection and discussion of their practice to ensure high-quality and evidence-based practice. It is the responsibility of any psychology service manager to ensure that their clients' needs are best represented and gained through recruiting the most appropriate professional based on skills, experience, competences and knowledge that best fits the work context and its requirements, not just solely on qualification title.

Note

1 DHP Professional Development Chair, Department of Health's New Ways of Working in Applied Psychology Lead for the DHP, Department of Health's Improving Access to Psychological Therapies Health Psychology Lead, and Expert Advisor in Chronic Respiratory Disease for National Institute for Clinical Excellence (NICE).

10

Health Psychology: The Missing Ingredient from Health and Safety?

Jenny Lunt

Raw Ingredients

With the able support of an experienced team of health and occupational psychologists and health scientists, I have, since 2003, been progressing a role for health psychology in health and safety. This is through my work as a psychologist at the Health and Safety Laboratory (HSL), which is an agency of the Health and Safety Executive (HSE). I began working as a researcher and have since progressed to being a technical leader, completed a professional doctorate in health psychology and obtained BPS chartered status. When I was first confronted with some of the challenges facing health and safety compliance and occupational disease prevention, the potential for applying health psychology in health and safety seemed obvious: namely, to use behavioural change 'know-how' to reduce risk-taking behaviour that cannot be engineered out of the workplace. I have also applied health psychology–based expertise to the retention of employees with health limitations at work, risk communication, sickness absence and developing a more holistic approach to managing well-being at work.

Through this chapter I hope to provide insights into why health psychology is relevant to health and safety, and areas where the evidence base needs developing to optimize its usefulness to employees' quality of life. The amount of time working-age adults spend at work, coupled with forecasts of an ageing population, means that health psychology as a discipline cannot afford to overlook the workplace as a channel through which it can affect change at a population level.

Health Psychology in Action, First Edition. Edited by Mark Forshaw and David Sheffield.
© 2013 John Wiley & Sons, Ltd. Published 2013 by John Wiley & Sons, Ltd.

The Mixing

The Health and Safety Laboratory is the main research arm of HSE. Accordingly, HSE has been the chief source of opportunities for applying health psychology to health and safety. Other government departments and the commercial sector also increasingly commission work through HSL. With a multidisciplinary workforce comprising of scientists ranging from physicists, to microbiologists, engineers, occupational physicians and psychologists, HSL affords ample prospects for multidisciplinary team working. HSL's work portfolio has reactive and proactive strands and includes accident and incident investigation; root cause analysis; standards development; and proactive research, training and consultancy concerning the causes and prevention of accidents and occupational ill health. Formal project management systems are used to deliver work to high health and safety standards, cost, quality and time.

Building capability in this area has required being proactive in identifying relevant existing opportunities and in creating new research opportunities. As momentum has built, so too has the opportunities for applying health psychology to health and safety. A large-scale literature review exploring psychosocial aspects of occupational asthma served as an initial catalyst (Lunt & White, 2005). From a growing recognition that traditional health risk assessment and management, based on dose response assumptions, does not fully lend itself to contemporary occupational health conditions with psychosocial factors intermingled in their aetiology, an extensive evidence synthesis then followed (Lunt, Bowen & Lee, 2005; Lunt, Fox, *et al.*, 2007). Often referred to as 'common health problems' (Waddell & Burton, 2004; Lunt, Fox, *et al.*, 2007) such conditions typically include stress, musculoskeletal disorders, anxiety and depression. This work examined the utility of the biopsychosocial approach to occupational health risk management, using expert consultation and literature reviews. Another key milestone arose from conducting a systematic literature review evaluating the effectiveness of behavioural-related preventative interventions for dermal and respiratory occupational diseases (Lunt & Lee, 2006). Collectively, these and other pieces of related work, such as identifying factors that affect dutyholders' decisions with respect to noise control and respiratory protection (Bell & Webster, 2011; Bell *et al.*, 2010), has provided an evidence base informing barriers and enablers to compliance in the workplace, solutions for improving compliance and barriers and enablers for staying at and returning to work with health limitations and corresponding solutions. We have since used this evidence base to directly help employers. This has included developing a web-based leadership and worker involvement toolkit for small and medium-sized construction enterprises, aimed at improving health and safety performance through behaviour change (Lunt, Bennett *et al.*, 2009; Lunt, Webster *et al.*, 2009). This has been designed so that construction companies can navigate it to ensure all the ingredients for behaviour change, as applied to industry, are addressed. As part of a wider collaboration, we are also producing a toolkit with the aim of enabling employees with health limitations to remain at work without resorting to sick leave. In a previous collaboration we helped deliver and evaluate a large-scale health promotion intervention (McEachan *et al.*, 2008).

More recently, we have combined our know-how at HSL to produce a holistic approach to well-being at work. We are developing measures for assessing an organisation's strategy with respect to occupational health and well-being management, and its alignment with 'good practice'. As a complement to the widely used safety climate measures (HSL, 2011a) we are operationalizing occupational health climate as a concept through developing a corresponding assessment measure. 'Occupational health climate' refers to staff perceptions of the seriousness by which their organization regards their health and safety. With our European counterparts within the Partnership for European Occupational Health and Safety (PEROSH) (Fishwick *et al.*, 2010; PEROSH, 2011), we are working to consolidate the 'business case' for well-being at work, including the need to maintain its appeal to employers during times of austerity.

Ways by which we have found health psychology to benefit health and safety can be captured by the following themes:

1. *Behavioural change*: Traditional approaches to promoting health and safety issues have been through awareness raising campaigns (e.g. HSE's 'shattered lives' campaign for slip and trip hazards) (HSE, 2011a). The evidence base underpinning social cognition models, implementation intentions, stages of change models,and the more recent theory-driven behaviour change taxonomies has helped us to convey to policy makers the other behavioural change components necessary for translating raised awareness into a sustained reduction in risk-taking behaviour by employers and employees. This has been particularly pertinent to reducing volitional risk-taking behaviour, and reads across both health and safety hazards.

2. *Risk communication*: As a facet of behaviour change, positive and negative framing and using persuasive and vivid messages have helped us to underscore the potential adverse consequences of noncompliance to self, colleagues and family (Lunt, Bennett *et al.*, 2009; Lunt, Webster *et al.*, 2009). Within our leadership and worker involvement toolkit we have used 'widow' and 'survivor' testimonies to mitigate complacency. Positive framing has merits in engaging those who are desensitized to the adverse consequences of noncompliance. The distinction between 'monitors' and 'blunters', reflecting a key distinction in the quantity of information people prefer on health risks, has emphasized the importance of providing detailed information as 'options'.

3. *Social norms*: Poor health and safety culture, which can be usefully summarized through the shorthand 'the way things are done around here', appears to repeatedly emerge as a root cause of accidents and incidents at work. For example, on an adjacent platform to Piper Alpha, perceived business pressures to keep pumping oil between platforms profoundly distorted key operators' risk perception, despite obvious flames (Human Engineering, 2005). Health and safety culture is manifest in leadership's behaviour (e.g. the consistency between leadership

action and rhetoric) that in turn signals to employees how seriously they should take health and safety. Ensuring that formal leadership and informal peer leaders role model good health and safety practices is a crucial component of any work-based behavioural change programme.

4. *Self-efficacy and response efficacy*: To avoid denial by its recipients, self-efficacy and perceived control serve as reminders that fear-provoking messages must be accompanied by guidance on how to avoid harm (Bandura, 1986). Similarly, it reminds us that the effectiveness of skills-based health and safety training, such as using personal protective equipment appropriately, will only be effective if employees believe that those skills will protect them from harm. For example, use of local exhaust ventilation by a paint sprayer may only occur if the worker believes that the system will reduce exposure to potentially asthmagenic paint spray. In addition, policy makers are increasingly espousing the motivating power of worker involvement in health and safety decision making as a solution for improving health and safety performance. Conceptually, worker involvement should provide a mechanism for enhancing workers' self-efficacy.

5. *Pain management*: Evidence-based models accounting for the subjective nature of pain can be used to explain why, for example, ergonomic interventions might not always yield the expected improvement on the prevalence and severity of work-related musculoskeletal disorder (MSDs) (Burton *et al.*, 2008). This disorder persists as leading causes of sickness absence (HSE, 2011b)

6. *Retention at work and early return to work*: Self-regulation models and other research on coping with chronic illness, including lay and expert differences in illness perceptions, has helped to inform the development of strategies for improving the prospects for people with health limitations to remain or return to work (Lunt, Fox, *et al.*, 2007). Developing adaptive illness perceptions, and 'workability' social norms, should help gear employers up to contending challenges stemming from ageing population and persistently high prevalence of 'common health problems'. The latter includes stress, anxiety, depression and MSDs. Creating a sense of dual responsibility for occupational health between employers and employees could also create working conditions more tolerant of health limitations. This would instill an 'internal locus of control' in workers, but also ensure employers observe their duty of care obligations.

7. *Health and social inequalities*: Flexible work conditions, worker involvement, equal opportunities policies and healthy lifestyle enablers are examples of routes by which employers can help reduce social inequality. Since social and health inequalities are strongly linked, initiatives for reducing health inequalities might consider an employer's inclusiveness.

8. *Psychoneuroimmunology*: In recent years, HSE has invested considerably in rolling out the 'Management Standards for Stress' (Mackay *et al.*, 2004). The link between work-related stress, as reported via HSE's stress indicator tool, and stress biomarkers remains largely unexplored.

9. *The biopsychosocial approach*: The biopsychosocial approach's value in explaining apparent anomalies that defy the biomedical model, such as individual

differences in symptom presentation despite common organic pathology, has attracted increased attention in health and safety circles in recent years. Its capacity in accounting for the multifaceted etiology and progression of contemporary occupational health conditions lends itself as a framework on which to base evidence-based 'holistic' approaches to well-being at work (Lunt, O'Hara *et al.*, 2007).

Hand-in-hand with developing health psychology capability in health and safety research has been the need to develop knowledge and technical skills within the team, and maintain motivation. Achieving this has been done through, for example: feeding back on success; providing constructive feedback; delegating according to skill levels; highlighting team members' achievements to others, and conveying a conviction that health psychology can make a difference to the quality of working life. Equally, networking opportunities have grown in number. Initially these focused on presenting at internal HSE conferences and meetings. These have now grown to include external contacts with academia, industry and policy makers, and presenting at trade conference and academic conferences internationally. It has also led to routine inclusion in multidisciplinary projects. We also now regularly run training courses on behaviour change and well-being for industry practitioners (HSL, 2011b). So that the reader does not have to take this account at face value, our work in developing this area can be found on HSE and HSL websites. Examples of relevant publications are provided at the end of this chapter.

The Cooking: Some Challenges

From developing this area, a number of challenges have risen to the surface that health psychology may need to tackle if it is optimize its potential influence. These are challenges that I continue to grapple with. As a play on the cooking metaphor these can be described according to 'palatability', a 'balanced diet', obtaining 'Michelin status' and' shelf life'. Challenges in overcoming industry barriers to behaviour change are detailed within the key debates box for this chapter.

Palatability

Even if technically flawless, we have learnt over time that a project will have limited impact if it's not communicated in a manner palatable to its target audience. For us, these are typically policy makers. Avoiding jargon, using plain English, bullet points, glossaries and boxes to summarise key points and even adopting an expansive writing style have served our cause. However, in a discipline in which peer journal publication requires technically imbued language, such skills can run counter to gaining peer recognition. An apparent tendency to protect health psychology's identity by 'mystifying' its work using perhaps unnecessary technical terminology may actually undermine its attempts to have greater sway with policy makers. As an illustration, the coalition government has set up a 'behavioural insights' team to explore the merits of behaviour change–related work as an alternative to introducing new regulation. It is behavioural economists who lead this.

Making our 'tools' (e.g. Lunt, Bennett *et al.*, 2009) palatable to employers has required us to extensively test their usability first. As forms of process evaluation, we carry out user trials with researchers acting as observers, issue usability questionnaires, conduct semistructured interviews during pilots and use simulated cases (Lunt, Bennett *et al.*, 2009). This is with a view to testing the tool's 'understandability', the accuracy of users' understanding of the tool's purpose and design, and their perceptions of the tool's utility. Funding parameters, and difficulties in isolating cause and effect, compounded by the scale by which interventions are carried out, can make impact evaluation a luxury in health and safety research.

As a way of standardizing intervention reporting and permitting more systematic accumulation of knowledge on what does and does not work with respect to behaviour change, health psychologists are advocating increased use of intervention protocols (e.g. Dombrowski, 2009). This is perhaps a tall order for health and safety research. The researcher has little control over how interventions are implemented by employers where interventions are rolled out on a national basis. In the same vein, an expectation to document how behaviour change programs were carried out, or close adherence to a prescribed approach as specified in a protocol, will undoubtedly be an unpalatable burden for many employers.

A Balanced Diet

Health psychology is founded on the biopsychosocial approach. In practice, however, it seems that explication of the causal pathways is imbalanced. It appears skewed to the psychobiological interface. Perhaps with the exception of the Whitehall II studies (e.g. Marmot, 2005), understanding of the mechanisms by which factors operating at the social level affect health outcomes appears limited. Yet it is at this level within organizations that the causes of occupational health issues are often rooted. For example, morale may influence health independently of stress. Under conditions such as high stress, as in the Second World War, and perhaps under conditions of austerity, morale seems to act as a buffer (Lunt, O'Hara *et al.*, 2007). Intuitively, morale seems to be heavily influenced by leadership, which in turn is a key driver of organisational climate. Without research into mechanisms, this is a largely conceptual argument. However, it is this lack of research into systemic pathways that thwarts our ability to target psychosocial-based intervention in the workplace. An all-inclusive intervention approach therefore becomes necessary, tackling anything that could range from communication practice, to supervisor skills, senior leadership values or production pressure. This might be more fail-safe, but it's not necessarily efficient.

As highlighted by the industry practitioners with whom we work, individually targeted behavioural change programmes seeking to improve health and safety performance are futile if the work environment does not facilitate individuals' efforts to change. Any enthusiasm generated by attending a course may soon be extinguished if met by an unreceptive and scathing team supervisor. This provides further reason for unpacking the ingredients of the social and physical work environment that affect behaviour. If efforts to produce behavioural taxonomies are to translate to the workplace, then such factors may need to be specified at a similar level of detail to that used for operationalizing individually focussed behavioural change components. Given its empowering role, worker involvement would be amongst these components. So too should subconscious antecedents of human error. Health psychology's behavioural change models are geared towards volitional decisions, which make them directly relevant to deliberate violations. However, they have less applicability to subconsciously generated human error. Situational awareness research, referring to workers' moment-by-moment awareness of their immediate surroundings, reveals strategies relevant to mitigating human errors, such as encouraging ongoing communication within a team. Subconscious variables might explain some of the variance in behaviour, which remains largely unaccounted for by behavioural prediction research.

In short, health psychology may need to give prominence to systemic influences on behaviour, and an individual's subconscious drivers, in order to affect change through the workplace. The workforce, after all, is a captive audience.

'Michelin Star' Status

At this juncture, the applied characteristic of our work should be obvious. While feedback from our customers and employers implies our work is useful, and its uses are far-reaching, its applied nature makes it more difficult for our work to meet the criteria necessary for peer-reviewed publication. Similarly, recruiting a properly powered sample can be an enormous burden, given the time burden participation may place on employees and employers. As previously indicated, the sheer scale of interventions, and consequent resource implications, can deter empirically evaluating work at appropriate levels of statistical power. More flexibility for the realities of applied research in peer review publications could engender a stronger 'community of practice' amongst health psychology practitioners and academics alike.

Shelf Life

The interdepartmental Health and Wellbeing Group (Health, Work, Wellbeing, 2001) is an obvious vehicle through which health psychology could raise its profile at a government level. Once obtained, that prominence would need to be sustained.

Territory challenges may stem from the attention that 'nudge' has received from government via the behavioural insights team (Cabinet Office, 2011). Developed by behavioural economists, 'nudge' refers to features of a 'choice architecture' that makes a preferred behaviour more attractive than other choices by acting on the sub-conscious. Types of nudges include heuristics, defaults, framing, cues and prompts and social norms. Placing healthy food options centrally within the line of sight on a food counter is an obvious example. Based on 'libertarian-paternalism' principles, nudge seeks to preserve freedom of choice but make selection of healthier behaviour more likely. Whilst its proponents are not claiming nudges as new, their packaging under the banner of 'nudge', and positioning as alternatives to legislation are novel. Perhaps because of its simplicity, low-cost implications and intuitive appeal, 'nudge' has gained a shelf position that health psychology might envy.

Other issues that health psychology would need to tackle in order to retain currency in health and safety research firstly include evolving risk communication techniques to stem underestimation of long-latency occupational health risks, typically occu-pational cancers. Exposure biomarkers could be used as early-warning indicators. Likewise, real-time exposure graphs of airborne hazards can provide instant feed-back on susceptibility. Secondly, Lord Young's review (HM Government, 2010) of the operation of health and safety law recommends consolidating the regulation bur-den on low-hazard workplaces. This may mean that intrinsically motivating such employers to realize improvements in health and safety performance will become all the more important. HSE also often recruits intermediaries such as local gov-ernment to help implement initiatives. If this trend continues, the evidence base on third-party influencing in this manner needs development in order to inform this area. Finally, if current predictions that employment will become more precarious come to fruition, as characterized by short-term contracts and transient working, the windows of opportunity for influencing will become ever more flux.

As a final point, much of the preceding has portrayed health psychology as the missing ingredient from health and safety. This is not the say that the reverse has some semblance of truth. As a conduit for protecting the health of working-age adults, health and safety could be a missing ingredient from the health psychology domain.

Key Debates in Health Psychology

Overcoming 'Real-World' Barriers

Based on our experience, applying behaviour change to contemporary in-dustry settings must overcome a range of practical barriers. Foremost is the challenge in affecting change in a transient workforce, as is currently the case

---

in the construction sector and seasonal work within agriculture. In the future, temporary contracts may become a more common feature of working conditions more generally. Want of a stable captive audience can therefore thwart 'upstream interventions' targeting culture, and ability to maintain change. Solutions for overcoming workforce transience include managing behaviour change programmes project by project, empowering project managers to implement strategies on the researchers' behalf; reducing the range of different companies that make up a 'supply chain' and adopting more prescriptive behaviour modification–based approaches. As globalization takes hold, and the proportion of the workforce comprising immigrant workers increases, workforce diversity will increase still further. Diversity may stem from linguistic differences and national cultural differences. It means that a given target audiences can hold a mixture of knowledge about the range and nature of health and safety risks. Diversity can be tackled by using 'pictures' to convey risk. Using 'point of use' pictures to prompt worker as to the correct course of action right at the moment when they undertake that action (Chinien & Cheyne, 2006) can transcend cultural differences. It can also be tackled by tailoring interventions according to a given project's health and safety cultural maturity. To illustrate, there is little point in trying to target individual workers' behaviour in a reactive culture that lacks an adequate health and safety management system and leadership buy-in. Another common barrier stems from lack of senior management commitment. Initiatives have little chance without the company boss's backing. Demonstrating the business case for health and safety improvements for senior management is crucial. Promoting the cross-issue relevance of behaviour change programmes to other company operations such as financial management or improving its 'green credentials' can lend weight. Obtaining a project client's endorsement can also add persuasive power in a 'results'-driven industry. Complex supply chains can distort behavioural change messages. A principal contractor's ability to affect practices in a 'third-tier' supplier (i.e. subcontracted by a subcontractor) has invariably thwarted the interfaces between suppliers. Including behaviour change programme expectations within supplier contracts can help control the resultant dilution in behaviour change messages. Ultimately, microsized businesses that comprise just one or two workers remain the hardest to reach for behaviour change programmes. For the 'man-in-the van', winning business is often contingent on creating a favourable impression with a householder. So long as they carry out a job to the householder's satisfaction, there is little incentive for them to adhere to good health and safety practice. Unless the public at large accurately appreciates the importance of health and safety, persuading microbusinesses to embark on behavioural change programmes may have little traction. This is a challenge that has yet to be overcome.

Acknowledgements

The author would like to acknowledge the active roles of colleagues Nikki Bell and Jane Hopkinson in raising the profile of this area. Thanks are also due to Victoria Bennett, Jennifer Webster and Nadine Mellor for their valuable input into related work.

References

Bell, N., & Webster, J. (2011). *Influencing dutyholders' behaviour regarding the management of noise risks*. Research Report RR866. Sudbury: HSE Books. Retrieved from http://www.hse.gov.uk/research/rrpdf/rr866.pdf

Bell, N., Vaughan, N., & Hopkinson, J. (2010). *Factors influencing the implementation of RPE programmes in the workplace*. Research Report RR798. Sudbury: HSE Books. Retrieved from http://www.hse.gov.uk/research/rrpdf/rr798.pdf

Bandura, A. (1986). *Social foundations of thought and action: a social cognitive theory*. Englewood Cliffs, NJ: Prentice Hall.

Burton, A.K., Kendall, N.A.S., Pearce, B.G., Birrell, L.N., & Bainbridge, L.C. (2008). *Management of upper limb disorders and the biopsychosocial model*. Research Report RR596. Sudbury: HSE Books. Retrieved from http://www.hse.gov.uk/research/rrpdf/rr798.pdf

Cabinet Office, Behavioural Insights Team. (2010). Applying behavioural insight to health. Retrieved from http://www.cabinetoffice.gov.uk/sites/default/files/resources/403936_BehaviouralInsight_acc.pdf

Cabinet Office. (2011). Applying behavioural insight into health. Retrieved from http://www.cabinetoffice.gov.uk/resource-library/applying-behavioural-insight-health

Chinien, V., & Cheyne, A. (2006). *Trojan horse health and safety messaging: an assessment of the long-term and behavioural impact on construction site operatives*. Research Report 505. Sudbury: HSE Books. Retrieved from http://www.hse.gov.uk/research/rrpdf/rr505.pdf

Dombrowski, S.U. (2009). Is the science and application of behaviour change changing? *Health Psychology Update*, 18, 22–25.

Fishwick, D., Lunt, J., Curran A.D., & Trainor, M. (2010) Wellbeing and work: a perspective from 8 European countries on common areas of understanding, national drivers for progress, and research needs. Paper presented at the Towards Better Work and Wellbeing International Conference, Helsinki, 12 February.

Health and Safety Executive (HSE). (2011a). Shattered lives. Retrieved from http://www.hse.gov.uk/slips/index.htm

Health and Safety Executive (HSE). (2011b). Sickness absence. Retrieved from www.hse.gov.uk/sicknessabssence/msd.htm

Health and Safety Laboratory (HSL). (2011a). HSL's safety climate tool. Retrieved from http://www.hsl.gov.uk/health-and-safety-products.aspx

Health and Safety Laboratory (HSL). (2011b). Health and safety training. Retrieved from http://www.hsl.gov.uk/training.aspx

Health, Work and Wellbeing (2011) [Home page]. Retrieved from http://www.dwp.gov.uk/health-work-and-well-being/about-us/

HM Government. (2010). Common sense, common safety. Retrieved from http://www.number10.gov.uk/wp-content/uploads/402906_CommonSense_acc.pdf

Human Engineering. (2005). *A review of safety culture and safety climate literature for the development of the safety culture inspection toolkit*. Research Report 367. Sudbury: HSE Books. Retrieved from www.hse.gov.uk/research/rrpdf/rr367.pdf

Lunt, J., Bates, S., Bennett, S., & Hopkinson, J. (2008). *Behaviour change and worker engagement practices with the construction sector*. Research Report RR660. Sudbury: HSE Books. Retrieved from http://www.hse.gov.uk/research/rrpdf/rr660.pdf

Lunt, J., Bennett, V., Hopkinson, J., Holroyd, J., Wilde, E., Bates, S., & Bell, N. (2009). *Development of the People First Toolkit for construction small and medium sized enterprises*. HSL Report WPS/09/05. Buxton: HSL.

Lunt, J., Bowen, J., & Lee, R. (2005). *HSE review of the risk assessment approach to occupational health: applying health models to 21ˢᵗ century occupational health needs*. HSL Report HSL/2005/57. Retrieved from http://www.hse.gov.uk/research/hsl_pdf/2005/hsl0557.pdf

Lunt, J., Fox, D., Bowen, J, Higgins, G., Crozier, S., & Carter, L. (2007). *Applying the biopsychosocial approach to managing the risks of contemporary occupational health conditions: scoping review*. HSL Report HSL/2007/24. Retrieved from http://www.hse.gov.uk/research/hsl_pdf/2007/hsl0723.pdf

Lunt, J., & Lee, R. (2006). *Systematic review of preventative behavioural for occupational dermal and respiratory hazards*. HSL Report HSL/2007/36. Retrieved from http://www.hse.gov.uk/research/hsl_pdf/2007/hsl0736.pdf

Lunt, J., O'Hara, R., & Cummings (2007). Which mask do you prefer? Changing occupational health behaviour. In J. Houdmont & S. McIntyre (Eds.), *Occupational health psychology: European perspectives on research, education and practice* (Vol. 2.). Nottingham: Nottingham University Press.

Lunt, J., Webster, J., Bell, N., Bennett, V., Hopkinson, J., & Sugden, C. (2009). *Behaviour change worker engagement toolkit for small and medium sized construction companies*. HSL report WPS/09/08. Buxton: HSL.

Lunt, J., & White, J. (2005). *Psychosocial and organisational factors affecting the development and control of occupational asthma: a critical review of the literature*. HSL Report HSL/2005/43. Retrieved from http://www.hse.gov.uk/research/hsl_pdf/2005/hsl0543.pdf

Mackay, C.J., Cousins, R., Kelly, P.J., Lee, S., & McCaig, R.H. (2004) 'Management Standards' and work-related stress in the UK: policy background and science. *Work & Stress, 18*(2), 91–112.

Marmot, M. (2005). Remedial or preventable social factors in the aetiology and prognosis of mental disorders. In P. White (Ed.), *Biopsychosocial medicine: an integrated approach to understanding illness* (pp. 39–59). Oxford: Oxford University Press.

McEachan, R.R.C., Lawton, R.J., Jackson, C., Conner, M., & Lunt, J. (2008). Evidence, theory and context: using intervention mapping to develop a worksite physical activity intervention. *Bmc Public Health, 8*, 326.

PEROSH. (2011) [Home page]. Retrieved from http://www.perosh.eu

Waddell, G., & Burton, A.K. (2004). *Concepts of rehabilitation for the management of common health problems*. Report prepared for UK Department for Work and Pensions. London: The Stationery Office.

11

Keeping Up Appearances in Health Psychology

Timothy P. Moss

When I tell people that I am a health psychologist, even amongst other psychologists from different subdisciplines, there is often confusion as to just what this entails – which is why a book like this is so welcome! In becoming, and staying, a health psychologist, I have often had to think and rethink what this area of psychology really encompasses. I now work as an academic health psychologist in a post-1992 UK University, doing research to develop our understanding of the role of psychological factors in psychological adjustment to health conditions, relating these to practical interventions and teaching health psychology. In particular, my work concerns resilience and well-being amongst those with visible differences, whether originated by burns, trauma, genetics or some other cause. In order to understand the ways in which I do health psychology now (which is of course only one of many ways health psychology is practised), it is perhaps useful to see the pathway which I followed to get here.

By the time I was an undergraduate, I had developed, along with what seemed most of my cohort, a determination to become a clinical psychologist. Fortunately, my University offered the opportunity of a sandwich year, and I secured a position in a clinical psychology unit. This enabled me to take my psychology out of the classroom, and I was able to experience the reality of family therapy, assessment and group work. At this point, though, I realized that my interest as a psychologist lay not in the routine application of established practice regimes with clients seeking support, but in understanding and investigating the underlying processes involved in such problems and interventions. It spelled the end – for a long time – of my ambition to be a practitioner in a therapeutic setting, and awoke an interest in developing a career in applied psychology research, which in turn became the foundation of a career in academic health psychology research and teaching.

Health Psychology in Action, First Edition. Edited by Mark Forshaw and David Sheffield.
© 2013 John Wiley & Sons, Ltd. Published 2013 by John Wiley & Sons, Ltd.

In the early 1990s, there was not an established discipline of health psychology, and very few people would have identified themselves as health psychologists. The BPS had not set a postgraduate syllabus or sought to accredit health psychology training. Consequently, the early postgraduate courses available were varied in content and conception. I spent a year studying towards an MSc in Psychology and Health, on a syllabus which current postgraduates in health psychology would barely recognize, while working as a research assistant investigating the cognitive changes following acute aerobic exercise. While both of these challenges were interesting, neither offered a clear career path. I thus made the pragmatic choice of the curious graduate with an aversion to 9-to-5 work, and cast around for a PhD topic.

Appearance Research: A Role for Health Psychology

A consultant plastic surgeon, based at Derriford Hospital, Plymouth, had recently contacted the supervisor of my undergraduate project, and presented him with a problem. He routinely dealt with patients with a range of appearance-altering physical conditions – from disease processes like cancer, to traumatic injuries and burns through to developmental differences in the size, shape and function of the human body. Some patients were referred purely on the grounds of wanting to change their appearance, and others as part of a wider process of medical interventions. He was regarded by his colleagues as an expert surgeon, and had been president of his professional organization. Nevertheless, there was an issue of psychology which remained unclear to him. Why was it, he wanted to know, that patients' well-being before and after surgical intervention did not seem to bear very close relation to their degree of physical difference, or the clinical outcome of surgery? Was there a simple psychological explanation which he could understand, in order to select suitable patients for surgery and predict psychosocial outcome? Together, they secured funding for a PhD, and when I was offered the chance to take this up, the direction of much of the following 17 years of research and teaching was set. There was clearly not a simple psychological explanation to be found, and in trying to determine some answers to it, somehow I became a health psychologist. The remainder of the first part of this chapter will provide an overview of some of the essential aspects of the work, and include illustrations of where health psychology as a profession fits in. I will attempt to show that health psychologists face many of the same challenges and problems as other psychologists in applied settings, as well as some of the unique and idiosyncratic issues of health psychology.

Conceptions of the Person in Health Psychology

If we examine the problem presented by the plastic surgeon, we can see that implicitly there is an assumption that patients[1] varied on some consistent dimension to do with psychosocial well-being. In order to understand how individuals varied on this dimension, by how much, and why, it was clearly important to define what this construct could be. It was at this point that the relevance of the 'biopsychosocial' model of health psychology became apparent. This was the new paradigm for health psychology, and remains for many an essential feature of the discipline. When I had worked in the clinical psychology department, clients were formally assessed and classified according to the current *Diagnostic and Statistical Manual* (DSM-III-R; American Psychiatric Association, 1987). In the plastic surgery unit, patients were classified on the basis of physical condition. In unpicking the psychological adjustment in relation to different appearance, however, there was no reason to believe that adjustment would be related to physical diagnosis, or that psychological diagnostic categories designed to identify mental health problems would be relevant. Consequentially, we made a conscious decision to look across diagnostic categories and work from a patient-led perspective on how their appearance affected their lives to best understand the concept of adjustment.

In taking this decision, we entered into a debate which has continued unabated in health psychology, and shows no signs of retreating now. To what extent should health psychology be a discipline which takes the individual, idiosyncratic and esoteric aspects of individuals' lives and experience as its fundamental subject matter, as opposed to applying generalizable, theory-led approaches, which would be directly applicable to policy and practice? Crossley (2001), among others, has strongly argued the case for the former. She suggests that in moving away from a close analysis of individual accounts, health psychology is losing the essence of its humanity, and allowing itself to ape the models of medicine and the natural sciences for less than honest reasons. In adopting even a biopsychosocial model, (as opposed to a biological model) of health, psychologists' quantification of human experience brought the danger of following a purely technical programme, depersonalising those with whom it came into contact. Crossley, and those adopting a similar perspective, would argue that the way that language is used to create subjective realities for people, and the way that this informs the functions and structures of wider society in relation to health, should be the subject matter of health psychology. At the other end of the spectrum in this debate lie those who feel the greatest contribution that health psychology can make is a carefully categorized and objective set of diagnostic and intervention criteria to inform individual practice and policy at multiple levels. For example, Abraham and Hampson (1996) have proposed a model of health psychology firmly based in pre-existing constructs of social-cognitive approaches to psychology. These are founded on an assumption that individuals have cognitive representations of reality which serve to guide their interactions with the outer world. Constructs such as self-efficacy, the self-concept and behavioural intentions are all part of this approach. All reflexive health psychologists must find a way through this dilemma.

For us, it meant deciding whether we examined patients' accounts of their appearance, and used this to understand the range of meanings that appearance has, and the social context in which 'appearance' is created, reflecting perhaps on the construction of gender, age and so forth in so doing, but have a research programme which was not based on any aim of producing an intervention. The alternative was to use existing psychological theory to create and test hypotheses around adjustment, with an explicit aim of generalizing findings, but accepting the risk of losing some of the subjective, personal and powerful nature of people's stories around their appearance. This decision was informed by three factors – the philosophical stance of the research team, the agreements already in place with the funding body and the ultimate research question posed by the surgeon in the first place. Given these, we chose to adopt an essentially realist stance, in which we would measure appearance adjustment, and then identify predictors of it. Essentially, this is the perspective that I have maintained since. Where I would perhaps differ from colleagues with an otherwise similar viewpoint is that I have maintained a belief in the value of subjective, idiosyncratic perspectives – and was able to incorporate this approach in an unusual way later in the research programme.

Developing Measures to Test Theories and Outcomes

Having established a standpoint from which to work, the first step was to develop a useable measure. While it is conceivable that through a collection of existing measures and a review of the literature, we could have identified scales to use, for example assessing depression or social anxiety, this would have been too presumptuous. Rather, as a first step, we asked patients coming through the plastic surgery clinic in the local hospital to describe the way that their appearance affected their life. This enabled us to collect a large pool of items covering the spectrum of emotional, cognitive and behavioural aspects of adjustment. Clearly, amongst these items there was a great deal of overlap and redundancy, as well as some esoteric statements (that, if we had been taking a Crossley approach, might have been the most interesting aspects!). We made an assumption that there was an underlying construct of distress and dysfunction in relation to appearance. On this basis, we presented the statements back to new patients, asking to what extent the statements were true for them. Alongside this, we asked patients to complete a range of other established measures. From this, we were able to identify statistically which were the key statements – the ones which differentiated good and poor adjusters, and which were related to each other in a meaningful way. These items together formed two scales – a long version, the Derriford Appearance Scale 59 (DAS-59, comprising 59 items), and a short version, with 24 items (DAS-24) (Carr *et al.*, 2005). The measure suggested strongly that adjustment to appearance was less about depression than we had anticipated, but was largely composed of social avoidance, fear of negative evaluation, shame and social anxiety. By going through the drawn-out process of creating this measure, we were at last able to run studies to try to identify why some people adjusted well to a different appearance to the norm, and others adjusted less well.

Having identified what we loosely called 'good' and 'poor' adjusters, we returned to a more exploratory approach. An important part of health psychology training is the development of practical skills with clients and participants. I spent long (and often difficult) hours in the interview suite in my University training in the skills of client work, following the basic model of Egan (cf. Egan, 2009). This facilitated my engagement with vulnerable clients in home and hospital settings, exploring their own stories and their psychosocial accommodation of their difference appearances.

The details of the studies that followed have been presented elsewhere. However, in short, we were able to confirm that, firstly, the surgeon's hunch was largely correct; the subjective view of appearance severity was strongly related to adjustment, whereas the objective level of severity only weakly so. What is more, the weak relationship between objective appearance severity and adjustment was not as anticipated – rather than the most, or even least, severely different looking patients being most poorly adjusted, it was those with a moderate level of adjustment. The explanation for this finding remains one of the loose threads of this research; we hypothesized that it was due to those with moderate levels of difference generating less predictable, more ambiguous social feedback. Secondly, we were able to demonstrate that the physical location and cause of an appearance difference were not nearly as influential as we (and others) had anticipated. Finally, we ran studies which demonstrated that the most important aspect relating to an individual's adjustment to their appearance difference is the contents and organisation of information in their self-concept (the emotional and information-based store of self-knowledge). We used a task which required participants to go through a rather long winded booklet, which provided information we were able to decode in terms of each patient's self-concept complexity, in terms of the organisational separation of appearance and non-appearance self-relevant information, and in terms of the relative importance of appearance information about the self compared to self-relevant information unconnected to appearance. This task enabled us to quantify idiographic perspectives, facilitating an assessment of subjective perspectives yet allowing us to compare across different participants. When synthesized, we could demonstrate that someone struggling with adjustment to their appearance would have a more generally negative self-view, which was organized in a more complex way. Furthermore, the information about themselves which was also to do with physical appearance was rated as more important by them, and also kept more separate from 'non-appearance' information about the self. This rather complicated set of findings essentially presented a profile, from a cognitive and emotional point of view, of a poorly adjusted individual. For this person, they would have negative views of themselves. The corresponding negative thoughts were also more likely to be associated with appearance, and additionally, be amongst the most easily brought to mind with the least prompting.

Applications of Health Psychology to Clinical Practice

One of the things I have realised about an academic career as a health psychologist is that despite planning, a large part of the direction is governed by opportunities which cannot be anticipated. It is through being known as someone interested in measurement that a number of projects have arisen that characterize a lot of my health psychology practice. Not all of the work has been submitted for publication, being done on a more pragmatic basis. Some examples of this are below.

Once again, this next project started with a problem posed by a colleague in clinical practice, as a clinical psychologist seeing in- and outpatients in a large hospital's plastic surgery department. She was aware from her therapeutic work that, for many patients, the issue of sexual intimacy was the major aspect of their lives impacted upon by appearance. For some patients, they felt that they could not even approach or speak to someone they were attracted to. For others, they felt that they could get to a certain level of intimacy but go no further. My colleague worked on a one-to-one level to help these patients find coping strategies and alternative ways of thinking about their situations, and, for many of them, improved the quality of an important aspect of their lives. However, none of the established measures in the field really enabled her to evaluate the success of intervention in this area. This was important for two reasons; firstly, she needed to ensure that she was not biased in her interpretation of the success of the intervention. Many well-meaning therapists fully believe in their work, despite it later being shown to be no better than placebo or demand effects (for example, think of some well-meaning but, it is often argued, misled homeopaths, prescribing water for what could potentially be serious health conditions). A proper outcome tool is the first step in being able to establish treatment efficacy. The second reason follows from this; if the treatment worked, she would be in a much stronger position to argue for continuation of funding for the service. My involvement was to work with her, and a health psychology trainee, to develop this measure. She created a pool of statements from her clinical experience, which we supplemented with appropriate statements inspired by generic measures of intimacy. This topic required a great deal of sensitivity. It was apparent that people had a hierarchy of intimacy – from entirely nonsexual contact, through behaviours which would be appropriate in a public setting (e.g. hand holding), to more intimate and personal behaviours including intercourse. This meant that standard test theory would be somewhat flawed; each item would have a different level of 'difficulty' relating to the level of intimacy referred to. We would not necessarily expect items to all predict each other equally. Consequently, the scale we produced owed more to Guttman scaling than a traditional Likert scale (cf. Guttman, 1950). The lessons from this work? To be prepared to shift from initial preconceptions about the nature of a problem; to keep focussed on the patient perspective as much as that of the clinicians.

Other similar projects include the development of a measure for young people, the Appearance Behaviour Checklist, a measure of appearance salience, CARSAL (the extent to which appearance is brought to mind as part of the working self-concept), and a measure of appearance valence (CARVAL). This suite of measures reflects a growing armoury for health psychology appearance researchers and practitioners who do not wish to be constrained by the conception of 'body image' (a discussion for another day).

There have been countless other developments from this research, straddling direct client/user psychological support, working with medics to support decision making and outcome assessment, as well as ongoing basic research. Needless to say, this work has also greatly influenced the direction and content of my teaching and training. The next section of this chapter lays out some of these developments, from the point of view of the competencies of a health psychologist as understood through the BPS health psychology curriculum.

Teaching and Training Health Psychology

One of the core aspects of health psychology practice, according to the BPS, is to teach health psychology, and train new health psychologists. A significant proportion of my working life now is taking up with programme management and delivery on an MSc Health Psychology, and teaching on a programme I ran until recently offering professional doctorates in health psychology. What I have learned from this is the tremendous appetite for the discipline amongst students; I regularly interview candidates for these programmes, and am often impressed by the ways in which they would like to bring health psychology into really diverse workplaces. I often field the query, 'What do graduates in health psychology do?' It is easy to see why this question arises; compared to other fields of applied psychology, the career route is less obviously mapped out, with health psychologists often working in jobs without 'health psychologist' in the title. I firmly believe that this is a strength of the discipline. Clearly, there would be a sense of security and more obvious community in a more recognized health psychology track within the NHS. However, the limitation of this is that it would place artificial boundaries on the settings in which health psychologists work. Currently, the graduates we have taught and trained from both Stage 1 and 2 programmes have found themselves doing health psychology in, for example, public health teams, in condition management programmes, in drug and alcohol services and in both basic and applied research. In this way, I see health psychology having a wider and more profound influence than it could within the artificial construction of a more consistent professional identity.

Regulation of Teaching and Training

One of the other core aspects of health psychology practice, from the BPS perspective, is 'professional skills in health psychology'. This covers a multitude of approaches and ways of working. The most explicit engagement I have with this is through work with the British Psychological Society and also with the Health Professions Council in their respective roles overseeing the UK training courses. The BPS health psychology training committee (BPS DHPTC) offers accreditation to new MSc and doctorate programmes, and makes regular visits to validate and later re-accredit these programmes. Recently, the statutory regulatory role in psychology has moved from the BPS to the Health Professions Council, and the broader discipline of psychology, as well as health psychology more specifically, is adjusting to this change. I act both as a member of the BPS DHPTC and as a visitor for the HPC. It is in this capacity that I have been able to engage with many courses, and take an overview of the existing provision in the United Kingdom. Of course, it has also been a hugely beneficial learning process, with an opportunity to see what works well and what courses are challenging. It is clear that almost all the UK health psychology programmes are sound; the process of BPS and latterly HPC scrutiny has helped course teams engage with and develop a set of useful standards of course delivery, from programme management to assessment to course content, within the context of individual course philosophies. Feedback to course teams has enabled them to identify their blind spots in existing practice, and also put pressure on their institutions where necessary.

While it is still too early to take a firm view on the impact of the HPC on psychology, it seems clear that the BPS has certainly helped programmes. However, I would also want to recognize that there is a danger that both of these bodies may be limiting the development of health psychology. The basic curriculum and scope of the discipline in the United Kingdom were established by the Division of Health Psychology, with some revisions over the past decade, most recently with a review of Stage 2 training being introduced into courses in 2010–2011. It is now more difficult to make basic changes to this codified version of what health psychology is. In meeting health psychology trainees at various stages of their training, as well as employers, my experience is that the curriculum is not always taking trainees where they want to go. Specifically, in the Stage 2 (post-MSc), practical aspect of training, there is far too little training on the facilitation of individual, community and population health changes. A combination of therapeutic and public health skills should be at the core of training. In my view, this would enable trainees to secure work more easily, and at a higher level. How is this related to my own practice? In the BPS and HPC roles I have, I am aware that I am supporting training regimes which I believe could be much better fitted with trainees' needs, but regulation is possibly preventing this, rather than facilitating the development of the discipline. I live with the choice of supporting good regulation around a compromised conception of the discipline, or stepping away and having less access to any future debate around this within those bodies. My essential optimism, based on the willingness of course teams I have visited to be innovative where possible, and the energy of trainees, combined with the increasingly apparent plethora of roles for health psychology, persuades me to stay.

Summary

In this brief snapshot of selected aspects of my progress through health psychology, there are a number of common issues that are worth sharing explicitly. The first has been the ongoing necessity and value of multi- and interdisciplinary working. Health psychology is best when it is hand in hand with medics, psychotherapists, other psychologists and policy makers. This means that health psychologists need to be multilingual in jargon and multicultural in work practices – but also that we have opportunities to operate and influence widely and deeply.

The second point relates to this; health psychology in the United Kingdom has, in my view, struggled for a distinct identity. Professional training and recognition through the HPC and BPS have institutionalized its existence, but the challenge of a delineated single career structure remains a real challenge. It is essential that those of us who identify as health psychologists are also advocates for the discipline externally, but also support each other collectively in the face of potential fragmentation and isolation.

Thirdly – writing this chapter has necessitated further reflection on what it means to be in academia in the United Kingdom. Research metrics (and thus, perhaps, research-led institutions) do not necessarily lend themselves well to applied psychology. In order to sustain health psychology within academia, it is necessary to demonstrate financial sustainability of research from external means, as well as a clear and strong recruitment record for health psychology graduates. As a result of this, we rarely have the luxury of what I have heard called, somewhat pejoratively, 'curiosity-driven research'. Instead compromises and choices of topic and approach are required. A clever new academic in health psychology would find a way of piggy-backing basic research onto a sustainable programme of applied work.

Finally, in taking an overview of some salient aspects of the last couple of decades, I have realized unmistakably that nothing is ever wasted. The discussion about a new theory at a conference 10 years ago, the lecture prepared to cover for a colleague's absence, the abandoned draft of a paper – all these and more have been there and ready to be useful when unexpected circumstances have arisen. Louis Pasteur (1854) famously said that 'Chance favours the prepared mind.' Being open to serendipity and having the faith that it will operate has been a difficult but rewarding part of being a health psychologist. I look forward to the next couple of decades of health psychology with interest and curiosity, and wonder what unexpected turns it will take.

Key Debates in Health Psychology

Positive Health Psychology: A New Direction

Returning to research; it is only years later when I reflect on the process of developing the DAS24 that I realize a huge bias that we were blind to at the time. We were entirely focussed on the negative aspects of adjustment, and the ways in which a different appearance impinged on life. What we had not explicitly considered were the ways in which people drew on strengths and resilience to adjust positively. The idea that having a different appearance could be a route to finding meaning in life and developing stronger relationships was, although clear now, not one which we had been prepared to consider. How had this blind spot developed? In part, through the expectations all the researchers brought with them from a history in the health sector, which despite the rhetoric of treating the 'whole person', has remained essentially an illness sector with a focus on pathology. Current work involves using ideas taken directly from the positive psychology movement, directed at human growth and 'nurturing what is best' (Seligman and Csikszentmihalyi, 2000) rather than pathology. The first of these is to consider the role of personal values in building resilience to altered appearances. Personal values are multifaceted, with a degree of cultural specificity, and include distinctions between, for example, transcendental and materialistic values. We would hypothesize that individuals whose value system is nonmaterialistic will find it easier to cope and manage with a visible difference, being more likely to see the challenges as an opportunity for growth. A second avenue of research arising from the positive psychology movement is to look at the way in which people are able to differently use their own strengths to enhance their resilience in the face of personal and interpersonal threat arising from difference appearances. Strengths, like values, have been carefully analysed to understand what basic categories exist. We would expect that we would see variation in adjustment based on the ability to use strengths such as compassion, courage, perseverance and insight. The challenge for researchers is to identify how strengths can be related to resilience, and how clients can be helped to use them most effectively. The ongoing work on strengths and values reflects only part of the shift in ethos to a positive psychological perspective; at the time of writing, I am convinced that there is a huge well of untapped potential for ways of developing theory and practice in health psychology using a positive perspective. However, health psychologists will be faced with a difficult task persuading others that a focus on positive health is as fundamental a challenge, and as central to the discipline, as an illness-based approach. Are we able to show that we can provide the personal, social and economic benefit necessary to obtain funding outside the academy? I believe that unless we are content to become illness psychologists, though it is a challenge we must face.

Acknowledgements

Many thanks to Dr Antonietta DiCaccavo – not only for comments on a draft of this chapter. Also thanks to the late Dr Tony Carr, and to David Harris MS, for their support, and to the editors of this book for their observations.

Note

1   I am using the description of the people concerned here as 'patients' knowingly, as this is how they were thought of by the health professionals that they came into contact with. The debate over the consequences this linguistic choice, as opposed to 'client', 'service user' or even 'consumer' is live and ongoing, but beyond the scope of this chapter.

References

Abraham, C., & Hampson, S. (1996). A social cognition approach to health psychology: philosophical and methodological issues *Psychology and Health, 11*, 223–241.

American Psychiatric Association. (1987). *Diagnostic and statistical manual of mental disorders* (3rd ed., rev.). Washington, DC: American Psychiatric Association.

Crossley, M. (2001). Do we need to rethink health psychology? *Psychology Health and Medicine, 6*(3), 243–255.

Carr, T., Moss, T.P., & Harris, D.L. (2005). The DAS 24: a short form of the Derriford Appearance Scale (DAS59) to measure individual responses to living with problems of appearance. *British Journal of Health Psychology, 10*(2), 285–298.

Egan, G. (2009). *The skilled helper: a systematic approach to effective helping.* Pacific Grove, CA: Thomson Brooks/Cole.

Guttman, L. (1950). The basis for scalogram analysis. In S.A. Stouffer (Ed.), *Measurement and prediction: the American soldier* (Vol. 4). New York: Wiley.

Pasteur, L. (1854). Inaugural lecture. University of Lille.

Seligman, M., & Csikszentmihalyi, M. (2000). Positive psychology: an introduction. *American Psychologist, 55*, 5–14.

Glossary

British Psychological Society (BPS): the professional body for health psychology in the United Kingdom, and is incorporated by Royal Charter.

Derriford Appearance Scale: a psychometrically sound and user-friendly measurement scale for assessing distress and dysfunction in relation to visible differences in appearance.

Guttman scaling: a scaling technique based on increasing item difficulty across the items which make up a scale.

Health Professions Council: the statutory body in the United Kingdom for regulating and registering professional psychology.

plastic surgery: the branch of medicine concerned with changing physical appearance through surgical means. Incorporates both reconstructive surgery, aimed at repair and restoration of appearance following disease or trauma, and cosmetic or aesthetic plastic surgery, which is aimed at 'improving' the appearance of people without any other objective medical need.

pool of items: a collection of potential items for inclusion in a measurement scale.

post-1992 UK university: a former Polytechnic, granted degree-awarding powers in 1992, usually with roots in vocational and applied teaching and research, and often with a more diverse student body in comparison to pre-1992 Universities.

psychosocial well-being: a positive psychological state, founded on positive emotional, behavioural and interpersonal functioning.

realist: a realist perspective works on the basis that phenomena in the world truly exist, rather than being the product of a social and linguistic process.

resilience: the psychological quality of resisting the negative consequences of traumatic or stressful events, even using this as a springboard for development or growth.

self-concept: the information structure containing the knowledge and emotion-based information about the self. It varies between individuals in content and organization. It has been implicated in many processes related to psychological well-being.

Stage 1 and 2 programmes in health psychology: Until recently (2009) to become a health psychologist in the United Kingdom, it was necessary to pass through three staging posts – firstly, achieving a psychology degree offering eligibility for the BPS graduate basis for registration, GBR (now graduate basis for Chartership, GBC). The second step entailed passing the 'Stage 1' qualification, the theory-based aspect of the training. This was either a BPS-approved MSc Health Psychology studied through a University, or the BPS equivalent studied independently. Finally, a prospective health psychologist would need Stage 2 training – either a BPS-approved professional doctorate in health psychology from a University, or independent Stage 2 training with the BPS. The advent of regulation by the HPC has changed this somewhat in terms of obtaining a legally protected title of health psychologist, but the existing courses by and large have remained in place.

12

Social and Political Health Psychology in Action

Michael Murray

Finding a Location

Perhaps one of the biggest challenges facing health psychology today is in expanding its role in moves to combat the substantial social inequalities in health in our society. Despite the wide range of policy initiatives introduced to reduce these social inequalities, they continue to persist and indeed may even be widening (Popay *et al.*, 2011; Mackenbach, 2011). If health psychology is to participate in attempts to reduce these inequalities it needs to develop a more social and political approach that explores the character of the social, historical and material context within which health develops and also develop ways of critiquing and challenging those social arrangements and practices that inhibit health and well-being.

Such an orientation informs some of the contemporary developments in critical health psychology (Murray, 2004) which in turn is informed by critical ideas in social psychology and the other social sciences (e.g. Gough & McFadden, 2001). Critical health psychology has drawn attention to the importance of the broader societal context within which health and illness are located. It has also emphasized the importance of multiple theoretical perspectives and research methods coupled with an awareness of how values shape our orientation. It stresses the importance of an ongoing process of critique and action coupled with a reflexive stance to our own research priorities and practices.

There is not one single approach within critical health psychology but rather a range of different critiques that are united by a rejection of the standard positivist orientation. As Billig (2008) recently commented in his work on the historical forebears of contemporary critical psychology:

Health Psychology in Action, First Edition. Edited by Mark Forshaw and David Sheffield.
© 2013 John Wiley & Sons, Ltd. Published 2013 by John Wiley & Sons, Ltd.

Whatever their differences, critical psychologists are nevertheless united by an opposition to mainstream psychology, which they consider too narrow in its focus and too rigid in its approach. (p. 17)

Billig distinguished between two main forms of criticality. The first is that of critical discourse analysis that exposes the role of certain power elites and discourses in sustaining social inequality and injustice. As part of this process of challenge, critical psychology is 'dedicated to helping provide voice [for those] groups who have been systematically exploited and whose voice is not generally heard' (Sampson, 2000, p. 3). However, earlier demands for providing voice have been augmented by critiques of the character of these 'voices' and demands for various forms of social action to challenge evidence of injustice and oppression. The second form of being critical is to criticize the discipline of psychology itself and to expose how 'its focus on the de-historicised individual, has failed to analyse how social inequalities have created many of the psychological phenomena that psychologists study' (p. 19).

In several previous papers my colleagues and I have stressed the importance of engaging in multiple forms of critique and action. For example, while welcoming the important developments made by critical discursive and qualitative work we have argued that 'sustained concern with language can divert attention from the broader material issues' (Murray & Campbell, 2003, p. 233). In a subsequent paper we argued for a more materialist approach to critique including an awareness of the sociohistorical context, the connections between the personal and the sociostructural, and the structural causes of health and illness (Murray & Poland, 2006). This attention to the material has also been taken up by other critics of what can be characterized as light forms of qualitative research. Thus Hook and Howarth (2005) in their commentary on a critical social psychology of racism and antiracism have argued:

We cannot presume an autonomous psychological individual above and beyond social/ material forces which constitute their subjecthood. For this reason, critical social psychological forms of analysis need to be *more* multi-disciplinary, *more* multi-perspectival than has traditionally been the case. (p. 510)

Critical health psychologists engage in various forms of social action designed to promote health and enhance quality of life. Thus they can work with individuals to explore the character of their illness experience and its social location but they can also work with collectives to challenge oppressive social relations. This does not mean that they ignore the broader structural factors that oppress people but rather their action is designed to draw attention to the myriad forms of social oppression. In previous publications we have stressed the importance of this critical approach to social action as being a means 'to promote analysis and action that challenges the restrictions imposed by exploitative economic and political relationships and dominant systems of knowledge production, often aligning [our]selves with broad democratic movements to challenge the social inequalities which flourish under global capitalism' (Campbell & Murray, 2004, p. 190).

Working with Older People

An example of some of these issues is our recent work with older people. There has been increasing public discussion about the growing number of older people in society. From the government perspective this is of concern because of the supposed increasing demand for access to a range of resources although this is debateable. But what do older people themselves think of this situation? In some previous work, we conducted detailed interviews with baby boomers about their perspectives on growing older (Murray *et al.*, 2003). From these interviews it was apparent that most wanted to maintain their independence and not to become dependent upon the state. In terms of how they viewed health, the most important feature was the ability to continue engaging in a range of social relationships.

There is a substantial body of research highlighting the importance of social interaction for health and well-being. Older people who live in disadvantaged neighbourhoods report more social isolation and loneliness (Fernandez-Ballesteros, 2008). They often live alone, with limited personal resources and fewer local opportunities for social interaction.

One project I am currently working on explores in some more detail what it means to be old in a disadvantaged urban community, the potential of involving older people in local social activities, and the practical and policy implications of such research. This interdisciplinary study is known as the CALL-ME project – an acronym for Community Action in Later Life (http://www.keele.ac.uk/callme). The project is part of the New Dynamics of Ageing research initiative, a large national programme of research on different aspects of ageing (http://www.newdynamics.group.shef.ac.uk). Currently over 40 projects are being funded through this programme ranging from the biological through to the arts-based.

Briefly, the CALL-ME project is located in four disadvantaged areas of one large city. Within each of these areas the project team has adopted a similar participatory approach which involves them in a reflexive cycle of research and action with older residents (see Brydon-Miller, 2004). In each area the key researchers began by exploring the lives of the older residents through a series of semistructured interviews, discussion groups and more informal conversations. From this initial fieldwork, the local area groups of researchers and residents then moved to develop a range of local community initiatives that offered enhanced local opportunity for social interaction. This usually involved them accessing some additional resources from the city council or some social agency and then working to develop the initiatives – these ranged from community gardening through to exercise classes.

In the area where I largely worked we developed a series of arts projects (Murray & Crummett, 2010). This use of the arts in community settings is something that I have been interested in for quite some time (see Murray & Gray, 2008). It is important to realize that this form of community arts is concerned with not just providing local social opportunities but also promoting discussion and action concerning larger questions around the allocation of resources. It is by orienting community arts both inwards and outwards simultaneously that its potential for change can be enhanced. As Meade and Shaw (2007) said:

> [Community arts has] a potential capacity for entering attentively into the experience of others, excavating and exploring the causes of flaws and wounds in society, thinking critically about structures and relations of power and acting creatively and collectively to transform the world for the better. (p. 414)

The initial interviews we conducted with the older people confirmed the extent of their social isolation and disengagement from formal social institutions. This degree of social isolation was subsequently confirmed in a survey we conducted of the residents using a standard measure of social involvement.

Reviewing the interview transcripts it was apparent that a lot of the conversation had focussed on the older residents' perceptions of their neighbourhood. Their experience of health and illness was immersed in this local social setting. They described their community in terms of decline and rejection. They perceived their community as distinct from neighbouring communities in terms of history, composition and access to resources. While certain physical barriers separated the communities, their separateness was also social psychological as was apparent in how they talked about the communities.

Following on from these conversations we worked with the residents to develop a series of arts projects. The reaction of the older people to these projects was very enthusiastic. The projects not only enhanced participants' self-esteem and wellbeing through creative artwork but also through developing local opportunities for social interaction and through challenging broader negative social representations of the community and its residents. An important part of this project was the exhibitions and public display which attracted large numbers of local people and press publicity. This was part of the process of taking the project out and engaging in broader public debate about resources in the neighbourhood.

Challenges and Joys

The life of the health psychologist working in community settings can be both exciting and frustrating. The most exciting aspect is the enthusiasm shown by the participants in the various projects. These are often people who have felt rejected and ignored by official agencies and can be apprehensive about outsiders. A lot of the initial work involves building relationships with the participants such that they are willing to discuss their lives and to consider new initiatives.

Thus research becomes a process of co-learning through social engagement. In his book on qualitative research, Kvale (2000) uses the term 'conversation' to describe the process of conducting an interview. Noting the Latin base of the term conversation as 'travelling with', Kvale stresses that an interview should also be a process of travelling with the other. However, the participatory action research project is more than travelling with the other; it is a process of working with the other to reveal their strengths, to identify obstacles and to work together to overcome those obstacles.

An example of how this collaboration can evolve and expand was the work by Ann Crummy in developing a community festival in a working-class neighbourhood in Edinburgh. In her personal account of the impact of this event Crummy (1992) concluded:

> The annual festival had proved to be the key to tapping and releasing the community's creative imagination and talent. Once released, men's and women's horizons widened. They became aware of the restrictive and damaging effect on family life of living in an area where there are only houses, scarce community facilities, little work and second class education. (p. 58)

Thus, it is not the initial project but the processes around the project and how it can build to larger projects that are important.

In reflecting on this process of community engagement it is important at all times to adopt a reflexive stance – personally, methodologically and theoretically. Critical psychologists are aware of their role in the research process and need to consider who is setting the agenda and who benefits from the research (see Key Debates box, this chapter).

There are also myriad frustrations in doing such work. These can be both practical but also theoretical. From a practical perspective such work can involve considerable expenditure of time and energy with what can seem to be limited impact. There is also the frustration of dealing with a range of social agencies which do not seem particularly sympathetic or interested in your research.

The interdisciplinary nature of the work involving different social and health researchers can also be challenging. This provides an opportunity to access a range of new theories and research skills, but it can also be problematic in terms of conflicting or overlapping perspectives and research approaches. An important aspect of the project is the involvement of a range of community partners. A key partner in our project has been the city council which has been committed to developing initiatives to improve the quality of life of older people throughout the city, especially those residents in poorer neighbourhoods. This provides an excellent opportunity to connect our research with practice and policy developments.

There are also methodological and theoretical challenges. In participatory action research there is considerable latitude in the sorts of data being collected. Working with individuals and groups over time provides an opportunity to develop a substantial corpus of information. The challenge is how to systematize and interpret this large data set. This form of research is not hypothesis testing but rather complementary development of theory and practice. A values commitment to social change underpins this research and provides an impetus during times of frustration. The focus on local social action has some implicit dangers if the researchers do not reflect upon the broader sociopolitical context. For the past 10 years or more, there has been a move to decentre the role of the state through the privatization of health and social services and the downloading of responsibility not only to the individual but also, increasingly, to the community. Thus communities that are already disadvantaged have the additional burden of being considered responsible for their condition. This becomes the new contemporary form of victim blaming. Previously, we argued:

> By locating the responsibility for health problems within marginalized local communities, such analyses serve as a smokescreen for governments who seek to reduce welfare spending [etc.]. (Campbell & Murray, 2004)

Health psychologists have an important role to play in promoting discussion of these issues. The answers are not straightforward and require ongoing reflection on our practice as well as a commitment to broader social change.

Filtering Health Psychology

On looking back over the development of the discipline of health psychology over the past 30 years I am struck by the continued dominance of individualistic theoretical models and a neglect of the bigger societal and structural issues. Back in the 1970s, before health psychology was formally established, there was a debate within social psychology about the direction of that discipline. At that time there was a series of publications concerning the so-called crisis in social psychology. In one of these, Moscovici (1972) criticized much of social psychology for its focus on small studies and its neglect of the big issues. At that time he posed the challenge:

> We must ask what is the aim of the scientific community. Is it to support or to criticize the social order? Is it to consolidate it or to transform it? (p. 23)

From the outset, health psychology tended to ignore these bigger questions and instead drew inspiration especially from the positivist perspectives of the attitude change models that were developing at that time. Fishbein and Ajzen's book on attitudes was published in 1975 and remains perhaps the most influential text in health psychology. It is interesting to look at how they framed their approach at that time:

> Generally speaking we view humans as rational animals who systematically utilize or process the information available to them. The theoretical structure or conceptual framework we have adopted assumes a causal chain linking beliefs formed on the basis of available information, to the person's attitudes, beliefs, and attitudes to intentions, and intentions to behaviour. (Fishbein & Ajzen, 1975, p. vi)

There has been much development and refinement of this conceptual model over the past 40 years but its assumptions are still endemic in the discipline (see Conner & Norman, 2005). Basically, it adopts an individualistic information-processing model which goes under the label social cognition. Its concern with social issues is usually operationalized in terms of perceived social norms.

Fortunately, more critical ideas have gradually developed within psychology and it is from these that I have drawn inspiration. These ideas are varied and cover both theoretical and methodological issues. This approach can range from concern with understanding the lived experience of those with particular health problems using detailed qualitative research through to various forms of action research designed to challenge the social and structural forces that contribute to ill health. There is increasing interest in the potential role of participatory action research. This entails involving research participants in a collaborative program of reflection and action.

'Set the Sails, I Feel the Wind A-Blowing' (*The Low Anthem*, 2009)

To close and to re-orient myself, I thought it would be useful to reflect back on the early days of health psychology and what I was doing then. Health psychology was formally established in the United States in 1978 and 8 years later as a section of the British Psychological Society in 1986. However, there were many psychologists conducting research on health and illness prior to that time. For example, in the late 1970s and early 1980s I was conducting a study on the social psychology of smoking among young people. The original design of this study was a large survey of teenagers. While epidemiologically the survey was very well designed, I quickly became disillusioned with its underlying positivist assumptions and pushed forward with an alternative approach. In 1981 I applied to the Medical Research Council for funds for an intensive qualitative study. It is useful to consider what I wrote in the original grant application:

> Much previous research into smoking has been cross-sectional surveys of the social and psychological correlates of the phenomenon. The smoker was conceived as a passive individual who responded by smoking when exposed to such stimuli as 'peer pressure' or 'positive beliefs about smoking' both of which were considered discrete measureable entities. . . . Recently social scientists have begun to develop an alternative methodology based upon a conception of man [*sic*] as a self-conscious actor who is not only aware of what he is doing but can give 'accounts' of his action (Harre and Secord, 1972). While it is agreed that the content of such accounts should not be accepted uncritically they can still provide us with an insight into the meaning of social behaviour. . . . Smoking should not be considered a neutral behaviour pattern emitted by passive individuals in the presence of certain stimuli but rather a social act which can have a variety of meanings in different situations. The task of the social psychologist is to identify the dimensions of these different meanings and situations. (Murray *et al.*, 1988, p. 5)

While I and others attempted in those days to promote a more critical social approach to the psychological study of health and illness, the positivist tenets of the American establishment set the course for the new health psychology. In part this also reflected the strong individualistic focus of much of clinical psychology. Today, we can see a resurgent interest in more critical ideas within psychology.

These reflect both the sustained sociopolitical turmoil underway internationally, as well as continuing debate within the discipline about the adequacy of mainstream approaches. Old ideas, however, do not fade away but continue to have currency and to dominate textbooks and training courses (e.g. Mielewczyk & Willig, 2007).

Discussion with younger health psychologists provides optimism. Only 12 years ago it was difficult to find contributions to a special journal issue on qualitative research in health psychology (Murray & Chamberlain, 1999); now it is almost mainstream. While a concern for personal success may discourage the adoption of critical ideas, debate in other disciplines and in the broader society encourages the asking of questions. The words of the American band, *The Low Anthem*, which I have quoted above, provide a fitting closure and opening.

Key Debates in Health Psychology – Need for Reflexivity

The dominant natural science approach within psychology has emphasized distance and objectivity. A more critical approach emphasizes the importance of reflexivity by which is meant a careful reflection on the role of the researcher in the research process. It also requires a reflection on the epistemological assumptions underlying the discipline. Science is pervaded by the prediction and control mantra of measurement and experimentation. An alternative approach is concerned with understanding and enhancement through active engagement and critique. As such, critical health psychology moves from the scientist practitioner model to that of the scholar activist. As a scholar the critical health psychologist draws upon a wide range of theories and research methods, while as an activist he or she is engaged in subversion and challenge to established truths and the promotion of various forms of action.

In terms of personal involvement, reflexive researchers need to consider their own role in the process. To what extent are they pushing for change that they define or change that is developed in collaboration with the participants? In terms of method health psychologists have historically favoured questionnaires but increasingly interviews and focus groups are now used. In some settings these methods are not appropriate and the researcher needs to reflect on their adequacy and to explore alternative ethnographic and arts-based approaches to develop an understanding of the everyday experience of health and illness. Finally, and at all times, the researcher needs to reflect upon their theoretical assumptions. Theories are not blueprints but rather guides to interpretation and potential action. We work with the theoretical frame rather than imposing it on the data. We also explore alternative frameworks that may increase our understanding of how people frame their worlds, their location in them and how they can be changed.

References

Billig, M. (2008). *The hidden roots of critical psychology.* London: Sage.

Brydon-Miller, M. (2004). Using participatory action research to address community health issues. In M. Murray (Ed.), *Critical health psychology* (pp. 187–202). London: Sage.

Campbell, C., & Murray, M. (2004). Community health psychology: promoting analysis and action for social change. *Journal of Health Psychology, 9,* 187–195.

Conner, M., & Norman, P. (eds). (2005). *Predicting health behaviour.* Buckingham: Open University Press.

Crummy, H. (1992). *Let the people sing: a story of Craigmillar.* Newcraighall, Edinburgh: Author.

Fernandez-Ballesteros, R. (2008). *Active ageing: the contribution of psychology.* Cambridge, MA: Hogrefe & Huber.

Fishbein, M., & Ajzen, I. (1975). *Belief, attitude, intention, and behavior: an introduction to theory and research.* Reading, MA: Addison-Wesley.

Gough, B., & McFadden, M. (2001). *Critical social psychology: an introduction.* London: Palgrave.

Hook, D., & Howarth, C. (2005). Future directions for a critical social psychology of racism/antiracism. *Journal of Community & Applied Social Psychology, 15,* 506–512.

Kvale, S. (2000). *InterViews.* London: Sage.

Mackenbach, J.P. (2011). Can we reduce health inequalities? An analysis of the English strategy (1997–2010). *Journal of Epidemiology & Community Health, 65,* 568–575.

Mielewczyk, F., & Willig, C. (2007). Old clothes and an older look: the case for a radical makeover in health behavior research. *Theory & Psychology, 17,* 811–837.

Moscovici, S. (1972). Society and theory in social psychology. In J. Israel & H. Tajfel (Eds.), *The context of social psychology: a critical assessment* (pp. 17–68). London: Academic.

Murray, M. (Ed.). (2004). *Critical health psychology.* London: Palgrave.

Murray, M., & Campbell, C. (2003). Living in a material world: reflecting on some assumptions of health psychology. *Journal of Health Psychology, 8,* 231–236.

Murray, M., & Chamberlain, K. (Eds.). (1999). Qualitative research [special issue]. *Journal of Health Psychology, 4* (2).

Murray, M., & Crummett, A. (2010). 'I don't think they knew we could do these sorts of things': social representations of community and participation in community arts by older people. *Journal of Health Psychology, 15,* 777–785.

Murray, M., Jarrett, L., Swan, A.V., & Rumun, R. (1988). *Smoking among young adults.* Aldershot: Gower.

Murray, M., & Gray, R. (2008). Health psychology and the arts: a conversation. *Journal of Health Psychology, 13,* 147–153.

Murray, M., & Poland, B. (2003). Health psychology and social action. *Journal of Health Psychology, 11,* 379–384.

Murray, M., Pullman, D., & Heath Rodgers, T. (2003). Social representations of health and illness among baby-boomers in Eastern Canada. *Journal of Health Psychology, 8,* 485–499.

Popay, J., Whitehead, M., & Hunter, D.J. (2011). Injustice is killing people on a large scale – but what is to be done about it? *Journal of Public Health Medicine, 33,* 148–149.

Glossary

epistemology: theory of knowledge.
individualism: a focus on the individual as the source of human action.
positivist: an approach to research that emphasizes natural science methods.
reflexivity: process of reflecting on research assumptions.

13

Tailoring Behavioural Support and Tailoring Health Psychology Careers

Felix Naughton

Introduction

Recently, when listing the conferences I had attended in relation to my PhD work for a fellowship application form, I was reminded how large the remit of health psychology is. In addition to attending health psychology conferences, I attended those focusing on cancer, primary care research, epidemiology, smoking cessation, behavioural medicine and public health. For my area of research, and most other areas within health psychology, there is considerable overlap with many other disciplines. Perhaps it is in part because of this overlap that there is some uncertainty regarding what health psychology is. Thinking about this overlap can cause one of two reactions. We can feel overwhelmed and head for disciplines that have clearer boundaries or we can embrace the broadness of health psychology. I have found great advantages in pursuing the latter course. It has enabled me to tailor my training and career trajectory according to my research and clinical interests. This has allowed me to build up my knowledge and experience on a number of different health topics, methodologies and research and clinical skills. A further benefit of working in a broad discipline is the opportunity to apply for funding from a wide range of funding bodies, work in a range of institutions and settings and teach a wide variety of students and health professionals.

My Background – What Led Me to Stage 2

I became interested in health psychology while working in IT for the North West Deanery, the institution responsible for the training of doctors and dentists in the North West of England. It was providing IT support and training to clinicians

Health Psychology in Action, First Edition. Edited by Mark Forshaw and David Sheffield.
© 2013 John Wiley & Sons, Ltd. Published 2013 by John Wiley & Sons, Ltd.

and colleagues on the use of a variety of computer-based technologies that got me interested in the way we interact with technology and how it can affect our behaviour. I realized that I was more interested in the process of IT use than the technological element. A brief chat with a colleague who had just finished a Master's in Health Psychology convinced me that this was the discipline for me. Fortunately, my first degree was in psychology so I enrolled on a Health Psychology Master's degree in 2004 and chose the course at the University of Bath as it included a 3-month placement.

I thoroughly enjoyed the MSc and found almost every area of health psychology we covered highly interesting. It enabled me to undertake some work on my area of interest and I undertook a review of the acceptability of telemedicine. One of the highlights was my 3-month placement with the Health Psychology Unit at the Gloucestershire Royal Hospital. During the placement I adopted a policy of saying 'yes' to every opportunity offered to me. The placement provided a platform for further tailoring my training over and above the Masters degree programme. This gave me some clinical experience of CBT programmes for pain management, cardiac rehabilitation and stroke rehabilitation. As I was particularly interested in improving my teaching skills, I enquired about potential teaching opportunities and ended up developing and delivering two short courses on bibliographic database searching. The placement also provided me with the opportunity of undertaking some clinical research; my MSc research dissertation was focused on the ostensible relationship between sleep quality and disability among individuals with chronic pain.

While I was not able to pursue my core research interest during the placement (which was shaping up nicely – the use of new technologies to promote and improve health), I was able to gain insight and experience of the clinical side of health psychology. However, my research desires were about to be satisfied. During the early part of my placement in 2005 I came across, applied for and was awarded a PhD place at the University of Cambridge, supervised by Professor Stephen Sutton, which was perfect for my interests – the development and evaluation of a computer-tailored text-message based intervention for pregnant smokers.

The PhD was a launch-pad for Stage 2 and the start of my health psychology career. As the different Stage 2 competencies rather succinctly categorize the work that I do, the next section is structured around these.

The Work That I Do

Research

The bulk of my time and efforts go into carrying out research. At my junior level, most of this research is in the area of my core research interest, though I am from time to time involved in some other studies. My PhD was funded for 4 years by Cancer Research UK; I started in October 2005 and I submitted in March 2010. Even though my PhD was funded for 1 year longer than usual, I still went beyond the funded time-period by the customary 6 months. However, as the PhD was funded for 4 years, the project was more ambitious than 3-year projects usually are. The project aim was to develop a computer-tailored intervention, using written and text message–based communications, for pregnant smokers, and undertake a trial to evaluate the feasibility of delivering it. The development work was guided by the MRC framework for the development of complex interventions (Campbell *et al.*, 2000). This consisted of four studies which mapped on to the framework's first three phases:

- A systematic review of the self-help intervention literature for pregnant smokers (Phase 0)
- An in-depth qualitative interview study to provide insight into prenatal smoking and identify potential intervention targets and barriers to behaviour change (Phases 0 and 1)
- A qualitative pre-test study of a pilot version of the intervention (Phases 1 and 2)
- A randomized controlled trial evaluating the feasibility and acceptability of the finalized intervention (Phase 2)

A reasonable proportion of the time taken to conduct these four studies was spent undertaking administrative and recruitment tasks such as meeting health professionals to discuss their involvement in the research, applying for ethics and R&D approvals, working on recruitment, trial management and, as always, some envelope stuffing. I also spent a great deal of time developing the structure and content for the computer-tailored 'expert system', though I was lucky to have a supervisor who could do most of the programming work. The remaining time was spent on the academic aspects of research – searching and reading the literature, study design, writing protocols, data collection, analysis (I found qualitative data analysis especially time consuming) and the write-up of the research. This also included presenting research findings at conferences, to health professionals involved in the research and to fellow academics at invited talks and seminars.

One of the major challenges I have found with developing a tailored behavioural intervention is developing the content. I think what surprised me most when I started development work was how little we know, to date, about what type of smoking cessation advice and techniques work best. A major part of any tailored intervention is matching participant characteristics to specific advice or feedback with the expectation that individualized advice will be more helpful to the individual than generic advice. However, we lack the evidence regarding how to best do this and lack insight into how smokers' beliefs, intentions and behaviour change over time and in response to intervention. Therefore, we have to rely on general guidance from theories and the literature in combination with intervention development research, clinical experience and intuition, and a significant amount of guesswork. This presents a particular challenge when you lack clinical experience (at this point I had not started working with smokers clinically and only had limited opportunities to gain guidance from those that did).

A practical challenge with undertaking research at all levels, though particularly at a doctoral level, is lacking the clout to get the health professionals involved in your research doing the things you want them to do. For me, getting midwives to help recruit for my studies meant a lot of cold calling, meeting with midwifery management and using any contacts I could lay my hands on. An obvious downside to this approach, which is unavoidable if you have no health professional collaborators, is that you have very little to bargain with when asking management to agree to their staff doing something for you, unless you have funding to pay for their time. Furthermore, and perhaps of more concern, is lacking the authority to resolve problems as they occur (e.g. health professionals not reliably inviting patients to take part in your study). This of course can affect the external validity of the research and slow recruitment down considerably. This was certainly an issue in my PhD research which I had to work hard at to resolve (the provision of chocolate certainly helping smooth the way). One mistake I made was not setting up a system whereby I could monitor exactly who was inviting clients to take part in the research and who was not. This could have been easily achieved by adding a code to each set of invitation forms given to a specific health professional and then working with any who had not successfully invited any clients to take part to explore how it could be resolved (e.g. further training).

Despite this last challenge, for me it has been the time spent with health professionals that has provided some of the greatest rewards in undertaking applied research. For example, I have found disseminating research findings to antenatal professionals at both a formal and informal level highly insightful. Who better to feed back to you on your research than the professionals who know your population the best? I also found that once the midwives involved in my research understood the whys and wherefores of it, they became very encouraging and interested to help. Meeting face-to-face with the health professionals that you are asking something from is something I found to be crucial, not to mention insightful, and often good fun.

Another aspect I particularly enjoy about the research I do is the feeling of identifying another piece of the jigsaw puzzle. Health behaviours are undoubtedly a vital element in determining people's health outcomes. But understanding these behaviours and how to change them can be fiendishly complex. Not only do we need to take into account people's internal environment, beliefs and goals, but also we need to consider these elements in a wider social and cultural context. However, complexity should not discourage investigation. Indeed, I feel a great sense of pride in being able to contribute towards this endeavour. The jigsaw may have a lot of small pieces, but it is highly satisfying to be involved in revealing the picture, not to mention a privilege of having the potential to help people along the way.

Teaching

Teaching is another area of my work that I get great satisfaction from. One of the main difficulties I have had with teaching work, however, has been finding enough of it. As I am part of the University of Cambridge School of Clinical Medicine and not a psychology department, I have had to work perhaps harder than most at seeking teaching work out. However, I think my experience reinforces one of the strengths of health psychology highlighted at the beginning of the chapter: its applicability to other disciplines.

Over the last 4 years I have coordinated a module on health promotion for an MPhil in Public Health with a public health colleague and supervised students taking an Introduction to Psychology module on a social and political sciences degree and medical students studying the social context of health and illness. For the health promotion module I have delivered lectures on models of health behaviour, health education and mass media health promotion and run practical sessions where students design interventions that aim to change a particular health behaviour for a specific target group. The topics for the psychology supervisions are various and can range from developmental psychology areas such as attachment and language development to classic social psychology areas such as majority and minority influence and the person versus the situation debate. Though these are mostly outside of the immediate remit of health psychology, there is significant crossover and students usually find the health psychology links particularly interesting. The range is fairly broad again for the supervisions with medical students and can include anything from the sick role and folk beliefs to the social and ethical dilemmas of new medical technologies. The supervision side of my teaching is particularly enjoyable. These typically are small-group teaching sessions (usually 3–4 students) where, after setting essays on particular topics, I encourage the students to discuss and explore these topics with each other. Running these 'supervisions', as they are called at Cambridge, have increased my teaching confidence. They have forced me to improve my 'thinking on my feet' skills and have given me the confidence to try out different types of teaching techniques.

As well as teaching students, I also very occasionally run training sessions for health professionals and fellow academics. For example, I refined and updated the bibliographic database-searching training course I developed during my MSc placement and delivered this to colleagues in my unit at the University of Cambridge. I also developed and delivered short courses on using the qualitative analysis software NVivo Version 8. I have found that when you look for it, interesting teaching opportunities often emerge. As well as helping me tailor my skill development, these opportunities have helped supplement my income during my PhD studentship.

A great benefit of teaching on different courses is that you get to interact with a variety of students with different types of knowledge and experience. The range can be quite large. For example, at the start of a week I have taught medical doctors from developing countries in Africa and South America studying Public Health, and later that week have taught UK students, who have just finished their A-levels or equivalent, studying social and political sciences. However, teaching a multitude of students a variety of topics in different formats requires a variety of teaching techniques. This exposes one of the bigger challenges I have faced in teaching; tailoring my teaching approach and using different teaching techniques effectively.

In an effort to address this challenge, I have read up about teaching and learning and also joined and attended a number of workshops organized by the Postgraduates who Teach Network (PGwT), set up to support psychology postgraduate students with teaching responsibilities. The PGwT workshops I attended were excellent (and free); I highly recommend them. However, I have been a little frustrated by the few opportunities I have had from my university to improve upon my teaching methods. In particular, they did not allow me, as a postgraduate, to attend most of their teaching-related training courses despite having teaching commitments. I imagine other universities have similar policies. I feel that being equipped with a teaching 'technique toolkit' would have helped me greatly.

Clinical Work

Apart from the experience I gained during my MSc placement, my clinical experience has been solely focused on smoking cessation counselling.

I started working as a smoking cessation counsellor for the Suffolk Stop Smoking Service in November 2009. Having completed 'Level 2' and 'Level 3' training I took over the running of a half-day clinic at a children's centre in Sudbury, Suffolk. This clinic is primarily for pregnant smokers, though we get a combination of pregnant and nonpregnant clients attending. The sessions are delivered on a one-to-one basis. An important element of the half-hour first session is to assess the client's smoking profile; their likely dependence to nicotine, their quitting motivation and confidence, their reasons for wanting to quit, the situations they find it hardest to resist smoking in or when they enjoy smoking the most and so on. After this, we discuss medication options. Nicotine replacement therapy (NRT) is offered to pregnant clients who have tried and failed to quit using willpower alone, and nonpregnant clients also have the option of taking Zyban (Bupropion) or Champix (Varenicline). After medication options are discussed and NRT vouchers or GP prescription letters have exchanged hands, clients are encouraged to set a quit date. Next we discuss the psychological and behavioural side of quitting. Often this involves talking about ways of enhancing their quitting motivation, depending upon their reasons for quitting, and getting them to start thinking about smoking as a habitual behaviour and how they might extinguish the associations they have made between internal and external cues and smoking. Finally, and potentially one of the most important elements of support, is giving encouragement. Follow-up visits provide an opportunity to further tailor the behavioural support to prevent relapse and to provide more encouragement and support to maintain their confidence and motivation.

I find the small amount of clinical work I do keeps me grounded in the reality of the complexities of behaviour. While models of health behaviour are useful when guiding the advice given to clients, I have come to appreciate the individual variation in how well particular psychosocial determinants appear to explain and account for motivation and behaviour. For example, for some clients their beliefs about the health outcomes of smoking seem to have a great influence on their motivation to quit, whereas for others it appears to be much less motivating. This difficulty in reconciling the difference between how individuals and groups behave exposes a weakness with many interventions that are not tailored to the individual, such as many of the leaflets and standardized health education programmes available. Individually tailoring these types of interventions using 'expert systems' can reduce the impact of this discrepancy to some extent, especially if they are informed by research, often qualitative, which identifies some of this variation. However, individually tailored interventions like the one I developed during my PhD still tend to be underpinned by theories and research based around how people behave at the group level and do not take account of individual variation. This issue is one that is currently difficult to resolve in the field.

Another dilemma of clinical work is that of accuracy versus engagement. The issue goes something like this. You have an obligation to provide accurate and evidence-based information and guidance to clients, but at the same time you have a duty to maximize their chances of successfully changing their behaviour. Sometimes by being strict with accuracy you can be in danger of putting clients off (Pregnant client: 'So will nicotine patches help me quit smoking?', Counsellor: 'We don't know, no one has yet done any research to answer that question';[1] Client 'Will I gain weight when I quit?', Counsellor: 'I'm afraid so, the average long-term weight gain among quitters is around 17 pounds and it's usually there to stay'[2]). On the flip side, by being too encouraging in the way you present information you could end up misleading the client (Pregnant Client: 'So will nicotine patches help me quit smoking?', Counsellor: 'Yes, taking NRT doubles your chances of quitting'; Client: 'Will I gain weight when I quit?', Counsellor: 'Although you may put on a few pounds initially, you can burn it off through a combination of diet and exercise'). The first two 'accuracy' answers reflect the state of the evidence and the last two both come from NHS smoking cessation information.[3] I am not trying to pick holes in the NHS advice provided, just give an example of the difficulty in going from the research world to the clinical world. Personally, and I am sure most counsellors are the same, I am more comfortable going down the strict accuracy route but with a large dose of plausible reassurance (e.g. Counsellor: 'Actually there hasn't been a great deal of research that has looked into NRT use in pregnancy, but there are some studies going on at the moment checking that it helps pregnant smokers in the same way that it has shown to help nonpregnant smokers').

These minor challenges aside, I find working as a smoking cessation counsellor highly rewarding. I have learnt a great deal from clients and feel I have a richer understanding of smoking and smoking cessation as a result of our interactions. I also really enjoy the rapport-building aspect, despite having to say to clients, when they have successfully quit smoking and their support has ended, 'I hope not to see you again!'

Consultancy

While it is both interesting and potentially career boosting to undertake consultancy work, from the small amount of consultancy work I have done I recognize how it can be a drain on the time you have left after meeting all the needs of your primary work commitments. This means being good at saying 'no' – though this is easier said than done.

My first consultancy project was with the Gloucestershire Royal Hospital Health Psychology Department (where I did my Masters degree placement). They had received a small amount of funding from the Alcohol Education and Research Council to explore why problem drinkers take around 7 years to access the treatment services after recognizing they have a drinking problem. The main aim of the project was to increase our understanding as to why this delay occurred and explore potential ways it could be reduced. My role was to consult with the other psychologists involved in the project to establish how we were going to address the aims of the project and then oversee the implementation of that work. Our approach was to undertake a qualitative study where we interviewed problem drinkers with varying levels of treatment experience to explore why they delayed help seeking. The findings were later disseminated back to the ultimate clients – the local drug and alcohol services. It turned out to be an engaging project, and I enjoyed the different role I had as a consultant rather than someone simply undertaking the research.

Since then I have undertaken some smaller more *ad hoc* bits of consultancy. This has been for several Stop Smoking Services and include exploring why pregnant smokers rarely take up NHS support to help them stop smoking and consulting on the set-up of an incentive scheme for pregnant smokers.

Although not strictly consultancy work, I have also served on the European Health Psychology Society's (EHPS) Synergy board for three years. Synergy was set up with a core aim of stimulating networking and collaborative research within the society, mainly through a 2.5-day workshop which precedes the annual EHPS conference. My involvement has included organizing the 2007 workshop which focused on internet-based health psychology interventions with another Synergy board member and holding the position of Secretary within the Board. As well as providing me with valuable organization experience, organizing the 2007 workshop enabled me to work with the workshop facilitators who are some of the leading experts in the field of internet-based behaviour change interventions. This is another example of how I have been able to tailor the work I do to match my research interests.

Reflections of Working in Health Psychology

Through my work experiences, I recognize how practically every element of health and health care has an important psychological component. From lifestyle choices to adjustment to chronic disease, our beliefs and goals regarding a desired health state or responses to a perceived health state have a bearing on our thoughts, feelings and actions, which in turn can progress or prevent ill health. I see health psychology as the leading discipline that seeks to explore, understand and potentially intervene to reduce negative psychological influences on health and to promote positive ones. As a consequence, I can see the huge value that health psychology can potentially provide to health care systems and public health around the world. However, there are several aspects of working in health psychology that can make it different from working in other fields.

I very much enjoy the opportunity of meeting and working with a variety of individuals, including academics, health professionals and study participants. I have learnt a great deal from them. However, one consequence of working with many different people, ironically, can be isolation. By not working with the same team of people for most of the time, my work has felt quite solitary. Usually when I attend meetings, visit teams involved in my research, undertake clinical work, attend training or deliver teaching, I do so with no discussion with my colleagues at my place of work, often not even my supervisor. This can leave you feeling like no-one really knows all of what you do. This is probably quite common in the field. On the bright side I feel this has helped me become more independent, feel more confident in the decisions I make and guidance that I provide and boosted my commitment to the field. But, it has shown me the importance of having a good support network both inside and outside of work life.

A further consequence of having a varied work life, especially where several of your roles are independent from each other, is that you often find yourself having to juggle quite a few pieces of work simultaneously. For example, in some weeks I have found myself having to do 10 hours of teaching work and a half-day smoking cessation clinic, attend several meetings, present some of my research work to fellow academics and still complete close to a full week's work on my primary research project. Realistically this means sometimes working on evenings and weekends. However, being good at planning your time can help you even out the peaks and troughs of work. For example, I sometimes 'bank' some additional research time during a quiet week that I can use to make life easier during a busy week. Senior academics are likely to have much more varied roles and have a whole raft of techniques to eke out every minute of every working hour, so they probably have plenty of useful time management advice to share.

Future Steps for Health Psychology

As we continue into the twenty-first century, individualization is becoming a common feature of our health care system; we have choice over our health care provider and can soon expect personalized drug treatments and genetic profiling for a clearer picture of disease risk. I can see computer-tailoring playing a valuable future role in health psychology interventions across all levels of health care. For example, with the rise in ownership of smart phones, many people are now carrying around minicomputers with the same resources as the PCs being sold at the start of this millennium. There is a huge number of applications that can be downloaded onto smart phones including ones which can help patients with long-term conditions keep track of their symptoms, triggers and medication use, ones that monitor physical activity levels using accelerometers and some that even allow users to scan the barcodes of food products to help them keep track of their daily calorie intake. By combining theory-based tailored behaviour change modules with new technologies, there is much potential for increasing the availability, sophistication and impact of health information and therapy without the reliance on or cost of one-to-one communication. Even with standard mobile phones, tailored text message support and advice has shown potential for delivering support and maintaining health-related communication conveniently. A further advantage with these types of mobile interventions is that they enable personalized or individualized advice and support to be provided in real time as a consequence of users feeding back on day-to-day changes in their beliefs, intentions and behaviours. However, it is important not to get too enchanted by the novelty of new technologies before they have started to demonstrate their value and popularity (most of us will remember the huge expectations for virtual reality in the early 1990s, but who has ever owned a VR set?). Furthermore, to better the existing interventions we have in more traditional formats, and to harness the potential of new media for intervention delivery, we need to improve the science of behaviour change.

Great steps have already been taken in respect to this last point. Work has been undertaken by Abraham and Michie (2008) and Michie *et al.* (2008) to develop a taxonomy of behaviour change techniques linked to theoretical constructs. This makes it feasible for researchers to describe the components of their interventions using the same language as each other. This could lead to the assessment of the effectiveness of particular techniques for particular behaviours, and potentially for particular individual characteristics, as part of systematic reviews and meta-analyses. In addition, there is a growing interest in health psychology in assessing behaviour within rather than between individuals using 'N-of-1' studies. This should provide a greater understanding of how beliefs, intentions and behaviour changes over time in response to different behaviour change techniques or interventions.

To me these developments represent the start of a new chapter in health psychology and behavioural science. Such advancement could certainly help to start address the challenge of knowing how to best tailor an intervention for the individual. If we can achieve this then rather than behaviour change interventions representing a 'hip shot', tailored support could much more accurately target behavioural determinants and become more like, and please excuse my computer game generation lingo, a 'head shot'.

Key Debates in Health Psychology

How important is it to adapt intervention content to the individual?

When it comes to persuading individuals to change their behaviour, it is generally assumed that the more relevant the information is to the individual, the more persuasive it will be – in line with the Elaboration Likelihood Model (Petty & Cacioppo, 1986). As a consequence, developers of computer-tailored interventions, aiming to persuade, painstakingly match individual characteristics to intervention content. Likewise, the information provided to individuals by behavioural counsellors that focus on persuasion is usually tailored to the client's beliefs and behaviours. But how important is it to adapt the content of persuasive communication? In an experiment, Dijkstra (2005) compared the behavioural impact of written smoking cessation information that was personalized (use of participant's name, brand of cigarettes etc.) but otherwise generic to nonpersonalized information that was adapted to several characteristics of the smoker (gender, self-evaluative outcome expectancies etc.). They found that personalization increased quitting activity more than the adaptation of content. Furthermore, they found that this difference in quitting activity was explained by how personally relevant the individual perceived the information to be. Other smoking studies have also demonstrated that the more personalized generic written information appears to be, the more it increases intention to quit (Webb *et al.*, 2005). While these studies are few in number and have focused on persuasive information rather than behavioural support, where adaptation is likely to be more important, they still raise important questions. Is the adaptation of content as important as we might think? When developing persuasive content, is it more important to ensure the individual *perceives* the information they receive as personally relevant rather than to ensure it is adapted for them? If so, given that personalization is much more straightforward than adaptation, a lot of time, money and effort could be saved. However, the increased efforts made by marketers of consumer products to personalize advertising materials, especially communications reaching us electronically, may well lead to personalization desensitization and an attenuation of this effect.

Notes

1   To date, only small trials of NRT for pregnant smokers have been conducted. However, a fully powered efficacy trial of NRT for pregnant smokers is currently underway in Nottingham, United Kingdom, led by Dr Tim Coleman, to address this uncertainty.
2   O'Hara, P., Connett, J. E., Lee, W. W., Nides, M., Murray, R., & Wise, R. (1998). Early and late weight gain following smoking cessation in the Lung Health Study. *American Journal of Epidemiology*, *148*, 821–830.
3   The NHS guidance does not distinguish between the efficacy of NRT for pregnant smokers and non-pregnant smokers. As pregnant women have been found to metabolize nicotine faster than non-pregnant smokers, there is reason to believe that standard NRT might be less effective for this group.

References

Abraham, C., & Michie, S. (2008). A taxonomy of behavior change techniques used in interventions. *Health Psychology, 27,* 379–387.

Campbell, M., Fitzpatrick, R., Haines, A., Kinmonth, A. L., Sandercock, P., Spiegelhalter, D., *et al.* (2000). Framework for design and evaluation of complex interventions to improve health. *British Medical Journal, 321,* 694–696.

Dijkstra, A. (2005). Working mechanisms of computer-tailored health education: evidence from smoking cessation. *Health Education Research, 20,* 527–539.

Michie, S., Johnston, M., Francis, J., Hardeman, W., & Eccles, M. (2008). From theory to intervention: mapping theoretically derived behavioural determinants to behaviour change techniques. *Applied Psychology, 57,* 660–680.

Petty, R.E., & Cacioppo, J.T. (1986). *Communication and persuasion: central and peripheral routes to attitude change.* New York: Springer-Verlag.

Webb, M.S., Simmons, V.N., & Brandon, T.H. (2005). Tailored interventions for motivating smoking cessation: using placebo tailoring to examine the influence of expectancies and personalization. *Health Psychology, 24,* 179–188.

Glossary

Champix (Varenicline): a partial agonist of nicotinic receptors designed as a smoking cessation medication.

Computer-tailoring and expert system: a computer programme which uses participant characteristics to individualize feedback.

Zyban (Buproprion): an antidepressant-based smoking cessation medication.

14

Working with Chronic Pain

Sue Peacock

Background

Upon leaving school, I was determined to be a physiotherapist, and had arranged to work as a physiotherapy assistant prior to going to university. I hadn't even considered psychology as an option. My experience working as a physiotherapy assistant was invaluable, in that it taught me about the politics of the NHS, but more importantly it taught me important people skills such as respecting dignity and showing compassion. One of my more tedious tasks actually turned out to be a turning point in my life. This task involved sorting out the referrals for out-patient physiotherapy, and I noticed that the same names kept appearing every few months, and I wondered why these people kept coming back and what we could do to help them so they wouldn't keep returning and I realized that these patients had chronic pain. I read a little around chronic pain and at this point decided that psychology was going to be the career for me, in particular working with people who have chronic pain.

Whilst at University studying my first degree, I made contact with a local psychologist who was running pain management programmes and worked as a volunteer helping her to run them. This eventually led to paid assistant psychologist work. Whilst studying for my MSc Health Psychology, I had to return to my post as a physiotherapy assistant to pay for my course fees. I used this opportunity to write my thesis on relaxation as a treatment method for phantom limb pain, as at that point one of my jobs was to run the amputee group. From there I moved into health promotion and was involved in various projects such as sexual health and workplace health promotion. At the onset of smoking cessation services, I was asked to set up

Health Psychology in Action, First Edition. Edited by Mark Forshaw and David Sheffield.
© 2013 John Wiley & Sons, Ltd. Published 2013 by John Wiley & Sons, Ltd.

the service from scratch in Luton Health Action Zone, which was successful and became a countywide service for the whole of Bedfordshire & Luton.

Meanwhile, whilst working in health promotion, I was offered the chance of working in a pain management department at Milton Keynes to develop their pain management programmes; to me this was a great opportunity. So I worked part-time in both health promotion and the pain management department. A few years later, I left health promotion to work part-time as a research assistant in pain management, whilst obtaining my PhD at the University of Leicester. This also involved being the 'Psychological Aspects of Pain' module leader for the MSc in Pain Management.

Now I work full time within the Pain Management Department, and have my own private practice, which includes a session in an Orthopaedic Medicine Clinic. This chapter will focus briefly upon my work in pain management.

What, Where, When and Why?

I am very fortunate in that there is a great variety in the type of work I do. My role covers patient contact such as in clinic with the Pain Consultants, individual clients, pain management seminars, pain management programmes and the support group. I line manage and supervise qualified and trainee health psychologists and the physiotherapist and nurse who run the pain management programme. I also write clinic letters and reports, and provide psychological support for staff working in cancer, renal, occupational health and other specialities. I am also involved in developing the psychological service throughout the hospital, and at a regional level in the NHS with the development of musculoskeletal treatment pathways.

Psychological factors have a wide-ranging impact on the perception of pain and its effects. There are fundamental psychological mechanisms that influence the perception of chronic pain, which in turn influence whether the patient decides to seek treatment or not, and responses to treatment.

Working alongside the Pain Consultants, in an out-patient hospital setting, I am often the first person who patients will meet when they come to pain clinic. We decided that it was important that all our new patients had the opportunity to speak to the psychologist and that it was perceived as 'normal', to get away from the stereotypes that you have to be 'mad or bad' to see the psychologist, or that the pain was 'all in their heads'. Sometimes this can prove tricky when it has been suggested to a patient when the reason for their pain isn't clear, and isn't showing up in MRI scans, so the patients feel as if they have been told that their pain is imaginary.

Almost all patients are suspicious of psychological issues and psychologists. I have found the best way to gain the patients' confidence is to outline the normal consequences of chronic pain and presenting the different traps chronic pain patients can fall into. For example, patients can slip easily into decreasing activity levels following well-meaning advice to 'take it easy'. This often leads to them withdrawing from activities they enjoy, hence follows a slide into depression and an increase in focussing on their pain. They perceive the pain alone, to be the barrier, whilst in fact now, many barriers exist. Most patients recognize themselves within these chronic pain traps and can begin to identify how they have become disabled with pain without any blame being implied. By avoiding blame, patients are often more willing to try treatments rather than becoming resistant and angry.

At this first session, my role also involves collecting information, using the concept of 'flags', which indicate psychological factors and obstacles to recovery, so we can decide as a team the best way forward to help this person with managing their pain. Firstly, I look at their pain history as this feels less threatening to them, so I enquire about their pain, how long they have had it, what do they think caused the pain, what tests and investigations have they had, what treatments have they had for their pain, what does their pain feel like, do these feelings and sensation change and if so, what causes it to change? This is important because it develops rapport, and also gives me an indication of what type of pain they might be experiencing. It gives me an idea of how they feel they have been treated by various health professionals and what they think about being referred to the pain clinic.

Following this, I then assess the impact that the pain is having on their social lives. Asking questions about the family; who lives at home with you? Are any of your family living locally? How do they feel about your pain? What do they do when you are in pain? Do you have any good friends or neighbours nearby? Are they able to help you out if needs be? Do you have someone to talk to about your pain? I ask this to get an idea of what social support, if any, they have. Interestingly in Milton Keynes, possibly because it is a new town (created by town planners almost from scratch in the 1960s), there appears to be quite a lack of social support. It also tells me how the patient's family respond to their pain; do they ignore it or are they overly solicitous?

Questions are asked around activities of daily living such as, are you able to manage the household chores? Is there anything you find difficult to do at home because of your pain? I ask questions about work and hobbies such as; are you currently working? If so, does your pain affect your ability to do your job? Are your employers aware of your pain? Do you have to take time off because of your pain? What hobbies do you have? Are these hobbies new hobbies that you have taken up since having your pain? Do you go out socially with friends and family? This information is useful because it shows us what their limitations are. If appropriate I can signpost them towards help and support, such as putting them in contact with the Disability Employment Advisor.

Thoughts and feelings are next on my agenda, often starting with a really general question such as; how does pain make you feel? Often this uncovers a whole range of issues, for example frustration with the various health professionals they have seen who can't find a cause for their pain, or if surgery hasn't gone as well as expected, or if they simply can't find the right pain relief. Patients can experience anger, grief, upset, anxiety, depression, stress and difficulty in their changing roles, such as a woman who feels she can't be a good mother because she can't do certain things such as keep the house clean and tidy or play active games with the children, or a man who has had to give up work and now his wife has to work, which he doesn't think is right. They often experience a strong sense of injustice. Many patients develop a fear of their pain, so they stop doing activities in case it makes their pain worse. Relationships between partners, families, friends and employers can become strained. Some worry about the financial implications of not being able to work, and their perceived shame and embarrassment of receiving welfare benefits. Most chronic pain patients worry about the coming years, and how they will cope with their pain in the future.

Lastly in this brief assessment, I enquire about their current pain self-management strategies. Self-managing is taking positive, planned action which reduces the 'luck' element in pain self-management. I might phrase this as 'I know that you have pain all the time, but what kind of things to you do to ease the pain when it is bad?' This is important so I can see if they are using active or passive coping strategies, and decide what treatments may or may not be helpful, in order to tailor our own interventions.

Within these assessment sessions my role covers giving information and advice ranging from giving out telephone numbers of the Citizens' Advice Bureau, the Carers' Project and the Disability Employment Advisor, to liaising with Social Services and Local Housing Associations. I dispel myths around chronic pain, the most common one being that hurt does not always equal harm. I try to reassure within the context of the patient and their pain experience, sometimes discussing various treatment options such as medication, medical interventions like injection treatments or complementary therapies and compliance to treatment regimes. When dealing with distress, I feel that it is important to give patients time to express themselves, and acknowledge that it is OK to be upset; it's important to distinguish distress caused by pain and disability from general distress. It is imperative to listen carefully and empathize, and also vital to remain detached from their anger or distress and remain objective. The professional decides what they can deal with, and what requires someone else, and refers on.

Following this brief assessment, I write up notes for the Pain Consultant who then sees the patient and makes the treatment decision based partly on their clinical judgement and partly on mine. This influences the treatment strategy for that particular patient, be it medical, psychological or both.

I strongly believe that self-management strategies should not be the last option in the treatment of chronic pain. Therefore, over time I have developed pain management seminars, which are two 1-hour group sessions which teach the basics of self-management such as understanding pain (reinforcing the role of psychological factors in maintaining pain), activity pacing, goal setting and relaxation. All new patients in the pain clinic are routinely referred to attend these sessions. Audit has shown them to be considerably beneficial in terms of patients' use of pain self-management skills. Pain management seminars are currently held in the hospital as an out-patient appointment; in the future I am hoping these will move into a community setting.

Those requiring more psychological intervention are offered a further appointment where I assess more thoroughly to see if they will benefit from individual therapy or the pain management programme. In this context I am looking at general suitability for pain management, to identify specific psychological targets for treatment and identify specific psychological obstacles to reactivation.

For those identified as having evidence of major personality disorders and/or substance abuse disorders, I ensure that, if required, they are known to the mental health team, as research suggests they are unlikely to benefit from pain management. Some patients face temporary obstacles such as an ongoing psychiatric condition, or comprehension difficulties due to their medication. Those with difficulties with comprehension due to posttraumatic cognitive impairment may benefit from a one-to-one approach rather than the pain management programme. Other reasons for offering an individual approach would be lack of confidence in group settings or poor English language skills.

Those individuals requiring an individual approach, for whatever reason, rather than the pain management programme, are offered further outpatient appointments. Specific conditions such as general anxiety disorders, anxiety related to pain, depression, stress, posttraumatic stress disorders, difficulty in adjusting to chronic pain, experiencing difficulties in relationships, pain catastrophizing, pain-related fears, self-efficacy, coping styles and strategies are often more effectively managed through individual psychology sessions initially. Often after individual psychology treatment sessions, suitable patients are willing to join the pain management programme.

Using cognitive-behavioural therapy (CBT) in pain management, I tend to draw on the primary objectives of treatment outlined by Turk and Okifuji (2003). These are

- To combat demoralization by assisting patients to change their view of their pain and suffering from overwhelming to manageable.
- To teach pain self-management strategies and techniques that help them adapt and respond to chronic pain and the problems resulting from it.
- To assist patients to reconceptualize themselves as resourceful, competent and able.
- To help them learn the associations between their thoughts, feelings and behaviour, and subsequently to identify and alter automatic, maladaptive patterns.
- To use these more active responses.
- To increase self-esteem and confidence and attribute successful outcomes to their own efforts.
- To help them anticipate problems proactively and generate solutions rather than fear them, which facilitates maintenance and generalization.

For those who find it difficult to adopt a CBT approach, 'mindfulness' and 'acceptance' seems to have a growing role in chronic pain. Mindfulness (McCracken *et al.*, 2007) is the practice of staying in the moment, spending more time present to ourselves, and our surroundings; not trying to change things but trying instead to accept the way that things are, for better or for worse. I have found this approach to be particularly effective with ethnic minority groups and those resistant to challenging negative thought processes. In my practice I also use hypnotherapy, sometimes for pain relief, but often to address needle phobias, promote positive self-esteem and confidence, and reduce anxiety. As with mindfulness this provides another tool for those who don't respond to CBT.

Our Pain Management Programmes (PMP) are held in a community setting and have been for the past 12 years, as I believe that for these group of patients, hospitals are often associated with disappointment and failed treatments, therefore we need to start afresh. Also, I think that a community setting reinforces the normality of chronic pain and decreases the reliance on formalized health care. We have a maximum of 10 people on each programme and all have completed the pain management seminars prior to being referred to the PMP.

The focus of psychological intervention using cognitive-behavioural principles in the PMP is to enhance the overall participation in the PMP by contextualizing people's emotions and reintroducing the biopsychosocial model of pain and disability as related to their experiences. It is key to addressing the stress–pain interface, as once these are recognized patients can start to implement changes and adopt appropriate self-management strategies. The basic management of emotions, cognitions and pain behaviour are taught; aiming to defuse anger, hostility and resentment using cognitive reappraisal.

We also teach stress management techniques such as relaxation, ranging from diaphragmatic breathing, to progressive muscle relaxation and guided imagery. Importantly as with all skills taught, we discuss how to implement it into daily life, and encourage them to do so. Of course when we first teach relaxation skills, some people experience difficulties such as initial self-consciousness, saying they can't relax (emphasizing the importance of practice!), and lack of time to practice so we usually adopt a problem-solving approach to this.

Cognitive restructuring is a major goal of the PMP. Patients need to learn that their thoughts about their pain and themselves can affect their levels of stress, pain and their behaviour. Typical thinking patterns of chronic pain patients include catastrophizing or 'all or nothing thinking' or 'hurt equals harm'. Often I have found it is easier to start these sessions by using case studies, as patients vary in their ability to identify their own cognitive errors. Once they are able to identify these, they can move on and examine their own using 'thoughts diaries'.

Having identified problems using case studies, we look at problem solving. Initially patients often need quite a lot of help with this. We tend to split the group into two, and 'brainstorm' as many potential solutions as possible. Sometimes if things are a little slow to get going, then we will suggest a completely inappropriate solution, which then facilitates patient involvement.

Patients are required to apply pain management skills in their daily lives, hence good communication including assertiveness skills are required for this. These can be difficult sessions as they have become passive, angry or withdrawn, or feel guilty. This session is towards the end of the course when the group members have established trust in each other, as these sessions often involve role play. We discuss the differences in expressing ourselves in passive, aggressive or assertive ways. We stress that assertiveness is a way of feeling more in control and less helpless in their situations.

Poor sleep is common in chronic pain, therefore we cover sleep hygiene. This involves making patients aware of the habits they have that might not be conducive to good sleep and trying to change them. In this session relaxation is included, with reinforcement in how to refrain from reacting to intrusive negative thoughts.

Family involvement is crucial, however it is sometimes a challenge to get them involved. We arrange evening sessions based on a 'Question Time' format, in that we have a panel (the pain team, plus a patient representative). Prior to the session we ask both patients and their families to send in some questions to us, which during the session we pick out and answer and invite patients and their families to comment. Usually this stimulates productive discussions.

A vital component of the PMP is relapse prevention, as the patients are only with us for 6 weeks. We ask patients to identify their goals, both short and long term. These will address specific areas such as medication use, management of flare-ups, targets for exercise and relaxation, the use of the health care system, return to family and other social activities, the potential to return to gainful activity such as paid employment or voluntary work, and areas specific to them such as improving communication skills with the family. These issues are followed up at the support group, as all patients are discharged from the pain clinic at the end of the PMP.

We set up the support group because after 4 or 5 years of patients completing the PMP, they started to come back to pain clinic: not because the pain had changed, but they wanted to see if there was anything new which might help. The support group is a very socially oriented meeting once a month. Either myself, or one of my psychologist colleagues attends the support group in case anyone has any issues to discuss around their continuing progress from the PMP. We have found that the support group acts as a 'safety net' and rarely do these people return to the pain clinic.

As part of my role, I run the Pain Drop-In Clinic with one of our pain nurses. Literally once a month any of our pain clinic patients can drop in, for a quick chat if they want some advice, or can make an appointment if they need a more in depth consultation. If their medication needs reviewing the pain nurse will do this.

Challenges and Joys of the Job

Service development is an exciting challenge, but also has its share of frustration. Over the years, as part of a supportive chronic pain team, I have been able to develop a successful psychology service. Sometimes this has been difficult especially having to write business cases and prove what you are doing is not only effective for your patients but is cost effective, in order to attract funding. Unfortunately there are no National Frameworks around chronic pain so there is rarely any available money. However, over time I have become better at identifying and obtaining various pots of money for new projects such as our chronic pain and sleep programme.

Trying to comply with waiting lists targets is difficult as the demand for our service regularly exceeds our capacity. Other challenges we face are putting chronic pain on the agenda at a local level. We run study days for colleagues working within the hospital and outside the hospital. In order to promote better communication between primary and secondary care, I have developed the Milton Keynes Chronic Pain Forum, which meets three times a year for educational purposes where we have a presentation about an issue in chronic pain and then discuss case studies, which has proved successful.

There is so much I love about my job and I don't really know where to begin; I see the purpose of my job to inspire, teach, support and empower people to transform their lives. Seeing people change their lives to have a more meaningful existence and prove to themselves that they can do things is really rewarding. I enjoy having the autonomy to run the psychology service as I see fit, within the realms of budgets and best practice.

My next challenge that I have been given is to develop a psychology service within the hospital, which I am hugely looking forward to.

How Health Psychology Is Interpreted through the Filter of My Work

As health psychologists, we know that pain is a complex perceptual experience influenced by psychosocial factors such as the meaning of pain to that person, beliefs, attitudes, expectations, emotions, the environmental and social context and biological factors. In both assessment and treatment we put theory into practice; without outlining the strengths and weakness, a few of the models used are explained below.

The biopsychosocial model is key in the development of cognitive-behavioural treatment for chronic pain. In chronic pain, this model assumes some kind of physical pathology or changes in the muscles, joints or nerves that generate nociceptive input to the brain. Perception interprets the nociceptive input and identifies the type of pain (i.e. dull, ache, burning and/or stabbing). Then through appraisal a meaning is attributed to the pain, based upon beliefs that people develop throughout their lifetime, which influence subsequent behaviours. Depending upon the appraisal process and these beliefs, the person may choose to ignore the pain and carry on, or refrain from all activity and assume the 'sick role'. In addition, their decision to adopt the healthy or the sick role is often influenced by both positive and negative responses from their significant others.

Patients' beliefs have a vital role in chronic pain. Literature suggests that beliefs are associated with psychological functioning, physical functioning, coping strategies, behavioural responses and response to treatment. Key beliefs to identify initially are the patients' attribution of the onset of their pain and fear and harm avoidance.

Health belief models attempt to link thoughts, emotion and behaviours, and can be applied to chronic pain. It is suggested that cognitive representations provide the basis for the coping responses for dealing with the health threat. Therefore, being faced with an unusual symptom (pain), or diagnosis from the doctor, the individual will construct their own representation, which in turn will influence behaviour, including help seeking and response to treatment. In addition to their appraisal of the situation, they will draw on their own expectations and beliefs about the different choices they have.

There is little research specifically in the use of HBM to pain management. The stages of change model applied to pain (Kerns and Rosenberg, 2000) is sometimes used, although my personal experience is that it lacks prediction of outcome. However, prior to the PMP, it is often a good starting point for patients to identify where they are in terms of change, and what is expected of them. Along with motivational interviewing, it is possible to move patients positively around the stages of change model.

Of particular use in pain management is the self-regulation model (Leventhal *et al.*, 1998). The patients' meaning of their pain is an important issue in pain management The SRM focuses on an individual's personal representation of their illness as a predictor of health treatment use. The SRM proposes that individuals' representations of their illness is comprised of how the individual labels the symptoms they are experiencing, the perceived consequences and causes of the symptoms for the individual, the expected time in which the individual would expect to be relieved of symptoms, and the perceived control or cure of the illness.

Self–efficacy theory (Bandura, 1977) refers to the individual's belief that they can do something and achieve the outcome they want. Pain self-efficacy beliefs are an important determinant of pain behaviours and pain associated disability. Self-efficacy beliefs can predict pain behaviour and also can be used as a mechanism of behaviour change.

Fear avoidance (Vlaeyen *et al.*, 1995) is often related to depressive symptoms and catastrophizing rather than chronic pain. Since this landmark study, there has been a large amount of research on the role of fear and anxiety on the development of pain associated disability. As fear and avoidance are major obstacles to rehabilitation and coping with chronic pain, especially following injury, it is crucial to recognize these.

As they are multiple influences on pain, unsurprisingly there is a wide variation in the way people cope with their pain. The main constructs of coping can be considered as coping styles including 'avoiders' and 'copers'; 'assimilative' and 'accommodative' modes. Strategies include 'active' versus 'passive'; 'adaptive' versus 'non-adaptive'; 'emotion-focussed' versus 'problem focussed'; 'avoidant' and 'attentional'; and we also pay attention to the efficacy of the coping strategies. It is key to remember that coping is a fluid process, which can change throughout the pain journey.

Since the development of the gate control theory (Melzack and Wall, 1965), there have been huge advances in the clarification of psychological factors in chronic pain. The challenge remains to investigate the specific influence of these factors and their interaction, and, most importantly, how do we translate this into clinical practice?

Where Health Psychology Is Heading . . .

I think that for health psychologists exciting times lie ahead, particularly in the field of long-term conditions and self-management, particularly with the shift towards managing long-term illness from the UK Department of Health over the past few years, and the need to save money in the NHS.

Health psychologists can offer so much within a hospital setting, such as pain clinics, support for diabetes, asthma and renal conditions, and intensive care; I think one of the exciting challenges ahead is for health psychologists to be working throughout the hospital environment, as an individual clinician, but more importantly as a member of the multidisciplinary team in all specialities including surgery. It is well documented that if patients are well prepared for surgery, then they have a better outcome and spend less time in hospital, thus providing a better experience for the patient and cost reduction for the hospital.

I think that with the changing political agenda and developments within the NHS, some of the work we do as health psychologists can be done in primary care in community based settings, particularly in managing long-term conditions, I believe that this is an area to expand our services into. In addition, as health psychologists perhaps we need to start to learn to 'market' our strengths and what we can offer a little more effectively, and carve out yet another niche for ourselves. Health psychologists seem to work in a biopsychosocial model rather than the narrow focus of the medical model, which provides huge opportunities not only in clinical practice but in also in research.

Working with long-term health conditions such as chronic pain requires us to have counselling skills, particularly for the individual work, and I would recommend health psychologists acquiring these. I believe that the future is looking brighter for health psychologists as employers are looking more at applied skills and competencies rather than job titles.

Key Debates in Health Psychology

Should Back Pain Be a Public Health Issue?

In both the orthopaedic medicine clinic and the pain clinic where I work, back pain is the most frequent reason for attendance. Back pain disrupts quality of life and accounts for enormous costs both to the individual, their families and the economy.

It is estimated that 80% of people will experience back pain at some point in the lives, whilst most will recover, some cases of back pain will result in long-standing disability and incapacity to work.

Back pain continues to be a major health problem around the world – one that costs the health care system a great deal of money. Studies show that there can be minimal pain but huge disability and vice versa: significant pain but low disability. Finding a uniform way to approach the problem of back pain is difficult with such a wide range of experiences.

Despite the evidence showing that the best treatment for the majority of back pain is to keep active, I am constantly amazed how many people I see have been told to take bed rest, hence reinforcing the potential for disability.

Should England follow the lead from other countries such as Australia, Canada, Scotland and more recently Wales and adopt back pain as an area of public health? Is it time for health psychologists such as myself working in chronic pain to join forces with our colleagues in public health to develop useful information in a variety of media such as the press, television campaigns and websites. Back pain (and indeed any other chronic pain) should be a national health priority particularly now with the benefit system is being reformed. By making it a national priority, it would ensure that there would be greater funding to prevent or minimize the impact of back pain on the individual and the wider community. It should also aim to address the development and progression of chronic pain, slowing the onset of complications that cause disability and encouraging self-management to reduce hospital admissions.

References

Bandura, A. (1977). Self efficacy: towards a unifying theory of behaviour change. *Psychological Review, 84*, 191–215.

Kerns, R.D., & Rosenberg, R. (2000). Predicting responses to self-management treatments for chronic pain: application of the pain stages of change model. *Pain, 4*(1), 49–55.

Leventhal, H., Leventhal, E.A., & Contrada, R.J. (1998). Self-regulation, health and behaviour: a perceptual-cognitive approach. *Psychology and Health, 13*, 717–733.

McCracken, L.M., Gauntlett-Gilbert, J., & Vowles, K.E. (2007). The role of mindfulness in a contextual cognitive behavioural analysis of chronic pain related suffering and disability. *Pain, 131*, 63–69.

Melzack, R., & Wall, P.D. (1965). Pain mechanisms: a new theory. *Science, 150*, 971–979.

Turk, D.C., & Okifuji, A. (2003). A cognitive behavioural approach to pain management. In R. Melzack & P.D. Wall (Eds.), *Handbook of pain management: a clinical companion to Wall and Melzack's textbook of pain* (pp. 533–542). Philadelphia: Churchill Livingstone.

Vlaeyen, J.W., Kole-Snijders, A.M.J., Boeren, R.G.B., *et al.* (1995). Fear of movement/(re) injury in chronic low back pain and its relation to behavioural performance. *Pain, 62*, 363–372.

15

Combining Practice and Academia as a Health Psychologist

Karen Rodham

Introduction: How I Became a Health Psychologist with a Foot in Both Practice and Academia

I began my psychology career in 1989 when I started my undergraduate degree at the University of Portsmouth. Three years later, I graduated with a respectable upper-second-class (Hons) degree and was looking for the next step. I successfully applied for a funded PhD in the same institution and embarked on my research career. My thesis focussed on how health professionals working in business coped with the conflicting demands put upon them by both managers and employees. On completing my PhD I worked as a lecturer for 4 years until I accepted a Research Fellow post at the Centre for Suicide Research at the University of Oxford. It was here that I really learned the craft of completing large-scale research projects. The project I was managing explored the coping skills of adolescents aged 15 and 16 years. My involvement in the project cemented my passion for researching how people cope when they are facing difficult situations.

When the funding for my post expired, I applied for a job lecturing in health psychology at the University of Bath. In all honesty, reading the job advert was the first time I had heard of the discipline of health psychology. As I read about the field in preparation for my interview, I began to realize that although I had not known I was a health psychologist – health psychology was in fact, what I had been engaged in throughout my research career. Joining the University of Bath was therefore where I finally worked out where my research interests fitted. Finding health psychology was like finding a professional home!

I immediately got involved with the Division of Health Psychology (DHP) and soon found myself taking on the role of Secretary for the DHP. Much later, I was the

Health Psychology in Action, First Edition. Edited by Mark Forshaw and David Sheffield.
© 2013 John Wiley & Sons, Ltd. Published 2013 by John Wiley & Sons, Ltd.

Conference President for the Division of Health Psychology and the European Health Psychology Society joint annual conference which was held at the University of Bath in 2008. Becoming involved with the DHP is something I encourage other health psychologists to do – I have found that it has been incredibly useful for meeting other academic and practising health psychologists from whom I have learned huge amounts about the discipline, its application and its future. For example, when I joined the DHP specialist knowledge list, I had the opportunity to comment on initiatives related to health policy, promotion, education and research. In doing so, I was able to raise policy makers' awareness of the issues important to health psychology as a discipline and to people who practice as health psychologists. I have also got to know a wide range of academic and practising health psychologists, many of whom have been kind enough to come and share their experiences with my Masters students. Finally, through attending the annual DHP conference I have been able to stay abreast of developments in both theory and practice which I have then incorporated into my own research, teaching and practice.

Although I thoroughly enjoyed my academic role, I was longing to find a way to combine this with the opportunity to practice. My chance came when the team of academic psychologists I was working with decided to contact local practising health professionals with the intention of establishing research collaborations. We suggested that as academic health psychologists we had expertise in research but often struggled to access patient populations; whereas they had access to such populations but perhaps struggled to incorporate research into their working commitments. We thought that combining our respective strengths might make a powerful collaboration and provide a great opportunity to engage in research. An unanticipated result from this mailing was that a consultant rheumatologist contacted me because he was interested in my focus on coping. He invited me to sit in on his patient appointments and it became apparent to me that if I were to work with his multidisciplinary team, I could potentially make a useful contribution to the patients' coping strategies. I was offered a trial, and the university agreed to second me for one day a week. Four years on, I am still combining my work at the hospital with my work at the university. This chapter will describe how I combine the practice and academic elements of my role as a health psychologist.

Practice

I am based in the Rheumatology Department at the Royal National Hospital for Rheumatic Diseases (RNHRD) – the hospital is known locally as the 'Min' because of its original name, 'The Mineral Water Hospital', and its links to the Roman Baths. The department offers a specialist service for adults who have complex regional pain syndrome (CRPS). The multidisciplinary team (MDT) I work with consists of a rheumatologist, physiotherapists, occupational therapists, a rheumatology nurse, a research fellow and a clinical research practitioner. The service includes a 2-week in-patient programme which offers a full multidisciplinary team assessment, patient-centred goal setting, concentrated physical rehabilitation and information and education about the condition.

CRPS is a painful debilitating condition which greatly affects an individual's ability to function and therefore impacts on their quality of life (Allen *et al.*, 1999). People who live with CRPS are often in extreme pain and experience vastly exaggerated reactions to normal stimuli such as the touch from clothes or a light breeze which can result in the stimulus feeling excruciatingly painful (allodynia). In addition to pain, the condition can cause other symptoms, such as swelling, temperature changes around the affected area, skin changes (colour, texture and temperature), increased sweating, intolerance to heat or cold and muscle spasms (Bruehl *et al.*, 2000; Turner-Stokes, 2002). Commonly affected sites are the hands, feet and knees, although it can be seen in other parts of the body too. There is currently no diagnostic test and consequently there can be a prolonged period of time before a confirmed diagnosis is made (Blake *et al.*, 2006). In addition, the duration of CRPS varies. In acute cases it may last for weeks followed by remission, but in more chronic cases the pain can continue for years; resulting in significant disability, loss of earnings and psychological distress. It is very difficult for health professionals to give patients definite information about their prognosis and as a consequence, patients may find their condition difficult to understand, cope with and come to terms with.

Our patients come from all over the United Kingdom and my role as health psychologist is to explore how CRPS has impacted on their life and to assess how well they are coping. The consultations can be emotionally draining for the patients because the appointment is often the first opportunity they have had to reflect on and talk at length with a health professional about their feelings. My listening skills are therefore of paramount importance.

I first meet patients at their out-patient MDT assessment day. This can be a very tiring day for them as they are assessed by each member of the team. This enables us to build up a complete picture of the different physical, medical and psychological challenges that the person with CRPS is facing. In terms of the psychology assessment, I tend to structure this meeting around five key issues. First, patients are often afraid that they have been referred to me because someone thinks that the CRPS is 'all in their head'. This perception arises because prior to diagnosis, they have commonly spent a long time seeing many different health professionals before being referred to the Min. This long road to diagnosis can lead them to doubt their own symptoms. Therefore asking patients why they think they have been referred to me allows me to explain and reassure them that my role as health psychologist is to explore how CRPS has impacted upon them with a view to helping them to find effective ways to cope with the challenges they face. It is also important to spend some time exploring what the patient's expectations are of the MDT. The Min has a reputation for being a CRPS centre of excellence and often patients arrive with exaggerated expectations of what our service can offer them. Ensuring that their expectations are realistic can help patients to engage more readily with the treatment and advice offered by the MDT.

Third, I explore how the impact that CRPS has had on them (e.g. employment, finance, emotions, relationships and practicalities). This enables me to build a picture of how much they feel their life has altered as they try to adjust to the limitations imposed upon them by CRPS. The fourth issue, 'coping' follows on naturally from this discussion and I explore what coping strategies patients have tried and how effective they have been. Finally we discuss the issue of support: specifically, to whom do patients feel they have in their network that they can turn to. Furthermore, because many patients tell me that although they could turn to someone, they prefer not to for fear that they will become a burden, I also explore whether there are barriers blocking them from making use of the support network available to them.

Following this first meeting, I am able to judge the individual's expectations of me and of the programme; how they feel CRPS has impacted on them; their coping strategies and their perception of support. For many, the impact of CRPS has been devastating and the possibility of attending the in-patient programme represents hope that they can begin to find a way forward with the support of the MDT. Sometimes after this first meeting, it is necessary for me to refer the patients for more in-depth psychological support than I can provide: my role is to see patients for their assessment and then again during the in-patient programme, but I am not able to provide ongoing support. Patients are referred on for further support via their GP. This process is completed in partnership with the patient concerned, with whom I will have discussed the possibility of further psychological support and obtained their agreement and consent prior to contacting their GP – there is little point organizing further input if the person concerned is unwilling to engage with the therapy. For those who are content to be referred, I write a letter to their GP explaining my reasons as to why I consider the person with CRPS would benefit from further psychological input and suggest the type of support that would be appropriate. The GP then sets in train the local processes that enable the therapy to be organized.

Usually the next time I meet the patient is when they begin the in-patient programme. During this meeting we will review the issues raised during our first meeting and begin to work together to address them. This may involve discussing implementation intentions, teaching relaxation skills and encouraging them to explore ways in which they could change elements of their behaviour. During the second week of the in-patient programme, we focus more attention on preparing for the return home.

As a team we are concerned about this transition from hospital (where there is lots of support and understanding) to home (where patients can feel very alone). Patients' anecdotal evidence suggests that the move from a hospital's supportive environment to their home environment impacts significantly on their ability to implement the skills that they have been taught whilst completing the in-patient programme. One patient summed up this transitional problem: 'It is very hard to move from a safe environment where you don't have to think about ironing, washing and so on. Whilst you are on the course, there is nothing to distract you from the tasks.' In response, we have recently completed a number of in-depth interviews with 'graduates' of the in-patient programme to find out more about how they coped and what the main obstacles to implementing the team's recommendations were. The analysis is currently underway and we intend to publish our findings both in the form of an academic paper and in summary form for our CRPS patient support group. Sharing our findings in this way ensures that we communicate with other health professionals as well as with our patients.

It is important to us that our practice is both evidence-based and informed by ongoing research within the team. For example, in an effort to gain greater insight into how people cope with CRPS, we obtained permission from a CRPS online support group to examine messages and responses posted on a message board (Rodham *et al.*, 2009). We hoped that analysing the way in which the message board was used would provide an opportunity to access users' descriptions of their experiences and in turn, offer insight into the online needs that this group have.

Online message boards have emerged as a potentially useful source of both information and support for patients. Some researchers have suggested that participating in online message boards can contribute to an individual's social isolation because the only interaction they have is with others in cyberspace (Finfgeld, 2000). However, the internet is increasingly an environment where social relationships are formed and networks are actually increased (Høybe *et al.*, 2005); something which is an obvious benefit for those who have reduced opportunities for social interaction in their 'offline world' as a consequence of mobility problems caused by their medical condition.

We found that users often mentioned that they had few people locally who they could turn to, or whom they felt fully understood them. Whilst having someone local to whom one could turn was the preferable option, the message board provided members with a useful substitute. The lack of local support was not necessarily simply a case of a lack of people to turn to, rather a lack of local people who were perceived to understand. This was exhibited in the belief expressed via the message board that only those who themselves had CRPS could truly understand the complexity of the condition. Similarly, members were able to receive recognition for their achievements, which in the offline world could be regarded as being insignificant ('it might not seem like much'). The sharing of achievements, skills and techniques, therefore, provided an opportunity for members' progress to be recognized. The process of engaging in this cycle of giving and receiving support appeared to contribute to the development of a feeling of community between members which was reflected in the respectful and sometimes humour-laced interactions. Given that many people who live with CRPS have considerable mobility problems which can lead to isolation, the message board seemed to provide users with an opportunity to connect with others albeit in an online environment.

Perhaps of most importance, it became apparent that amongst a small sample of users, being referred to a specialist at hospital was regarded as being the first step on the route towards a cure. Users of the message board who posted on this issue harboured high hopes of recovery. Patients' hopes and expectations play an important role in how they understand and cope with their conditions; furthermore, such expectations may influence patient compliance and motivation (Lacroix *et al.*, 1990; Turk, 1990). Similarly, Habib *et al.* (2005) suggest that one of the consistent predictors of drop out from multidisciplinary treatment programmes is discrepant expectations. It is for this reason that I now explicitly spend time at the start of my first meeting with a patient exploring their expectations.

Thus the analysis of the message board has provided potentially useful information for health professionals working with this patient group. That patients may come to the health service with unrealistic hopes and expectations highlights the need for health professionals to explicitly and sensitively explore the beliefs that a patient holds regarding their treatment. This is vital, for, whilst it is important hope should not be taken away from this group, if incorrect or unrealistic expectations are left unchecked, effective communication and successful patient engagement with treatment programmes will be difficult to achieve.

Academia

In my role at the University of Bath, I am involved in the three staples of academic life: teaching, administration and research. I teach on the Masters in Health Psychology (currently the only masters in health psychology to offer a full-time summer placement where students work in a range of settings). The two units for which I am responsible concern the application of health psychology principles to research and to practice. One unit takes students on a journey from developing a research question, reviewing the literature, choosing a method and methodological approach, considering the ethical implications of their research and, finally, writing a research proposal. The other unit focuses on health psychology in practice. Given my dual academic and practice roles, I am well-placed to teach this unit which largely explores the application of health psychology interventions. In addition, practising health psychologists are invited to share their experiences of applying health psychology in the 'real world' with our students. I believe that these two elements of the programme pull together all the theoretical input that students have had and demonstrate how health psychology can be put into practice. This is absolutely vital in terms of preparing our students for the placement element of the Masters degree.

One of my administrative roles is that of admissions tutor for the Masters in Health Psychology and I deal with queries and applications for our programme throughout the academic year. I interview all applicants that appear to meet our entrance criteria. The interview is a key part of the selection process, for it enables us to ensure that applicants do have a basic understanding of health psychology. There are still a small number of applicants that make an assumption that health psychology is simply another name for clinical psychology, and it is important to rectify this misunderstanding as early as possible. We see the interview as a two-way process and recognize that it is not just about us deciding who we can offer a place to, but also an opportunity for the applicant to meet us and check that what we are offering meets their expectations.

My second administrative role involves my membership of the Psychology Department ethics committee. All staff and students planning research are required to apply for ethical approval from the committee before commencing their study. This is an interesting and sometimes challenging role because it can throw up difficult issues with which we have to grapple. A key benefit for me is that I am much more aware of the exciting variety of innovative research that the department is engaged in.

The third strand of my role as an academic concerns research. My research focuses on exploring how people cope with difficult situations: I have published on the topic of stress at work, pain, deliberate self-harm and the use of internet message boards as a mechanism to aid coping (Adams *et al.*, 2005; Osborn & Rodham, 2010; Riley *et al.*, 2009; Rodham *et al.*, 2007, 2009). As I mentioned above, it was my interest in coping that led me to my current NHS role. It is important to me that the research I engage in does not just have theoretical application; I also want to ensure that my work has practical application and will make a difference to those whom I study.

As well as engaging in my own research, a significant part of my role as an academic involves the supervision of doctoral students. I value this element of my role because it provides me with an opportunity to share my research knowledge and experience with the next generation of academics. The doctoral journey is a difficult one and requires a lot of support and guidance from the supervisor, particularly in the initial stages, but the reward is great as the students develop their confidence and become independent researchers in their own right.

I see my role as an academic as being focused on four key elements: conducting and reporting my own research in order to contribute to knowledge and practice in the field, fostering interest in health psychology through teaching and research, cultivating the research skills of doctoral students and, in short, developing the next generation of academics and health psychologists.

Challenges and Joys

Challenges

As with any career there are issues with which one has to grapple. For me, there is one key issue which revolves around raising awareness of what health psychology is and what it can contribute. It is frustrating that health psychology is still a relatively unknown discipline; however there are more and more students graduating with masters and doctorates in health psychology and subsequently working in the field. This means that awareness raising is something which is happening naturally as a consequence of their presence in the work environment. In addition, I find that the leaflets designed by the DHP for raising awareness of the role of health psychology have proved invaluable in this process.

Another challenge I faced when I began to practice was finding a suitable colleague to offer me practice supervision – at that time I was the only health psychologist in the hospital. As a result of my work with the DHP I was aware of other health psychologists who were practising in similar fields in different parts of the country. Together we have developed an informal peer supervision arrangement. We meet three or four times a year and share good practice: for example we present cases we have found difficult and outline how we addressed the difficulties. Members of the group then share their perspective and sometimes offer suggestions for other methods or approaches we could consider for the future. We also provide informal telephone and email support for one another between our meetings if it is required. Having this form of support has been invaluable for me in terms of improving my practice and my continuing professional development.

Finally, working as both an academic and a practising health psychologist is proving to be a steep but interesting learning curve. Inevitably it is difficult to contain the hospital job to a Monday and the university job to Tuesday through to Friday. As a consequence, a key skill I am fast developing is time management! However, my two roles complement one another very well and I am able to incorporate real-life examples from my practice work into my teaching, whilst implementing research findings into my practice to ensure that what I am doing with my patients is 'evidence-based'. Therefore I am able to apply theories and principles of health psychology in my interactions with patients whilst continuing to research the area that interests me the most: how people cope with difficult situations, in this case, the diagnosis of CRPS.

Joys

I think that in identifying the 'joys' of my role, they all condense into one issue – my opportunity to be a facilitator. Thus, helping my patients to develop the tools and skills that will enable them to cope better is an extremely rewarding aspect of my job as a practising health psychologist. Similarly, teaching the next generation of health psychologists and therefore having the opportunity to shape the future of health psychology is something I really value. Seeing the students learn, grow, develop independence and ultimately go out and practice is something I regard as a very special part of my job. It is very gratifying when our graduates keep in touch and tell us about the exciting areas they are now working in. I see it as vital to maintain contact with our graduates because they very quickly become role models for our current students. Finally, being in a position to offer 'work experience' to trainee health psychologists in my practice role at the hospital is something I take seriously, I try to take one health psychology trainee on placement each year because it an opportunity for them to see how theory does (or doesn't) work in practice.

Future of Health Psychology

What would make a huge difference would be to secure funding for Stage 2 training. There is a need for parity between the career routes for health and clinical psychologists. Health psychology trainees are currently disadvantaged because they have to fund themselves, whereas clinical psychologists earn a wage and have their course fees paid for by the NHS whilst they train. Furthermore, compared to clinical psychology posts, fewer health psychology posts are advertised. In addition, although many people employed in the NHS have qualifications in health psychology, they may not be employed with that job title – this can be disheartening for individuals who have invested a lot of time and money in achieving the Stage 2 Health Psychology qualification. Nevertheless I feel very positive about the future of health psychology – I believe that we are reaching the point where there is a critical mass of trained and practising health psychologists. Furthermore, the Scottish branch of the DHP has recently had major success in that they have developed a pilot of NHS funded, 2 years full-time Stage 2 training posts for health psychologists. What this means is that more health professionals will come into contact with health psychologists and begin to understand the wealth of skills we have to offer.

Key Debates in Health Psychology

What Can I Do with a Qualification in Health Psychology?

A common question I am asked, both by my students and by applicants considering studying health psychology concerns the issue of finding work as a health psychologist once qualified. In the first instance I will direct the enquirer to the Division of Health Psychology website – here they will find detailed information about what it is that health psychologists do and the different environments in which health psychology can be applied. In addition, this site has a link to current jobs being advertised.

A further issue to consider is that compared to for example, clinical psychology posts, there are fewer health psychology posts advertised (Newson & Forshaw, 2009). This is an issue which is also raised on the Division website, where it is noted that 'there is a wide-range of jobs available, although they are not always advertised as health psychology posts'. Thus in addition to the current inequity in training (a trainee wishing to complete the Stage 2 health psychology qualification will have funded their own study, whereas a clinical psychologist working towards Chartership will be earning a salary for the duration of their training), our newly qualified health psychologists are in the unenviable and frustrating position of needing to be creative in their applications for posts not explicitly aimed at their profession.

However, being creative is often successful. I know of a number of colleagues and ex-students who have applied for posts not aimed explicitly at health psychologists who have managed to explain why a health psychologist would be just as appropriate in role, and by mapping their skills as a health psychologist onto the 'desired' and 'essential' skills listed in the job description, have managed to convince the potential employer of this fact. This is illustrated by a quote from a health psychologist which is presented on the DHP website:

> You could be a pioneer and make your own career path. . . . You will have opportunities that other disciplines don't. Creatively identifying jobs where Health Psychologists can have an impact. You could be working in research, developing treatments to help people change debilitating behaviours. You could be using research to re-design health services so that they are more effective. You could be on the front line working with people with chronic illness to help them take charge of their lives, or cope day to day. . . .

My role at the 'Min' is a case in point, in that prior to responding to our advertisement, my current MDT colleagues had not heard of health psychology, whereas now they are keen to secure the continued input of a health psychologist with their patient group.

I believe that as health psychologists we have a duty to play an active role in promoting the discipline of health psychology to potential employers. The DHP do this very well with their printed resources and outreach events. At the university we endeavour to highlight the potential role that health psychology can play when we are seeking new placement opportunities. We continue to demonstrate the added value a health psychologist can contribute through our existing placement links and furthermore, as academics, we can publicize the role that health psychology can play by sharing our research widely, through different publications. It is also important to ensure that as well as presenting our work at health psychology conferences, we also do so at conferences aimed at other health professionals. Conferences are an excellent platform for showcasing the theoretical and applied work of health psychologists.

I believe that although this is currently an issue of concern for our trainees as well as our newly qualified health psychologists, this is a situation which is in the process of changing. As the number of health psychologists grows, so too does awareness of the discipline and what it can offer, and in turn jobs explicitly aimed at health psychologists will become more common.

References

Adams, J., Rodham, K., & Gavin, J. (2005). Investigating the 'self' in deliberate self-harm. *Qualitative Health Research, 15*(10), 1293–1309.

Allen, G., Galer, B.S., & Schwartz, L. (1999). Epidemiology of complex regional pain syndrome: a retrospective chart review of 134 patients. *Pain, 80*(3), 539–544.

Blake, D., Lewis, J., McCabe, C., & Taylor, C. (2006). *Insights into pain and suffering: a guide to neuropathic pain and complex regional pain syndrome, known as reflex sympathetic dystrophy.* Oakham: RSD UK Charity.

Bruehl, S., Harden, R.N., & Sorrell, P. (2000). Complex regional pain syndromes: a fresh look at a difficult problem. In *62nd annual assembly of the American Academy of Physical Medicine and Rehabilitation* [Conference proceedings]. San Francisco: AAPMR.

Finfgeld, D. (2000). Therapeutic groups online: the good, the bad and the unknown. *Issues in Mental Health Nursing, 21*(3), 241–255.

Habib, S., Morrissey, S., & Helmes, E. (2005). Preparing for pain management: a pilot study to enhance engagement. *The Journal of Pain, 6*(1), 48–54.

Høybe, M.T., Johansen, C., & Tjørnhøj-Thomsen, T. (2005). Online interaction: effects of storytelling in an internet breast cancer support group. *Psycho-oncology, 14*(3), 211–220.

Lacroix, J.M., Powell, J., Lloyd, G.J., Doxey, N.C.S., Mitson, G.L., & Aldam, C.F. (1990). Low back pain factors of value in predicting outcome. *Spine, 15*(6), 495–499.

Newson, L., & Forshaw, M. (2009). Health psychologists in the NHS. *Health Psychology Update, 18*(2), 30–33.

Osborn, M., & Rodham, K. (2010). Insights into pain: a review of qualitative research. *Reviews in Pain, 4*(1), 2–7.

Riley, S., Rodham, K., & Gavin, J. (2009). Doing weight: pro-ana and recovery identities in cyberspace. *Journal of Community & Applied Social Psychology, 19*, 348–359.

Rodham, K., McCabe, C., & Blake, D. (2009). Seeking support: an interpretative phenomeno-logical analysis of an internet message board for people with complex regional pain syndrome. *Psychology and Health, 24*(6), 619–634.

Rodham, K., Gavin, J., & Miles, M. (2007). I hear, I listen and I care: a qualitative investigation into the function of a self-harm message board. *Suicide and Life Threatening Behaviour, 37*(4), 422–430.

Turk, D.C. (1990). Customizing treatment for chronic patients: who, what and why. *Clinical Journal of Pain, 6*(4), 255–270.

Turner-Stokes, L. (2002). Reflex sympathetic dystrophy – a complex regional pain syndrome. *Disability and Rehabilitation, 24*(18) 939–947.

Glossary

allodynia: pain experienced from a nonpainful stimulus such as touch or even sound.

complex regional pain syndrome (CRPS): a painful debilitating condition. Symptoms include pain, swelling, temperature changes, muscle spasms and allodynia. Also known as reflex sympathetic dystrophy (RSD).

16

Health Psychologists in Action – Working for the Pharmaceutical Industry

Katja Rüdell

This text is an introduction to the work that I do as a researcher in the pharmaceutical industry and offers a basic overview of my role. Many health psychology colleagues have previously asked me about my role in industry, and so I am delighted to put my insights into a published document and make it available for greater dissemination. I will follow the outlines of the other chapters describing what my colleagues and I do, where and when we do it and why the work is important, following the challenges and joys of the role we do, the interpretation of health psychology in our work and the direction in which it is heading. Prior to this, I have included a brief summary of my personal background and my motivations to join the industry in the first place as this is a question that is also often asked when I give introductory talks about my role.

Personal Background and Why I Began to Work in the Pharmaceutical Industry

I was born and raised in a small town near Cologne in Germany. I considered studying medicine in Germany, but then enrolled for an undergraduate BSc degree in Psychology in England. Before the start of my studies, just after completing my school exams, I had a serious accident that kept me in hospital for 3 months and in receipt of physiotherapy and other medical treatments for a further 8 months. In 1995, I began studying psychology at Royal Holloway and New Bedford College, University of London where I listened to an introductory lecture about health psychology from Professor Lynn Myers (now at Brunel University) which got me very excited about becoming a health psychologist. I felt a career in health psychology would enable me to combine my interest in medicine and health care in general whilst focussing on

Health Psychology in Action, First Edition. Edited by Mark Forshaw and David Sheffield.
© 2013 John Wiley & Sons, Ltd. Published 2013 by John Wiley & Sons, Ltd.

the patient perspective with which I had a lot of experience. I then decided to embark on the MSc in Health Psychology at University College London. I gained valuable hands-on experience of working as a health psychologist when working in a smoking cessation clinic at the Camden and Islington Smokers Clinic and whilst working there I received a studentship to study for a PhD at Barts and the London Medical School. The PhD aimed to develop an assessment method for illness perceptions that would work across culturally and ethnically diverse groups. Following this I coordinated with the Tobacco Dependence Unit at the Royal London Hospital the last few months of the Varenicline (a stop-smoking medication from Pfizer) clinical trials and then moved on to a lecturer post in health psychology at the University of Kent. In 2007, I was asked to consider a position at the Global Outcomes Research department at Pfizer. My previous exposure to the pharmaceutical industry removed some of the inhibitions that many other health psychologists seem to have when it comes to encounters with pharmaceutical settings. My initial interest in joining the pharmaceutical industry was fuelled by the desire to expand on my knowledge of psychological assessment across cultural groups and be assigned to an international organization that would enable me to expand my knowledge in this area.

The What, Where, When and Why

I work in an international team of six health psychologists in the Patient Reported Outcome Centre (PRO) of Excellence, Market Access department of the Primary Care Business Unit at Pfizer. Our main task is to advise on the use of Patient Reported Outcome (PRO) tools firstly within the development of new pharmaceutical agents (medications) but also after they have been licensed for use by patients determining how to best evaluate any additional value or treatment benefit it may bring to patients. PROs describe outcomes assessment that require patients' input and are sometimes characterized as subjective 'soft' outcomes assessment contrasted with 'hard' outcomes such as mortality or morbidity. As PRO specialists, we act as consultants with particular expertise in symptom, functioning and health-related quality of life (HRQL) assessment, as well as in the measurement of treatment satisfaction and treatment preference. Our role involves significantly advising teams in relation to planning, implementing and analysing PROs in clinical trials. To understand the process within which we work it is probably best to provide a quick and simplified outline of pharmaceutical drug development.

Drug research and development begin with chemistry where various elements which are potentially seen as interesting and therapeutically meaningful for use in medical settings are combined and patented – this is, in most companies, called the 'discovery phase' or also 'pre-clinical work'. Following this is an exploration of how to translate the knowledge about the molecule into a compound and bring it into a format that is both tolerable to humans and easy to digest, store and so on. The safety and tolerability of these new compounds is firstly tested on animals and healthy human volunteers in toxicology studies. After establishing that the compound is not causing any harm, the compound will then move into what is described as the 'clinical phase'. During the clinical phase, each compound is supported by a group of scientists who are brought into evaluate the compound from various perspectives. These normally include a medical doctor/clinician, a protocol manager (who is an expert in operationalization of study designs and manages the implementation of protocols for the various studies that evaluate the compound), a project planner (who outlines the timing of the studies), a medical statistician (who advises on sample size and statistical analyses), a regulatory lead (who interacts with the official regulatory authorities that evaluate the process formally and externally), a toxicologist (who advises on the safety of the drug), data managers (who bring in the from various sites across the world into a centralized database), study managers (who liaise with the protocol but have a more direct link to the various sites), pharmaceutical scientists (who evaluate the consistency of the compound) as well as other functions including the outcomes research team who evaluate the compound for its societal, economic and humanistic value – this is where we come in.

The R&D process is divided up into a test on healthy volunteers for safety in Phase I, Phase II where the compound is tested on a smaller sample of patients for safety and initially efficacy in the intended population (IIa) and globally run adequately sized randomized controlled clinical trials to continue to assess the safety and efficacy of the compound, which will also include 'dose selection' (Phase IIb). Finally, in Phase III an established likely marketable dose, or sometimes two doses, are evaluated in a minimum of two globally run adequately sized randomized controlled clinical trials – two trials are necessary to show replicable evidence that the medication works. At the end of a successful phase III program, the drug is filed for approval with regulatory authorities (e.g. the European Medical Authority, or EMA, and the US Food and Drug Administration, or FDA) for registration to be marketed. After filing, additional studies are often conducted to determine further benefits which are called IIIb or IV trials. The whole process from patenting the drug to bringing it to the market takes approximately 15 years and on average costs between $500 million and $1 billion. However, fewer than 1% of compounds will make it through this lengthy and careful evaluation process to filing with regulatory authorities. As there is a high investment and a big portfolio of compounds, a pharmaceutical company needs to carefully select which compounds will be taken forward and invested in. Each compound is patented upon conception and is therefore protected by intellectual property and patent laws until it reaches the loss of exclusivity (LoE) stage. The time from launch to LoE is what is known in the industry as the drug's life cycle – during which it can be applied to different groups of patients and the industry obtains optimal financial reimbursement for the drug development process. This is often followed by generic drug development which derives from the previous agent a chemical similar compound which must show bioequivalence to the originator compounds within a region of 80–125% in terms of efficacy, and comparable safety.

The PRO CoE, is situated within the outcomes research section of the market access division which includes various groups (pricing and reimbursement, health technology assessment, health economics and evidence-based population research).

Our group is drawn in to perform a rigorous evaluation of the compounds and consultation to the development teams during phase II, III and IV. We are most busy in Phases II and III of the drug development process where the efficacy of the doses of the compound for the patients is determined, but we may also get involved in earlier phases of the drug development in therapeutic areas where the primary outcome is patient or caregiver reported (e.g. pain, neurosciences and sexual health) or later when the drug is available on the market.

Examples of tasks we might undertake in each phase:

Phase I (review the impact of the condition on a patient's life and review the relevance of PRO instruments in a pharmaceutical compound's life cycle):
  □ Begin to understand the particular patient population under investigation. This may involve patient interviews which usually are conducted by external research organizations.
  □ Start to review the relevant therapeutic literature and critically appraise the instruments that may be useful to evaluate our compounds in our clinical trials.
  □ Visit and speak with experts in the area.
  □ Conduct focus groups to discuss the impact of the disease on the patients.
Phase II (pilot test the efficacy and safety of the drug in relatively small clinical trials involving the patient population):
  □ Finalize the critical review of available instruments (and when appropriate publish) and recommend one for use.
    □ Pilot the instrument in early clinical trials.
  □ Alternatively, consider the development of a new PRO:
    □ Generate items from analysis of focus group and patient interview transcripts.
    □ Review (with experts and patients) the items for appropriateness and language clarity.
    □ Validate the instrument during early clinical trials.
    □ Advise on appropriate psychometric analyses to be conducted to determine validity, reliability and sensitivity to change of the instrument.
  □ Generate Hypotheses of the compound's effects on PROs.
  □ Conduct cultural and linguistic validation of the instrument, if required.
  □ Consider, review and assess the PRO administration mode – we develop, use and test PRO assessment on paper, mobile phone, personal digital assistant and the internet or over the standard telephone interactive voice response systems (IVRS).
  □ Finalize PRO strategy and discuss with European and US regulatory authorities regarding the rationale and method of PRO assessment.
Phase III (large-scale clinical trials to demonstrate efficacy and safety):
  □ Implement a PRO strategy in large-scale clinical trials.
  □ Write the PRO sections of the clinical protocol.
  □ Write the statistical analysis plan.

□ Present the PRO evaluation rationale and guidelines to the study investiga-
tors around the world involved in running the clinical trials.
□ Implement the PRO publication plans.
□ Report the PRO results at internal and external meetings.
Phase IV and other studies (including methodology studies):
□ Additional studies are conducted to generate further evidence regarding the
medication.
□ Methodology studies (noncompound) are conducted to determine the
value of assessment methodologies independent of individual drugs.
□ PRO validation studies are sometimes run to determine psychometric prop-
erties (reliability, validity and responsiveness (sensitivity)) of PROs.
□ Support outcomes research studies that require PRO input and expertise.

All of the tasks above are carried out by a group of dedicated PRO specialists who
have a good sense of the patient perspective on health care, knowledge of clinical
trial implementation and knowledge of instrument development and psychometric
evaluation. We are generally assigned to specific compounds which may be in different stages of drug development so the tasks we do are usually quite varied. Our
work requires a good deal of knowledge, experience and sometimes persuasion skills
to train and educate the teams on the value of PROs in clinical trial development.

The reason why our work in industry is necessary and important is related to an
increase in pharmaceutical and other health interventions being made available for
treatment. This is accompanied by a population that is living longer and budgets
for health care being limited. Health budget pressures combined with a crowded
market place increase the need to show a marked improvement of health status and
outcomes often over and above the drugs that are already available in generic form.
These outcomes need to be generated by using rigorous scientific assessments to
warrant further investment internally by the pharmaceutical organizations and also
to justify appropriate reimbursement for the costly development process.

Challenges and Joys of My Role(s)

I have outlined the joys and challenges of the role as I see them in a table below. On
most days, the joys outweigh the challenges of the role, but that does not mean that
it is an easy position and to everybody's taste. Compared to my previous work in an
academic setting this role is more varied and interesting whilst being very challenging
at the same time. It requires a high level of flexibility in relation to managing research
projects, liaising and negotiation with project teams, using various different means
of communication and a reasonable amount of travel. Contrary to generating your
own research profile and research projects it is mostly true that research projects in
industry are mostly externally generated. The research question is asked by an agency
or determined by other external driving forces. At the same time the environment
is quite ideal for someone with an interest in research in patients' perspectives like

myself and I make sure that the patients' views of medication are part of the drug development process. Personally, I sometimes miss working in university settings, but this is mostly related to the lack of contact with younger health psychologists, but I have continued to mentor young psychologists here and outside of my work place. We also sometimes offer placements to expose more young health psychologists to work in the pharmaceutical industry as an alternative route to NHS or academic settings.

Joys	Challenges
Important role in supporting external and internal decision making for investment in new drugs that can really show increased patient benefit	High level of personal accountability to make the right decisions as companies' investment (cutting potentially beneficial interventions) may also depend on the patient-reported benefits of the medicine
Working within an environment where the health psychology expertise and knowledge is recognized and appreciated	Working within a huge organization or corporate environment
Working within a team of highly skilled and knowledgeable health psychologists and having a constant dialogue with groups of highly qualified scientists (clinicians, statisticians, economists)	Working to challenging timelines and often across different time zones
Working in a regulated research environment where the highest level of scientific rigour is required and extensive funding and state-of-the-art assessment of the patient perspective is justified (e.g. precise electronic technology enables assessment of illness and treatment perceptions on a daily basis)	Workload/daily activities involving many meetings and teleconferences and that are mostly controlled by a range of external (e.g. regulatory authorities who may determine that a drug is not appropriate) and internal (e.g. the decision to halt compound development) factors
Permanent, full-time research position independent of grants or publications	Working in the private sector is responsive to market forces which may change more quickly than the public sector
Frequent travel	Frequent travel
Working within an organization that operates internationally – working with individuals from different cultural groups	

How Health Psychology Is Interpreted through the Filter of My Own Work

Health psychology is currently not recognized by name through the filter of the pharmaceutical industry, and appointments specifically requesting a 'health psychologist' are rare or non-existent. However, the appointments sections of pharmaceutical companies generally target 'outcome researchers', which usually means health economic expertise but does also involve PRO assessment and development. The term PRO specialist is growing as its own a specialism and more specific roles for PRO specialists (mostly health psychologists) are now being set out. Also, many pharmaceutical organizations do not have specific health psychologists or outcome researchers in house; but work with contract research organizations such as United Biosource Corporation (UBC), MAPI Values, Oxford Outcomes and specialized academics in patient-reported outcome development and strategy. Opportunities for working with such organizations abound due to the increasing amount of treatments that are available; but the label 'health psychologist' may not be frequently applied.

The skills of health psychologists – the recognition of the importance of the patient perspective on illness, the research focus, statistical skill and understanding of quantitative and qualitative research methods – are however highly valued through the filter of the pharmaceutical industry. This may be as PRO specialists or more generic outcomes research appointments; as well as other job opportunities such as clinical protocol leads, study managers and with appropriate specialization as clinicians. An important prerequisite for working in the research and development sector of the pharmaceutical industry is a detailed knowledge of the complexity of research from inception, implementation and operationalization through to careful evaluation. Contrary to the belief of some people who have limited understanding of the pharmaceutical setting, the role does not (or at least not in our organization) require letting go of professional integrity and does not foster the development of Machiavellian substandard research approaches. Those that do develop health interventions know that it is a very challenging and difficult task to come up with an intervention that works well. In most circumstances, it takes many people many years to do, so once such a task is achieved there is a great desire to make it available to all people and get acclaim for the benefit of the intervention. The pharmaceutical industry is very heavily regulated and this inhibits one-sided and unbalanced intervention promotion and marketing. While generally too little is known about why health interventions actually work (including drugs, placebo, psychological interventions and counselling), the pharmaceutical industry has been setting standards (and has been set external standards) to explain much more clearly what works, how and with whom. With more health psychologists moving towards the development of health interventions on either an individual or group level, learnings should be expected to occur in both directions (i.e. from the health psychologists involved in pharmaceutical organizations to the health psychologists working with nonpharmaceutical interventions, as well as the other way around).

Where Health Psychology Is Heading

New health care interventions are ever increasing with only a limited amount of funds available for all. Pharmaceutical companies, as well as other stakeholders in developing interventions, have to demonstrate efficacy, safety and quality of their interventional compounds, devices and procedures to regulatory authorities before they can be made available to patients. Due to the limited funding and the ever-increasing availability of new and better health care treatment methods, there will be even more attention to the way these interventions work, and what each method provides as additional benefit to the patient. Quality of life improvements, as well as epidemiological outcomes such as morbidity and mortality, are key in determining the value of such interventions. Indeed, the National Institute for Clinical Excellence (NICE; http://www.nice.org.uk/newsroom/features/measuringeffectivenessandcosteffectivenesstheqaly.jsp) in the United Kingdom makes recommendations that interventions are to be funded only if they can demonstrate that the time that the benefit in terms of a patient quality of life is outweighed by the costs using a threshold of £30,000 per life-year gained. Therefore, it is important to plan and show the benefit and value of a new health intervention. When I review this field of the industry and the number of job offers for outcome researchers, along with the phone calls my colleagues and I receive on a regular basis, I believe there will be a growing need for well-trained epidemiologically oriented, health psychology outcomes researchers with broader interests for example in public health policy. The majority of people join the industry after a few years working in academia, the NHS or one of the contract research organizations.

Whilst we are sought-after experts, my main concern for my field and where we are heading is to do with greater recognition of the patient perspective and clarity of how health care decisions (in the individual consultation or in public policy) are made that affect patients first and foremost. Although there is widespread agreement amongst the medical community and regulatory authorities that there should be an increasing use of patient-reported outcomes (including health-related quality of life) to establish the benefit of treatment for patients directly, a recent review conducted by MAPI Research Institute found that particularly in the United States, there is limited acknowledgement of broader health-related quality of life information on medication labels. In addition, there seems to be even less patient relevant information used in determining the price of medication and the decisions of payers to make medication accessible to all patients. It seems that whilst the medical community, including the great efforts of health psychology, has made great advances towards embracing the biopsychosocial model of health and illness, the biomedical model still often prevails when funding is concerned. A greater transparency of what health interventions (clinical, counselling, pharmaceutical or web-based behavioural support) patients truly prefer and want, and for what reason, would in my view enable doctors to make much more appropriate assessments when allocating treatments to patients.

There are so many conditions that still need effective interventions. For example, in respiratory conditions, adherence rates vary, with between 10% and 90% of patients being classed as non-adherent. The high end of this spectrum points to an enormous amount of resource unnecessarily wasted both in terms of economic costs, but also in terms of humanistic costs. In human terms, doctors and nurses spend lots of their time prescribing and evaluating treatments that patients are seemingly neither able to understand nor are satisfied with and in turn non-adherence results. Transparency of what works from the patient perspective could, in my view, only improve adherence and that, in turn, should improve health outcomes. Increasing our knowledge and understanding of patient perspectives on treatment and health care and determining high-quality standardized outcome assessments in my view is therefore imperative for the future. Generating more evidence about the patient perspective can be used to educate various stakeholders about the benefit of treatments and could give the patients increasing responsibilities and autonomy in their treatment. In the United Kingdom, there are some changes in practice such as the PROMs initiative to evaluate treatment outcomes for surgery (hip and knee replacement, hernia and varicose veins) using patient-reported outcomes (http://www.ic.nhs.uk/proms). On a European level, there are also a few initiatives such as the Innovative Medicine Initiative (IMI) which manages the administration of funding large new pan-European projects. This is partially funded by public funding from the European Commission (EC) and partially by the European Federation of Pharmaceutical Industries and Association (EFPIA). One of these projects involves developing better outcome measures for COPD patients – the PROactive project. PROactive assessments are going to be used to assess treatment efficacy across the industry and in academic settings (http://www.proactivecopd.com/index.php). These are hopefully what we can consider the seedlings which will grow over time. In conclusion, I'd like to point out where as there are so many more patients than doctors (and I include myself in the patient group) it lacks common sense to me that most decision making whether it concerns the individual patient who is discussing treatment options with their doctor and or policy decisions as to whether treatment options are to be used within a health care system are based around so many non patient based endpoints or effects. On the contrary, what does make sense to me is that as patients we all should ensure that the patient perspective on treatment benefit is taken more often into account.

Key Debates in Health Psychology

Determining a Meaningful Outcome for Patients from a Health Intervention

Health interventions, including health psychological group interventions, individual clinical interventions and those that are provided by the pharmaceutical industry, are often tested quantitatively in randomized controlled trials to rigorously determine their efficacy and safety. The assessment of the benefit of the intervention is therefore often judged by statistical standard inferences that define significance. A common debate among those working in outcomes research is whether what is statistically significant is also clinically important or meaningful to the individual patient. A further question is how to determine the threshold at which it is advisable for a patient and society to invest in a new intervention.

Not all interventions are likely to be meaningful and effective to all patients at all times, but the discussion centres on which value or a threshold of values a particular interventions should aim for. Take for example a randomized control trial where the patient mean improves from a pain rating at baseline of 5 on a 0–10 scale (where 10 is the worst imaginable pain and 0 no pain) to a rating of 4 by the end of the treatment – is this a reduction that is meaningful and desirable for the individual patient? How can we determine whether a statistical significant mean difference translates into something that is meaningful to patient?

Ideally, also one knows the value or threshold *a priori* to the scientific evaluation of the intervention and this can be determined by including a measurement of meaningfulness in an intervention trial where patients rate whether they feel they have improved or deteriorated since beginning the treatment (using a scale). What is then often examined is the point from which a patient feels that he has neither improved nor deteriorated to a patient's sense of the most minimal sense of improvement. It is explored which range of values is given by the group of patients who do not change and how this compares to the patients who have felt they have minimally improved. The difference between those two is viewed as what is the minimally important difference and hence the determination of meaningful is hereby assigned by another quantitative measure of meaningfulness. This method is commonly referred to as an 'anchor-based method'.

An alternative method is distribution-based approaches, which determine the value based on the statistical variation of the outcome assessment scores. Here the meaningfulness is often assigned to standard deviation from the mean or other distribution assigned values. When comparing these two values, it can be that both approaches produce different values or thresholds of meaningfulness.

A question therefore exists and needs to be further clarified for consensus in the scientific community – what is the best method for developing meaningful outcomes for intervention assessment, and what is the relationship that we should seek between anchor- and distribution-based approaches? I think that this ongoing debate in outcomes research is a useful consideration for the development of interventions and also their evaluation as per randomized clinical trials and that this consideration should also be utilized more often in health psychological research. It may be important to also query whether these statistical methods are indeed providing the optimal answer to what is meaningful change to the patient.

Glossary

discovery: phase of research where pharmaceutical compounds get incepted and patented.

life cycle: drug development process.

patient-reported outcome (PRO): outcomes of health-related interventions that are self-reported symptoms, function, health-related quality of life, satisfaction with treatment and treatment preferences.

research and development (R&D): phase of research where pharmaceutical compounds gets examined in humans.

17

The Rapid Growth of Health Psychology in Medical Schools and Clinical Practice

Harbinder Sandhu and Shilpa Patel

Health psychology is a growing and dynamic discipline which has had a huge impact on research and teaching in medical schools across the country. Dr Harbinder Sandhu (Registered Health Psychologist and Assistant Professor of Health Psychology) and Dr Shilpa Patel (Registered Health Psychologist and Research Fellow) have several years of experience of working within a medical school setting and more recently experience of combining a clinical role with an academic post. After completing Professional Doctorates in Health Psychology, they have continued to apply Health Psychology in clinical practice (within the area of chronic pain management) and also in research and teaching. Dr Sandhu's research interests include communication in health care (clinician–patient interactions) and patient outcome. Dr Patel's interests include chronic pain management and, in particular musculoskeletal pain. Both fields are widely researched within a medical school setting. Health Psychology is also applied in medical teaching and other health related topics to undergraduate and postgraduate students. In this chapter we will highlight how Health Psychology is fast growing within medical education, research and clinical practice, drawing on our experiences, challenges and rewards.

Health Psychology Research in Medical Schools (Chronic Pain and Health Care Communication)

Management of chronic conditions is an important part of health psychology practice. In particular, low back pain is a common and costly condition. Accurate data on the cost of low back pain come from 1998 where the condition cost £1 623 million in

Health Psychology in Action, First Edition. Edited by Mark Forshaw and David Sheffield.
© 2013 John Wiley & Sons, Ltd. Published 2013 by John Wiley & Sons, Ltd.

health care alone (Maniadakis & Gray, 2000). The indirect costs associated with lost production and wage compensation add an additional £10 668 million per annum (Maniadakis & Gray, 2000). Research has shown patients with pain conditions face a number of barriers when it comes to returning to work (Patel *et al.*, 2007), therefore in the current economic climate these figures are likely to be much higher.

In 2009, the National Institute for Health and Clinical Excellence (NICE) introduced the low back pain guidelines for the early management of persistent nonspecific low back pain (Savigny *et al.*, 2009). These guidelines suggest patients with nonspecific low back pain that has lasted for more than 6 weeks but less than 12 months should be offered a course of exercise, manual therapy or acupuncture. Patients can be offered another of these three treatments if the originally chosen one does not produce satisfactory improvements. Following these treatment choices the patient can be referred to a more intense combined physical and psychological intervention. Although the guidelines recommend patients should be given a choice (Department of Health, 2004), by taking their needs and preferences into account, there is no guidance on how to help patients make the best informed decision. Therefore, we question how patients make decisions about their back pain treatments and whether we can help improve the informed shared decision-making process.

Current research aimed to address this issue is a Research for Patient Benefit programme in which Dr Patel is a co-applicant, looking at informed shared decision making within a physiotherapy department in light of the NICE low back pain guidelines. The aim of this pilot randomized controlled trial is to develop a Decision Support Package to help physiotherapists and patients with the decision-making process (Patel *et al.*, 2011). If patients have had the opportunity to discuss different treatment options before selecting the treatment they feel would be most beneficial for them, then there is a possibility that they may perceive better treatment outcomes (Preference Collaborative Review Group, 2008). As this is a pilot study, it focuses on the effects of our decision support package on patient satisfaction. We are currently in the intervention design phase of this study. In the future we would hope to carry out a larger randomized controlled trial powered to look at effects on clinical outcomes.

Crucial to the decision-making process is the interaction between the health professional and patient. Clinician–patient communication is the heart of the consultation and fundamental to determining the processes and outcomes (Travaline *et al.*, 2005). Effective communication will allow clinicians to gather information from the patient which then informs diagnostic and treatment decisions (Hawken, 2005). However, what is actually meant by 'effective communication'? A wealth of research shows that adapting a patient-centred consultation, where a partnership is built between the clinician and patient, the patient is able to express their concerns and ask questions, the clinician informs the patient enabling them to develop a good understanding about their condition and is then able to participate in a shared decision-making process leading to better health outcomes. This includes higher patient satisfaction and adherence to treatment advice as well as having a better understanding about their condition and the ability to self-manage, which is extremely important in chronic conditions (Ha *et al.*, 2010).

When conducting research in this area it is important to consider a range of methodological issues. For example, to really capture the nature of the interaction between the patient and clinician, most studies use either videotaped or audiotaped consultations which are then coded and analysed. The majority of studies are conducted within a primary care setting where a standardized consulting room can be used to capture the consultations. However, recent studies have also found differences in communication styles amongst different clinician groups in other health care settings such as emergency care (Sandhu *et al.*, 2009; Dale *et al.*, 2008).

In a study examining consultations skills between Senior House Officers (SHOs), Specialist Registrars (SPRs), General Practitioners (GPs) and Emergency Nurse Practitioners (ENPs) with patients presenting with a primary care–type problem within an inner-city emergency department, it was found that ENPs and GPs had a similar consulting style placing greater emphasis on patient education and counselling-type talk compared to SHOs and SPRs who did less of this talk. Furthermore SHOs spent a greater proportion of their consultations gathering information asking more open and closed questions to patients. Overall ENPs had significantly higher associated patient satisfaction scores (Sandhu *et al.*, 2009) compared to other groups. The study clearly demonstrates the feasibility of recording consultations in a busy emergency department, using a standardized room and recording equipment as well as highlighting key differences in communication styles amongst the different clinician groups, and suggests the need for further study in this area to explore the impact on patient health outcomes and across other emergency departments.

The future of health care communication and back pain research includes addressing issues such as improving patient outcomes across a range of conditions and health care settings. We know managing and treating patients with back pain can be challenging, particularly because the existing treatments have small to moderate effects. Treating all back pain patients as a homogeneous group means that treatment effects are diluted. If we are able to target the best possible treatment to a defined subgroup of patients, we are likely to achieve better treatment outcomes. Dr. Patel is currently involved in a funded National Institute for Health Research programme grant aiming to develop a repository of high-quality randomised controlled trials for low back pain to try and identify subgroups that would benefit from particular treatments. This approach will hopefully lead to better treatment outcomes and also wider health and societal savings.

Health Psychology Teaching in Medical Schools

As mentioned above, our research interests fall within key areas of health psychology. They are also key areas of applied teaching. As health psychologists, we are also frequently asked to deliver guest lectures on a range of courses including MSc in Health Psychology and Professional Doctorate programmes. The ability to promote awareness and knowledge among other health care professionals is also an important skill. We are involved with training other professionals about a range of topics including chronic pain, its mechanisms, the application of the biopsychosocial model, motivational interviewing in a clinical setting, application of behaviour change, research methods and communication skills.

Within Warwick Medical School, Dr Sandhu is the module lead for Health Psychology on the MBChB degree. As highlighted by the General Medical Council (in *Tomorrow's Doctors*, 2009), one of the outcomes for medical graduates is to apply psychological principles, method and knowledge to medical practice. This includes having an understanding of the theoretical frameworks that explain health behaviours and beliefs, illness perceptions and beliefs and psychological aspects of behaviour change. Within this role it is therefore important to draw on cutting-edge, up-to-date research and theoretical frameworks including the transtheoretical model of behaviour change, the theory of planned behaviour, Leventhal's self-regulatory model and the health belief model and apply them to medicine. Recently, a core curriculum for psychology in undergraduate medical education produced by the Behavioural and Social Science Teaching in Medicine (BeSST) Psychology Steering Group (2010) has also been an influential guide in promoting a 'systematic and evidence-based curriculum for psychology in a medical curriculum'.

The Core Curriculum outlines key topics which are relevant to teaching psychology in medicine which includes Psychology – Core Knowledge, Psychology for Professional Practice, Psychology – Contribution to the Educational Process and general psychology topics including Leadership, Selection and Appraisal and Organisational Change. The curriculum is easy to follow and divides each topic into sections with key issues and a brief example. However, the challenge still remains of integrating such material within the existing medical curriculum and building case studies to illustrate key topics. The Core Curriculum provides a good foundation for this.

Teaching medical students is a very rewarding activity, however it can also be demanding. The biggest challenge is delivering the health psychology module in a way that is relevant and integrated with the other biomedical science modules. This is a crucial part of the teaching and is important in trying to overcome the stereotype that some students may hold of 'Health Psychology' being seen as one of the 'softer subjects' (Ayers and de Visser, 2010). By using clinical case studies and encouraging students to apply knowledge and plan a patient care pathway taking into account psychology and social issues, students are able to develop a better understanding of the clinical application. More recently a textbook designed specifically for medical students entitled *Psychology for Medicine* has been published by Susan Ayers and Richard de Visser (2010). This text is an excellent source for medical students as it covers key topics within psychology related to medicine including, Psychology and Health, Basic Foundations of Psychology, Body Systems and Healthcare Practice. Each chapter is directly relevant to the medical field with clear learning objectives, summary boxes, figures and case studies. The case studies illustrate patients' experiences in relation to the different topics discussed as well as illustrating the application of psychological theory, models and techniques in clinical practice. The chapters also include a clinical notes section with recommendations for use of the psychological theory and techniques in medical practice as well as short activities and questions to help students consolidate their learning. It is very encouraging to see the publications of such texts and one would hope that the future teaching and learning of psychology in medicine will become more relevant and applicable by students.

Teaching communication skills is also another important application of health psychology within medical schools. This includes facilitation of role-play sessions, where students are given the opportunity to conduct a consultation with a simulated patient and get feedback from observers (peers and the group facilitator). Assessment is then done by videotaping the consultation and using a standardised marking scheme, which captures the content of the discussion as well as process of the consultation.

However, there is debate as to whether recording consultations can alter the consulting behaviour of the clinician and therefore is not a true reflection of the consultation process. This is an interesting debate; but there is little research which actually shows that videorecording of consultations does influence clinician behaviour. Research within the area of health care communication will continue to grow and expand into different clinical settings and across a range of health care professionals.

Another application of health psychology teaching is a newly developed course within Warwick Medical School on Understanding and Facilitating Health Behaviour Change for which Dr Patel is the Course Director. Behaviour change is an important part of health psychology (Michie & Abraham, 2004), and this is acknowledged by the last Government who introduced Health Trainers (Department of Health, 2004). The certificate course is aimed at a broad range of health professionals from the health and social sectors who work with patients or clients where they wish to promote behaviour change. The certificate will introduce health professionals to core concepts in health psychology by taking them through a journey of establishing relationships in clinical practice and applying a patient-centred approach, accepting and overcoming resistance to behaviour change, examining readiness to change by exploring self efficacy, feelings, beliefs and values, planning for action and subsequently evaluating behaviour change.

Application of Health Psychology in Clinical Practice

The management of chronic conditions, such as long-term pain, can be challenging for health care professionals. Pain has been defined as 'an unpleasant sensory and emotional experience associated with actual or potential tissue damage, or described in terms of such damage' (International Association for the Study of Pain, 1979, p. 250). Having completed the Professional Doctorate and worked in an academic environment it felt like a natural step to branch into clinical practice that would, in turn, inform our continuous teaching and research. For example, working clinically has allowed us to gain insight into the patients' and health professionals' experiences and perspectives, which subsequently helps to inform research questions and the development of interventions to meet these needs.

Our Role as Health Psychologists in the Pain Clinic at Milton Keynes NHS Foundation Trust

Working with patients with long-term pain is a very taxing yet a rewarding role. Many of the patients we see suffer from a long-term pain condition, some without a definitive diagnosis. Probably the biggest challenge is helping patients understand the principles of self-management and coming to terms with the notion that this is a long-term condition that will require self-management and that there is not a 'magic cure'. Our efforts are, therefore, focused on managing the pain more effectively to allow patients to have a good quality of life. Often patients can find this hard to accept which can lead them on a path where they are looking for a diagnosis and hopefully a cure. This is not usually a fruitful journey. When we see patients our first barrier to overcome is the stigma associated with being referred to 'a psychologist'. We are often asked, 'Do you think this pain is all in my head?' This is our opportunity to educate patients on our role and also reassure them that we believe their pain is real. Once we have overcome these barriers and built a rapport with the patients, the most rewarding part is seeing them adapt their way of thinking and start to embrace self-management techniques.

As health psychologists, we deliver pain management seminars and pain management programmes to patients suffering from long-term pain conditions. We work in a multidisciplinary team of health professionals including pain consultants and acute and chronic pain nurses. The aim of the seminars is to provide patients with a broad outline of self-management techniques they can use in everyday living. These techniques are described to them and in some cases demonstrated. Patients are given a follow-up appointment to review their progress. The pain management programme is a more detailed and intensive programme delivered over 6 weeks. The programme is based on cognitive-behavioural principles and is delivered by a multidisciplinary team. Both of these interventions are delivered as group interventions, primarily because they provide a useful forum for patients to share experiences as well as learn from each other.

From our experience, working with groups of patients requires good facilitation skills. For example the patients that we see during the seminars are seen for two 1-hour sessions, which means the group does not always have enough time to gel. Therefore within this hour we try to create an atmosphere where patients feel relaxed and are able to share their experiences and give feedback amongst the group. The techniques we use to achieve this include carefully arranging the layout of the room. Chairs are placed in a circle with both the health psychologist and pain nurse as part of that circle. This is also done on our pain management programme. In some sessions rather than creating an expert part of the circle, the health professionals split and sit within different parts of the circle. We give all patients the opportunity to speak, encouraging the quieter ones as well as managing the more vocal members of the group. Members of a group can be quite easily led by one negative comment or opinion. Working with chronic pain patients, this can often be negative opinions towards health professionals, the future, other people's perceptions of them as pain patients and accepting changes in their life due to their chronic pain condition for example not being able to do what they used to do. To overcome this we often ask patients to reflect and focus on the positive aspects, the things that they can do, rather than the things that they can't do and allow other patients in the group to offer positive feedback or encouragement.

At the beginning of the pain management programme we set ground rules that ultimately come from members of the group. This allows the group to develop mutual respect for each other and avoid the risk of the session becoming a 'moan and groan' group. Although it is inevitable that patients will express negative opinions related to self management of chronic pain, we overcome this by allowing members of the group to explore their ambivalence encouraging patients to look to the future.

We also see patients on a one-to-one basis. This is either for a 'history-taking' session or thereafter a tailored therapeutic session. Patients will discuss with us a range of issues related to their chronic pain, including family, work, social and sometimes other health-related matters. In comparison with working in a group, one-to-one consultations give us the opportunity to explore in greater detail issues that are pertinent to the patient.

Our Thoughts: Health Psychology, the Past and the Future

This chapter has so far focused on how health psychology has been applied in a medical school environment in both the field of teaching and research combined with the clinical application of chronic pain management. To some extent the chapter highlights the diversity and successful ways in which health psychology is growing, however we feel there is still some way to go before we are truly appreciated for the range of skills we can offer across different health conditions.

When choosing health psychology as a profession there were only a few universities that offered health psychology as a masters programme and even fewer offering it as a Stage 2 training programme. We have to admit there were doubts when we started this journey and we would often discuss with each other whether going down the health psychology route was the best career move? Doubts we had included questions as to what were the career prospects after completing Stage 1 and Stage 2, which was the best option for Stage 2 training, in other words, was it doing the professional doctorate which seemed to have more day-to-day structure or was it best to undertake a PhD and complete Stage 2 through the BPS qualification?

After long discussions, research and talking with course tutors we both decided that actually health psychology was an up-and-coming area and this is what was actually exciting about it. As for the Stage 2 training, this was a bridge that would be crossed when the time came! During the MSc in Health Psychology it seemed that there were a lot of efforts being made to promote health psychology for example through the Division of Health Psychology and also the development of small network groups such as the East Midlands Health Psychology Network (EMHPN). Attending bimonthly meetings was a great way to network with other health psychologists in the area and keep up to date with training and current news. It was also an opportunity to speak to the more senior, experienced members of the network and to ask and learn from their experiences and what difficulties and challenges they had faced in their careers.

As we have progressed and become more experienced as psychologists we have now become members of the Midlands Health Psychology Network (MHPN) committee. This network reflects the expansion of Health Psychology across the Midlands as a whole. Annually we run continued professional development (CPD) events. Past events have included research methodology used in health psychology to applied techniques used in clinical practice. The network also holds an annual conference which has a diverse programme showcasing the latest health psychology research, keynote speakers and gives Stage 1 and Stage 2 students an opportunity to present their work in a friendly environment. We have expanded the network to social-networking sites such as Facebook, which has given us an easier and quicker way to keep members up to date with news, events and meetings. We often get asked, 'How would you set up such a network?' and 'What are the biggest challenges?' It is difficult to answer these questions as the original members of the committee have now stepped down. However we can draw from our current experiences of taking over the committee and taking the network forward. One of the biggest challenges is the time and commitment required from each committee member. We all take on our committee roles in addition to our academic and/or clinical roles. The present committee comprises of seven members, each taking on a specific role including marketing, maintenance of the website and Facebook pages, management of memberships, the mailing list and general administrative and treasury duties.

Open and honest communication is essential and regular committee meetings are important either face to face or through teleconference. There is sometimes difficulty in getting a time and date when all committee members can meet due to the various demands we have in our day-to-day jobs. However we do have regular e-mail contact that allows us to share ideas and keep up to date with any issues as well as an opportunity to air any concerns and discuss how to overcome these.

Having a Health Psychology Network is important and we have had enquiries from other regions in the country who are also trying to set up similar networks asking for advice. As more and more networks become established we feel it is important that the networks communicate with each other. We all have the same goal and that is to promote health psychology and allow networking and collaboration and keeping members up to date with information, current news and developments regarding Stage 1 and Stage 2 training.

Health psychology brings with it the opportunity to work in a range of fields including academia, NHS, private organizations, charities and as private practitioners. Many health psychologists have set up private practice offering health psychology interventions to a broad range of patients. We feel this is very inspirational, and with current NHS changes this may lead to new opportunities where we as health psychologists can sell our key competencies.

One of the things we really love about health psychology is the variety and flexibility of working areas that come with the discipline. The clinical areas of working resemble those that are common health problems that affect the general population, most of these being long-term conditions requiring self-management to some capacity. It is these conditions that often bring big costs to the NHS and society in general. For example, our clinical area of chronic pain, which affects a large proportion of the population, invokes costs for both health care services (in treatment and continuous investigations) and society (in lost working days and sickness absence). Therefore, it is very satisfying when we are able to see positive changes in patients' self-management and quality of life. This is challenging and sometimes not always possible; we have to remember we cannot 'cure' or 'fix' everyone, but if we can give them the tools to allow them to help themselves that is still a positive step forward.

The health psychology community is still relatively close knit, where many professionals know and interact with each other, which is crucial in any growing discipline. We are hopeful that as the discipline grows this collaborative and supportive nature will still remain. Having this support network will allow the discipline to have an influence on health policy and practice.

The health psychology journey has not been trouble-free; there have been times when we have doubted whether this has been the right route to take if your long-term career plans are to hold a combined clinical and academic post. Particularly in the early stages of our training we would often be asked 'What is health psychology?' which was not as easy to answer as was initially thought. There has been and still is limited knowledge amongst other health professionals about the role of health psychologists in the NHS. The division of health psychology has attempted to promote awareness by developing leaflets for other health professionals, which was a useful first step. Further promotion of the discipline is required particularly as we enter a period of uncertainly with commissioning of services. Health psychologists need to be at the forefront, clearly stipulating the services and competencies they hold to deliver these. We also need to question how well primary care services are aware of the role of health psychology; can we increase this awareness particularly amongst GPs who may ultimately commission services?

One of the other challenges we have faced in the discipline is the assumption that health psychologists are *academics*. Yes, it is true that we hold strong research and teaching competencies, but many of us also have clinical skills gained either while in training or thereafter. This has made it difficult for us to compete with clinical psychologists who clearly have a clinical basis to their training. We therefore feel the decision to add interventions as a compulsory component to the Stage 2 curriculum is a positive move and will allow people like us, who were in academic placements, to gain more clinical opportunities.

Are the jobs really there for health psychologists? This is a common question we are asked, particularly by trainees. We feel the jobs are there for people with the core health psychology competencies; the challenge here is to look outside of the box at jobs other than those labelled 'health psychologist'. There are very few jobs advertise with that title, therefore if you search just for that then the job market does not look very promising. However, taking the initiative and looking at posts where health psychology may be applied there are better prospects. Likewise, jobs advertised for clinical psychologists may also be applicable if a person can demonstrate that they have the core competencies to deliver that role. Therefore a shift towards competency-based learning is positive for health psychology. We feel that it would be a shame for there to be tension between two key fields of psychology, clinical and health, where they both clearly offer different strengths and unique qualities. On a positive note, we feel there are more research jobs being advertised which specifically ask for a background in health psychology.

Conclusion

Overall, health psychology has played and will continue to play a key role in medical schools throughout the country. Our clinical and academic mix has informed the planning and development of research ideas as well as curriculum development and teaching of health psychology in medical practice. This is an exciting time for health psychology and the growing influence it is having on health care policy and public health development.

Key Debates in Health Psychology

Health psychology plays a crucial role within medical schools, from both a research perspective and within teaching. There are several key issues within health psychology that have emerged from our chapter, however we feel that teaching health psychology to medical students, the hows, the whys and the whens of it, needs further exploration.

The How

How do we teach medical students such a complex and varied topic such as psychology? Traditional lectures in which information is given about the basic psychological theory are crucial, but then the biggest challenge is incorporating the application! Is this achievable in a lecture theatre? Are group work or short assignments more appropriate where students have an opportunity to discuss and share ideas? Crucial to such learning, whether it be in a lecture theatre or in the form of small-group work, is the use of case studies to illustrate the application of psychological theory in clinical practice. Clinical cases could represent a range of different conditions and each tackling a different aspect of health, illness and well-being. However, when using such cases it is important that we do not lose sight of evidence-based teaching. The cases should allow students to draw from relevant psychological research where they are able to apply what they learn and read about! As the application of psychology grows so

---

will the number of cases produced, ideally an electronic shared resources where all medical schools and institutions across the country could share and develop case studies, teaching ideas and support would make such teaching more successful. However time, funding and resources impede on such a resource.

The Why

Why teach psychology in medicine? This is also an interesting challenge that those who teach psychology within medical education face. Overcoming student perceptions that psychology may not actually be directly relevant to medicine is clearly a challenge that needs to be overcome in the early stages of teaching the module. Again the use of case studies to illustrate points is important here but also creating learning objectives that are clear, concise and relevant to medicine. There will always be a few students who come to the first lecture with the misconception of the 'soft subject', and so the challenge is to start thinking about how can we overcome these barriers? How do we demonstrate that psychology is in fact a science?

The When

The final issue in this debate is the when: when should psychology be taught within medical education? Year 1, 2, 3 or 4, or incorporated across the medical curriculum? The key challenge is to integrate psychology with the social and biomedical subjects whilst still having the unique identity as psychological theory and application. Questions that need to be thought of are: does it matter when psychology is taught? Are students more receptive to psychology once they are out in practice seeing patients? Should it be taught at the beginning to lay the foundations, or should it be spread across each year of the degree? There are no right or wrong answers to these questions or any of the questions raised in this debate. Psychology in medicine is becoming an increasingly relevant and important topic, as it becomes more and more recognzed and standardized within medical education it should bring with it the respect the discipline deserves!

References

Ayers, S., & de Visser, R. (2010). *Psychology for medicine*. London: Sage.
Behavioural and Social Sciences Teaching in Medicine (BeSST) Psychology Steering Group. (2010). *A core curriculum for psychology in undergraduate medical education*. Newcastle,

UK: Higher Education Academy Psychology Network and Subject Centre for Medicine, Dentistry and Veterinary Medicine.

Dale, J., Sandhu, H., Lall, R., & Glucksman, E. (2008). The patient, the doctor and the emergency department: a cross-sectional study of patient-centeredness in 1990 and 2005. *Patient Education and Counselling, 72*, 320–329.

Department of Health. (2004). Choosing health: making healthy choices easier. Retrieved from http://webarchive.nationalarchives.gov.uk/+/www.dh.gov.uk/en/Publicationsandstatist ics/Publications/PublicationsPolicyAndGuidance/DH_4094559

General Medical Council. (2009). Tomorrow's doctors. Retrieved from http://www.gmc-uk.org/education

Ha, F.J., Anat, S.D., & Longnecker, N. (2010). Doctor–patient communication: a review. *The Oschner Journal, 10*, 38–43.

Hawken, S.J. (2005). Good communication skills: benefits for doctors and patients. *New Zealand Family Physician, 32*, 185–189.

International Association for the Study of Pain. (1979). Editorial – the need of a taxonomy. *Pain, 6*(3), 247–252.

Maniadakis, N., & Gray, A. (2000). The economic burden of back pain in the UK. *Pain, 84*(1), 95–103.

Michie, S., & Abraham, C. (Eds.). (2004). *Health psychology in practice.* London: BPS Blackwell.

Patel, S., Friede, T., Griffiths, F., Lord, J., Thistlethwaite, J., Woolvine, M., & Underwood, M. (2011). Study protocol: Improving Patient Choice in Treating Low Back Pain (IMPACT–LBP): a randomised control trial of a Decision Support Package for use in physical therapy. *BMC Musculoskeletal Disorders, 12*, 52.

Patel, S., Greasley, K., & Watson P.J. (2007). Barriers to rehabilitation and return to work for unemployed chronic pain patients: a qualitative study. *European Journal of Pain, 11*, 831–840.

Preference Collaborative Review Group. (2008). Patients' preferences within randomised trials: systematic review and patient level meta-analysis. *British Medical Journal, 31*, 337:a1864.

Savigny, P., Kuntze, S., Watson, P., Underwood, M., Ritchie, G., Cotterell, M., Hill, D., Browne, N., Buchanan, E., Coffey, P., Dixon, P., Drummond, C., Flanagan, M., Greenough, C., Griffiths, M., Halliday-Bell, J., Hettinga, D., Vogel, S., & Walsh, D. (2009). *Low back pain: early management of persistent non-specific low back pain.* London: National Collaborating Centre for Primary Care and Royal College of General Practitioners.

Sandhu, H., Dale, J., Stallard, N., Glucksman, E., & Crouch, R. (2009). Emergency nurse practitioners and doctors consulting with patients in an emergency department: a comparison of communication skills and satisfaction. *Emergency Medicine Journal, 2*, 400–404.

Travaline, J.M., Ruchinskas, R., & D'Alonzo, G.E. (2005). Patient–physician communication: why and how. *Journal of the American Osteopathic Association, 105*, 13–18.

18

The Lived Experience of a Qualitative Health Psychologist

Rachel L. Shaw

Starting Out

I became a Chartered Health Psychologist[1] in 2004; arriving at this place in my professional career involved several twists and turns and it isn't the route I expected to take when I embarked on this journey fresh from A levels aged 18. I chose French, English language and geography at A level and intended to read French and linguistics at university. However, I didn't quite make the grade for my first-choice university and ended up opting for De Montfort University's BSc Psychology of Human Communication with French instead. This turned out to be the best thing I ever did! Psychology of human communication covered both linguistics and psychology and so satisfied my desire to study linguistics but it also introduced me to psychology. At the same time I was keeping up my French. Perfect.

From the outset, I was fascinated by psychology. I was intrigued by the 'staple' subdisciplines of developmental and social psychology although I was less enthused by cognitive psychology and statistics. I also enjoyed sociolinguistics and psycholinguistics. What really grabbed me were the modules which were to the traditionalist a little 'off the wall' and possibly perceived to be out of place in a psychology programme; I remember in particular *Mind, Meaning and Discourse* and *Film Studies*, both convened by Dr Dave Hiles. We thought it was fantastic that we could watch a film on a Wednesday afternoon and call it work; it was this inauspicious beginning that inspired my doctoral research and I'll never forget the significance of narrative illustrated in the classic 1987 Rob Reiner film, *Stand by Me*.

Mind, Meaning and Discourse began with Dave standing at the front of the lecture theatre with a wooden spoon and asking us what it was. Eventually, once we'd

Health Psychology in Action, First Edition. Edited by Mark Forshaw and David Sheffield.
© 2013 John Wiley & Sons, Ltd. Published 2013 by John Wiley & Sons, Ltd.

overcome our inherent student apathy toward the dreaded interactive lecture, people began to shout out things like 'booby prize', 'wedding present', 'wedding anniversary' (the fifth wedding anniversary is represented by wood), 'puppet' (once dressed – like they used to feature on *Blue Peter* when I was growing up) as well as the obvious, 'cooking utensil'. Dave was illustrating that multiple meanings of the same object co-exist and that different people might attribute different meanings to the same object, event or feeling. In short, he was demonstrating the postmodern assumption that reality is not static or unitary but fluid, dynamic and intersubjectively constructed in a way that is bound by time and place. This spoke to me because throughout the earlier modules I had questioned the generality of theories presented and wondered how we might consider the cultural, historical and personal context within our study of human experience and behaviour. This different approach seemed to offer a possible way of answering these questions.

Another key moment for me, which consolidated my interest in the conceptual foundations of psychology and the sociology of scientific knowledge, was the final-year module, *Conceptual Issues in Psychology*. This module introduced me to Kuhn's (1962) notions of paradigms and scientific revolutions and I began to realize that science (particularly but not exclusively when directed at the human subject) is not an objective fact-finding exercise but a complex journey of discovery that takes place within the sociopolitical and historical climate; science is not neutral or value-free but the product of human interaction and interpretation. This brief flirtation with philosophy sparked a deeper interest in the epistemology of psychology which led me, via Reason and Rowan's excellent (1981) *Human Inquiry*, to Wilhelm Dilthey's distinction between the natural sciences and the human sciences: 'nature we can explain, man [*sic*] we must understand' and to Donald Polkinghorne's (1988) *Narrative knowing and the human sciences*.

Since then, I have had a passion for a psychology that takes a human science approach and prioritizes meanings, subjectivity and context. Giorgi (1970) called this a phenomenologically sensitive psychology, Jonathan Smith has referred to it as experiential psychology, and many others understand it as qualitative psychology.[2] My commitment to qualitative methods in psychology is the one constant in my career. Since my undergraduate final year research project I have used qualitative methods and through the years have become known as a qualitative psychologist.

You may be forgiven for wondering what this has to do with health psychology, but it was my expertise in qualitative methods that introduced me to subject. My first postdoctoral research post was in the Health Services Research Centre[3] at Coventry University. I was employed on the Breastfeeding Best Start randomized controlled trial. My role was split into three main tasks: overseeing the data collection and qualitative analysis of interviews conducted with mothers taking part in the trial; managing midwives' involvement in recruitment at antenatal clinics and delivering the intervention on the postnatal ward; and carrying out a series of focus groups with midwives following their participation in the trial to explore their experience of it. Applying qualitative research techniques to this real-world scenario was an excellent footing on which to develop my research profile.

Finding My Niche

One thing you notice as a student and early career researcher is that academics tend to specialize and this can be in one particular substantive topic (e.g. diabetes), or perhaps in one area of work (e.g. behavioural interventions in primary care). The challenge I faced was deciding which specialism would suit me. For a while I didn't really feel at home in health psychology; when I was in training, health psychology hadn't entered my world. Nevertheless, for several years following my PhD I did primary and secondary research in health psychology. As a doctoral student I had immersed myself in philosophy and tussled with the complicated constructs of phenomenology including intentionality (which has nothing to do with intending to do something), the life-world and Heidegger's (1962) Dasein (there-being or being-in-the-world). As a postdoctoral research associate these were things that rested in the back of my mind while I began to answer the more mundane yet critical questions, such as how to persuade midwives to recruit young pregnant women to an interview study about their infant feeding choices in a 10-minute slot which is already full to the brim with essential information (and that's without even touching on the midwives' own beliefs about breast and bottle feeding).

I soon began to learn about the National Health Service; its oblique systems, lack of resources and the sterling efforts required by its staff. Working in this context was a reality check that woke me up to thinking about research questions that matter to real people. My next challenge was to find a way of marrying that applied focus with my expertise in qualitative methodology. This wasn't immediately obvious and it took a while for me to gain the confidence to position myself (as I do now) as a qualitative health psychologist who can offer something worthwhile to a research team.

The value of qualitative methods – known for their ability to make sense of the messiness of human experience – in the complex and pressurized context of the health service was almost self-evident: qualitative research is iterative, designed to deal with the real world; it produces in-depth, subjective accounts from which we can ascertain the cares and concerns of individuals (whether patients, practitioners or carers); it enables us to explore how people feel and how their health beliefs are negotiated and constructed dependent on their personal relationships, everyday interactions with people around them and with society at large. In short, qualitative research can look beyond the surface and explore people's beliefs and the decisions they make by asking them to reflect and tell stories about things that have happened to them. By treating people as experts of their own experience, we show them respect, prioritize them and are able to see the world as if we were in their shoes. It is not always easy to see things from someone else's perspective and so it is not surprising that health care professionals and patients often interpret things differently and have different expectations about the outcome of a consultation. Similarly, we know that individuals do not act in isolation; decisions we make, especially those that might impact on our own or our family's health, are often influenced by a whole raft of things including the economic, social and political climate, our religious beliefs, the cultural practices we engage in, the family traditions we have always partaken in, our educational level and our role(s) in society (for instance as a professional, parent, political representative or voluntary worker).

Once we accept as fundamental our inherent interconnectedness with the world in which we live, we begin to realize that to understand health and illness experience we need to understand the person-in-context; I believe the only way we can do that effectively is to employ qualitative research methods either on their own or in conjunction with other approaches (including large scale-surveys, experiments and randomized controlled trials). Hence, I found my niche. I am a qualitative health psychologist who works to make sense of individuals' experiences of illness: I explore the factors that come together to make up people's health beliefs and how they impact on their health management; I pay attention to the context in which health is managed and so take as a priority the need to understand the experiences and beliefs of carers, other family members and health care professionals as well as patients; and finally, because constructs of health and illness are contingent on the stories that circulate in the media, I investigate the content and functionality of the media and people's interactions with it, especially the internet, news media and 'celebrity culture'.

The Work of a Qualitative Health Psychologist

As summarized above, my objective in the work I do is threefold: to understand people's experiences of health and illness and what those experiences mean to them within the context of their everyday lives; to make sense of the interrelationships between patients, health care professionals and carers or family members to help the individuals involved see things from a different perspective and therefore understand each other better; and to describe current practices as experienced by different stake-holders to establish examples of best practice which will help all involved. This is a particularly ambitious (and probably never ending) project which I have chipped away at during the years but it is one that I am committed to and genuinely believe is worthwhile. Alongside this substantive project is a secondary objective: to raise the profile of qualitative research methods in health psychology and within the hierarchy of knowledge. To achieve this aim, I am committed to qualitative methods training and showcasing the benefits and successes of qualitative methodology within a discipline whose focus is to make sense of human experience and behaviour. Consequently, I am engaged in a number of different activities as a qualitative health psychologist.

One example is a qualitative interview study with patients and health care professionals involved in the DESMOND randomized controlled trial, which I conducted with colleagues at the University of Leicester (Ockleford, Shaw, Willars & Dixon-Woods, 2008). Our remit was to explore patients' experiences of the group education intervention in self-management for patients newly diagnosed with Type 2 diabetes and to gather health care professionals' accounts of delivering this intervention or standard care and their experiences of working with diabetes patients. We found differences of opinion about the group format of the intervention, demonstrating that health care professionals and patients don't always see eye to eye about the most effective method of consultation; some patients preferred doing their own research and negotiating appropriate treatment and lifestyle changes, while others preferred the traditional didactic approach; this wasn't necessarily associated with demographic factors such as age. We also found that an individuals' acceptance of their identity as someone with diabetes impacted on their readiness to accept the severity of the disease and the longevity of lifestyle changes made in accordance with professional advice. The trial's 3-year follow-up results also observed a significant difference between the intervention and control groups' illness beliefs: scores for patients' beliefs in coherence, timeline, personal responsibility and seriousness were significantly higher in the intervention group. This example demonstrates how qualitative and quantitative research can work together in a complementary way. The questionnaire data from the DESMOND trial had identified personal responsibility and seriousness as constructs affected by the intervention; through our qualitative work we were able to provide further detail and suggest that it was patients' readiness to accept a change in the way they viewed themselves (i.e. as a person with diabetes), together with their beliefs about the seriousness of the condition that impacted most strongly on their ability to manage their condition. What we gain from the qualitative work is a sense of how illness beliefs might be functioning in relation to a person's identity and outlook, which emphasizes the need for appropriate interpersonal relationships between health care professionals and patients so that practitioners can get to know their patients and therefore make informed choices about the best way to manage their care. Of course, what qualitative research often shows is that there are no shortcuts in developing effective and satisfactory health services. Group education can have wonderful effects on people (and some participants in our study particularly valued sharing their experiences with others) and there are obvious benefits in terms of resources (finance, time, staff) but it doesn't suit everyone. Nevertheless, because qualitative research prioritizes the person it reminds us of the need to respect individuals and the importance of maintaining personalized care within the NHS.

A second area of my work involves the media. I am interested in how health issues are framed in the media in order to favour one particular message over alternatives and have worked with my colleague, David Giles at the University of Winchester, to develop Media Framing Analysis as a method for analyzing media content that focuses on qualitative analysis of narrative, character construction and portrayal, language use, and the generalization (or repetition) of historical and cultural phenomena (Shaw & Giles, 2009). One study examined media representations of celebrity drug use, using Amy Winehouse as a case study, with a view to exploring what young people make of celebrities like Winehouse and how stories of illegal and destructive behaviour might impact on their own beliefs systems and sense making in relation to drug use (Shaw, Whitehead, & Giles, 2010). The Media Framing Analysis revealed a sudden shift in messages portrayed in the news media and an especially rapid fall from grace for Winehouse; initially Winehouse's behaviour was framed with a nostalgic tone as that of a typical 'rock star', but within a year news reports seemed to become impatient with Winehouse's recklessness and cast her as a hopeless case who should sort out her problems. Indeed, the young people who took part in focus groups in this study had also tired of Winehouse's alleged drug use and apparent inability to take control of her behaviour. Nevertheless, the issue did spark a debate about the media's role in society and its potential impact in terms of glamorizing drug use. One focus group revealed mixed views among the young people who participated, Sam[4] remarked:

> It's just glamorizing it, it's not making it look bad.

To which SJ replied:

> They do make it look rank [unpleasant] though. I don't want to look like Pete Doherty and Pete Doherty has no money, Amy Winehouse's husband is in prison, how is that glamorizing it?

This study illustrated young people's ability to critically appraise what they read in the media amidst fears of 'copycat' behaviour influenced by early work in behavioural modelling. The key benefit of carrying out in-depth qualitative analyses of both media content and group discussion data about that content is its sensitivity to the nuances within human understanding. The media data demonstrate the apparent unceasing cycle of idolization quickly followed by scandal and vilification and they are important in health psychology because they represent the pervasiveness of celebrity culture within contemporary society and its potential to impact on individuals' health beliefs.

A clear cut example of the power of the media in relation to health beliefs and decision-making behaviour is the infamous measles–mumps–rubella (MMR) and autism debate. I carried out a Media Framing Analysis of news stories following the press release in 1998 about Andrew Wakefield's research which tentatively suggested a link between the MMR vaccination and autism (Shaw, 2005). This quickly led to a radical drop in uptake of the vaccination as well as a subsequent increase some years later in (sometimes fatal) cases of measles. Consequently, I believe it is imperative that health psychologists approach health concerns within their social and cultural context and that part of this task is to understand the function of the media in generating discourses of health and in contributing to the frame of reference individuals use when making decisions about their own and their family's health.

Thirdly, the exponential growth of the internet and websites devoted to health has led to the birth of a new field in health psychology, ehealth. The internet has the potential to radically change the way we function in relation to our health; it is possible to seek advice and support from health professionals and others with the same condition, to self-diagnose, and to buy self-testing kits and treatments online. The key challenges provoked by these virtual consultations and peer- or self-diagnoses are concerned with the validity of information and the accreditation of products available. A focus group study with health care professionals and members of the public carried out by Louise Donnelly as part of her doctoral programme (which I supervised) demonstrated that increased internet access can lead to a decline in expert authority; participants felt capable of making sense of health information online and in some cases used this to challenge their GP in a way they wouldn't have done without the internet (Donnelly, Shaw & van den Akker, 2008). Furthermore, some individuals felt empowered by the availability of information online and found it served them better, mainly due to its convenience, than using traditional health services. This notion of the virtual patient and its implications for health management I think are crucial in future health psychology research and are certainly high up on my own research agenda.

Finally, I will illustrate the potential impact qualitative health psychology can have on the real world. The examples above illustrate the close links between the research I do and the lived experience of individuals in contemporary society; the focus on everyday experience and people in context is a major strength of qualitative methodology. Furthermore, qualitative research in health psychology can reveal flaws or omissions in current practice and help inform the design and implementation of new systems. Working from an evidence base in developing health care systems is paramount and historically, the 'gold standard' of evidence used in this way comes from systematic reviews of randomized controlled trials testing drug or behavioural interventions. Nevertheless, other types of evidence including that generated by qualitative research has been recognized for some time and is beginning to filter into the consciousness of funding bodies, policy makers and practitioners. Indeed, carrying out metasyntheses of qualitative evidence seems to be in vogue. Several of my PhD students are doing a metasynthesis alongside a more traditional systematic review of quantitative evidence and a number of training courses are now available in methods for conducting metasynthesis. Furthermore, I have written a chapter on this very subject for a textbook on qualitative methods for psychologists and psychotherapists (Shaw, 2011). This increased recognition of qualitative research demonstrates its new found significance within the hierarchy of evidence and together with continually growing proportions of qualitative research published in health services research, medical and health psychology journals consolidates the place of qualitative methodology within the scientific community.

A more direct way in which qualitative research can impact on the real world is to obtain funding from the NHS, charities or private companies involved in health care research and/or drug development that invest in applied scientific research within the health care setting. For example, I currently have two PhD students working on programmes of research of this nature. Christian Borg Xuereb is part-funded by Bayer Healthcare[5] to carry out a phenomenological study of patients' and physicians' experiences of living with or prescribing warfarin. Christian's research is a sister project to a randomized controlled trial of a psychological, educational intervention for atrial fibrillation patients on warfarin run by fellow PhD student, Danielle Smith. Both are working with clinical supervisor Dr Deirdre Lane and are based at a local hospital; I am Christian's academic supervisor and Danielle's is Prof Helen Pattison. Christian's work is closely linked to National Institute for Health and

Clinical Excellence (NICE 2006) guidelines for managing atrial fibrillation and his in-depth qualitative research has two objectives: to explore patients' experiences and beliefs in order to make sense of their decisions to accept or decline warfarin and to determine the rationale behind physicians' decisions whether or not to prescribe warfarin in particular circumstances. Managing potential risk is paramount in this area: the key concerns are overcoming patients' worries about the risk of stroke and bleeding and enabling physicians to feel confident in explaining those risks in a way that patients can understand in order to make a decision about appropriate treatment. Getting into the 'nitty gritty' of both patients' and physicians' perspectives on warfarin and risks will therefore help devise effective strategies for risk assessment and decision making that will benefit both patients and physicians.

Adrienne McCabe is funded by a West Midlands Nursing, Midwifery and Allied Health Professions Research Training Award, and her research is set in a Paediatric Intensive Care Unit. Adrienne's work follows on from her previous work which developed a Paediatric Early Warning System (McCabe & Duncan, 2008). Her doctoral research takes a phenomenological approach to explore nurses' and doctors' experiences of unexpected life-threatening events on the paediatric ward; within this Adrienne is investigating the methods of feedback and debrief that are in place as well as any related time off work, stress or distress experienced with a view to developing strategies to prepare nursing staff for such events and designing appropriate systems for providing feedback, debrief and support. Alongside this, Adrienne is involved in other tasks including an international survey of current practice for preparing staff for an unexpected life-threatening event as well as a systematic review of the literature. This programme of research will feed into further postdoctoral work which will develop and test an intervention to prepare and support staff in these circumstances. If successful, this intervention has the potential to be rolled out nationally and therefore have considerable impact on nurses' everyday experience, training and job satisfaction as well as on the care of patients and their families.

Other equally important areas of my work include training and consultancy. As introduced above, the objective underlining these activities is to promote the benefits and successes of employing qualitative methodology in health psychology research. This is a valuable enterprise due to the growth of qualitative health psychology and the related increased demand for both training in qualitative methods and applied research taking a qualitative approach. A good example of consultancy in the shape of research is a tender we won to carry out a qualitative evaluative study of the cardiovascular screening programme within the Heart of Birmingham teaching Primary Care Trust (HoBtPCT). Alongside quantitative analyses of biomedical and questionnaire data, HoBtPCT required an in-depth qualitative study of patients' and health care professionals' experiences of being involved in the screening programme. In addition, they required a systematic literature review of qualitative and quantitative evidence about the success or otherwise of cardiovascular screening programmes elsewhere. A great benefit of qualitative health psychology is its ease of application to the real-world setting which, together with our expertise in systematic reviewing, is attractive to organizations that commission research. As a team within the Health &

Lifespan Psychology Research Group at Aston, we are able to market our skills set and attract such consultancy work which both further develops our track record and raises our profile in the sector.

I also carry out consultancy work in the form of designing and delivering short training courses in qualitative research methods. I have done this in a variety of ways. I have delivered bespoke training courses in qualitative methods under the auspices of Community Pathways CIC (a consultation and research company that employs local people to carry out research and consultancy within the region) as well as for organizations such as the Health Research & Development Unit (part of the East of England NHS Research and Development Support Unit). Mostly, I offer one day training courses in Interpretative Phenomenological Analysis (IPA) here at Aston University. These courses provide Continual Professional Development (CPD) for practitioners in health, education and social work, doctoral or contract researchers, academics and others interested in developing their research skills. IPA has become a particularly attractive method in health psychology and the courses I run have attracted delegates from across the United Kingdom as well as from Ireland, Australia and Canada. Delivering these courses is a really enjoyable part of my job; I meet people from diverse fields doing fascinating research in a range of disciplines. I value this work because it keeps me in touch with the world outside health psychology; I find mixing in interdisciplinary circles is a great stimulation for developing research ideas of my own.

On top of this CPD training, I have also been involved in work to develop online resources for teaching qualitative methods in psychology, a project funded by the Higher Education Academy. Resources such as these will benefit both students and lecturers which will help build capacity in the shape of future qualitative researchers. I feel that work of this nature is worthwhile and part of my duty as an expert in the field. I am after all an educator and so am committed to the advancement of knowledge and skills especially when they contribute to the profile of qualitative health psychology.

Summing Up

The life of a qualitative health psychologist is a busy one! It is also varied, creative and inspiring. I have taken as read (perhaps in error) my involvement in undergraduate and postgraduate teaching and attendance at national and international conferences as these are the activities which feature most prominently (especially the former) in the life of a lecturer. Instead I have focused on those activities which characterize my passions and commitment to qualitative health psychology. Being a qualitative research in psychology often comes with a feeling of marginalization from the mainstream in the typical 'outgroup' sense. However, I no longer feel the need for continual justification for using words instead of numbers in the work I do. Great leaps have been made in recent years with thanks to people like Prof Jonathan Smith, Prof Michael Murray, Prof Kerry Chamberlain and Prof Lucy Yardley among others, all well known for their commitment to qualitative methods in health psychology. It is a vibrant field of which I am happy to be a part. In fact, I would go as far to say that as a qualitative researcher I feel at home in health psychology.

Key Debates in Health Psychology

I've just had an MSc Health Psychology student come and talk to me about a project idea: he is interested in asthma among young people from low socio-economic backgrounds. The dilemma he posed to me was whether to opt for a project about illness representations using Leventhal's Commonsense Model of Self-Regulation of Health & Illness as a framework or an experiential project which takes Heideggerian phenomenology as its theoretical background. My response (somewhat to my own surprise): the two aren't mutually exclusively; in fact one could argue that their objectives would be the same even though the methods used might differ substantially. After I'd told the student to go off and do some reading and to come back when he's got a clearer idea of his specific research question (which will – in theory – help determine which approach and methods will be the best fit), I found myself reminiscing about the realization I had many years ago that interpretative phenomenological analysis (IPA) is all about cognition! As a student I took an instant dislike to cognitive psychology and anything associated with it. Now, as a more mature qualitative health psychologist I know that studying cognition isn't limited to the infamous computer analogy or information-processing flowcharts; on reading Jerome Bruner's work, I realized that cognition put another way is meaning making. This notion of meaning making appealed to me because of its focus on meaning but also because it attributed agency to the individual who makes meaning (i.e. makes sense of something).

I believe that a key concern of health psychology is to understand the ways in which people make sense of things. This is a view that was clearly shared by many others as health psychology began to grow and develop, evidenced by the dominance of illness representations and social cognition models, including the seemingly omnipotent theory of planned behaviour, in health psychology research. My 'Eureka' moment brought home to me the closeness, in objectives at least, between historically distinct approaches. It also left me feeling bewildered about the (im)possibility of ever bridging the epistemological divide between the 'traditional' health psychology models and the 'new paradigm' approaches which used qualitative methods.

Recently, I have become more optimistic about this venture. Lucy Yardley's work promoting Dewey's pragmatism in an attempt to draw attention to the multifaceted nature of knowledge (and by extension the multiple methods which might produce scientific knowledge) has also advanced this debate from previous iterations about mixing methods. Like Lucy, I think we need to go beyond the idea of mixing methods, which can lead for example to 'watered-down' qualitative studies tagged onto the end of a large-scale survey which are neither use nor ornament. Instead, we need to think of ways of being creative and designing truly integrative projects. To do this we need to peel away the barriers between positivism and interpretivism and engage with their assumptions at a basic level to identify the essence of their objectives. This I envisage as an epistemological dance rather than the wrestling matches of yesteryear; taking to the floor with an air of openness and a shared desire to achieve a sense of knowing may help us feel the music in our bodies and start us moving to the same rhythm.

Notes

1   At the time this was a title awarded by the British Psychological Society (BPS) which was superseded in 2009 by the Health Professions Council's (HPC) protected titles of Practitioner Psychologist and Health Psychologist. The title Chartered Psychologist is still valid for those Chartered by the BPS without an applied specialism or in addition to the HPC specialist title.
2   Qualitative psychology usually incorporates a far broader range of methods, however, including those focusing on discourse such as conversation analysis and discourse analysis. Experiential psychology does not study language in its own right; instead, its objective is to use language as a path to making sense of lived experience.
3   Now called the Applied Research Centre in Health and Lifestyle Interventions.
4   Pseudonyms are used to protect participants' anonymity.
5   Christian's PhD is funded jointly by an Investigator-Initiated Educational Grant from Bayer Healthcare and University of Birmingham's Centre for Cardiovascular Sciences, Sandwell and West Birmingham Hospitals NHS Trust.

References

Burden, A.C. (2010). Rapid response: to show the benefit of targeting cardio vascular disease screening. *British Medical Journal, 340*. doi:10.1136/bmj.c1693. Retrieved from http://www.bmj.com/content/340/bmj.c1693/reply

Donnelly, L.S., Shaw, R.L., & van den Akker, O.B.A. (2008). eHealth as a challenge to 'expert' power: a focus group study of Internet use for health information and management. *Journal of the Royal Society of Medicine, 101*, 501–506.

Giorgi, A. (1970). *Psychology as a human science: a phenomenologically based approach*. New York: Harper and Row Publishers, Inc.

Heidegger, M. (1962/2004). *Being and time*. Trans. J. Macquarrie & E. Robinson. Oxford: Blackwell.

Khunti, K., Heller, S., Skinner, T.C., Gray, L. J., Dallaso, H., Realf, K., Carey, M., & Davies, M. (2010). Randomised controlled trial of the DESMOND structured education programme for people newly diagnosed with type 2 diabetes: follow-up results at three years. *Annual Professional Conference of Diabetes UK,* 3–5 March, Liverpool, UK.

Kuhn, S. (1962). *The structure of scientific revolutions.* Chicago: University of Chicago Press.

McCabe, A., & Duncan, H. (2008). National survey of observation and monitoring practices of children in hospital. *Paediatric Nursing, 20*(6), 24–27.

National Institute for Health and Clinical Excellence (NICE). (2006). *Atrial fibrillation: the management of atrial fibrillation.* NICE Clinical Guideline 36. Developed by the National Collaborating Centre for Chronic Conditions. London: National Institute for Health and Clinical Excellence.

Ockleford, E., Shaw, R.L., Willars, J., & Dixon-Woods, M. (2008). Education and self-management for people newly diagnosed with type 2 diabetes: a qualitative study of patients' views. *Chronic Illness, 4,* 28–37.

Palmer, R.E. (1969). *Hermeneutics.* Evanston, IL: Northwestern University Press.

Polkinghorne, D.E. (1988). *Narrative knowing and the human sciences.* New York: State University of New York Press.

Reason, P., & Rowan, J. (1981). *Human inquiry: a sourcebook of new paradigm research.* Chichester: John Wiley and Sons Ltd.

Shaw, R.L. (2005). Can we communicate health risk without causing hysteria? Making sense of the MMR scare. Oral presentation at the Critical Health Psychology Conference, 29 March–1 April, Sheffield, UK.

Shaw, R.L. (2011). Identifying and synthesising qualitative literature. In D. Harper & A. Thompson (Eds.), *Qualitative research methods in mental health and psychotherapy: an introduction for students and practitioners.* Oxford: Wiley Blackwell.

Shaw, R.L., & Giles, D.C. (2009). Motherhood on ice? A media framing analysis of older mothers in the UK news. *Psychology & Health, 24*(2), 221–236.

Shaw, R.L., Whitehead, C., & Giles, D.C. (2010). 'Crack down on the celebrity junkies': does media coverage of celebrity drug use pose a risk to young people? *Health, Risk & Society, 12*(6), 575–589.

Wakefield, A.J., Murch, S.H., Anthony, A., Linell, J., Casson, D.M., Berelowitz, M., Dhillon, A.P., Thomson, M.A., Harvey, P., Valentine, A., Davies, S.E., & Walker-Smith, J.A. (1998). Ileal-lympoid-nodular hyperplasia, non-specific colitis, & pervasive developmental disorder in children. *The Lancet, 351,* 637–641.

19

Health Psychology in Sickle Cell and Other Long-Term Haematological Conditions

Veronica Joan Thomas

Establishing a Health Psychology Service in Sickle Cell Disease

In November 1997, I was appointed as a health psychologist to work within the sickle cell team at Guys and St Thomas' NHS Trust. This post was the first of its kind in the country, which arose from the growing recognition of the need to take account of the psychological concomitants of sickle cell disease (SCD). The current service evolved from the randomized controlled trial that I undertook to evaluate the efficacy of cognitive-behavioural therapy (CBT) in patients with SCD and was shown to be effective in reducing pain, depression and anxiety and frequency of hospitalization and duration of hospital stay (Thomas *et al.*, 1999, 2000, 2001). CBT has also been shown to be a cost-effective intervention (Thomas *et al.*, 2001) being associated with a cost saving of £2000 per patient per month.

In starting the service, a needs assessment was undertaken. According to NICE, a 'Health needs assessment (HNA) is a systematic method for reviewing the health issues facing a population, leading to agreed priorities and resource allocation that will improve health and reduce inequalities' (NICE, 2005, p. 6).

The Psychological Needs of People with Sickle Cell Disease

SCD is a group of inherited blood disorders associated with sickling of the red blood cells There are over 9000 people living with SCD in London, and of these there are approximately 600 adults and 450 children on the Guy's and St Thomas' Foundation Trust GSTFT patients' register, and numbers are predicted to increase.

Health Psychology in Action, First Edition. Edited by Mark Forshaw and David Sheffield.
© 2013 John Wiley & Sons, Ltd. Published 2013 by John Wiley & Sons, Ltd.

SCD is the most prevalent genetic disorder worldwide and it primarily affects people of African and Caribbean origin as well as small numbers of people from the Mediterranean, Middle East and India. It is characterised by unpredictable and extremely painful episodes (called a 'crisis'), caused by the occlusion of blood vessels by abnormal, sickle-shaped red blood cells. This can result in chronic anaemia and tissue destruction, causing both acute and chronic organ damage (Charache *et al.*, 1989). Complications resulting from SCD include acute chest syndrome, severe damage to hip and shoulder joints, strokes and multi-organ failures from multiple episodes of crises (Serjeant, 1992). These acute and chronic complications contribute to lifelong suffering for patients with SCD (Gil *et al.*, 1989). Further, these patients live under the threat of early and sudden death related to the disease.

What Does Coping with SCD Entail?

As the disease is hereditary, being present from birth, it impacts on all social, educational and employment achievements and, consequently threatens the integrity of quality of life. It is a multisystem problem that can give rise to disability. Individuals with SCD may suffer psychologically and socially as well as physically due to pain and other symptoms. Frequent hospitalizations for pain interrupt family and peer relationships, key socialization, acquisition of social skills and educational achievements, and the disruption, isolation and distress that these may produce are significant (Barakat *et al.*, 2007; Thomas, 1996; Thomas *et al.*, 1999, 2001, 2009). This can lead to negative psychological consequences in the form of depression and health anxiety. These in turn can impact on behaviour and can cause frequent hospitalizations, prolonged admissions and the development of challenging behaviour in a few people.

The shortened life span and the lifelong suffering associated with the physical complications naturally have psychosocial ramifications. Individuals vary considerably in their ability to cope with the majority of people coping very well, leading active lives and being psychologically well-adjusted (Gil *et al.*, 1989; Thomas, *et al.*, 1999); a minority of this patient group have been found to be poorly adjusted with high levels of anxiety and depression (Gil *et al.*, 1992; Thomas *et al.*, 1999). Passive or negative coping styles have been found to be associated with increased health care utilization and hospital admissions (Gil, *et al.*, 1992; Anie *et al.*, 2002); low levels of self efficacy are associated with poor adjustment and more physical and psychological problems (Edwards *et al.*, 2001; Thomas *et al.*, 2001). In terms of illness beliefs when assessed on an illness perception questionnaire, SCD patients show poorer illness identity and greater illness chronicity, and believe pain control to be predominantly subject to chance events rather than personal control or 'powerful' doctors, compared with patients with renal disease, for example (Thomas, Serjeant *et al.*, 2001).

In addition to these physical and psychological consequences, the attitudes of health professionals concerning the provision of adequate pain relief, a lack of knowledge about SCD and a lack of cultural awareness do exacerbate things further. This has often resulted in stereotypical beliefs, which on occasions have led to the misinterpretation of the behaviour and expressions of this patient population. Clinical practice is based not just on knowledge and data but also on conscious and unconscious attitudes, belief systems and prejudices (Shapiro *et al.*, 1997). In some cases continuing mistrust and stigmatization by health professionals have led to:

- Invalidation of their legitimate pain and medical needs;
- Increasing levels of hostility and helplessness in the professionals caring for these patients;
- Increasing levels of negative attitudes in health care professionals towards SCD patients.

In SCD, one of the big trigger factors for sickle cell crisis is stress and patient stresses are linked to the following issues:

- Coping with pain
- Adjusting to symptoms and incapacities
- Managing emotional and social consequences
- Maintaining effective relationships in and outside of hospital
- Coping with long-term condition issues across the development and negotiating life challenges at specific stage of the development
- Managing lifestyle issues

Therefore, in my daily work my aim is to ensure good outcomes and experiences for people with SCD including maximum health and well-being, control over what happens to them, confidence in managing their own condition and using services, good relationships with professionals and access to convenient, efficient services that meet their needs and preferences.

Traditional Approaches

In the past, the main approach to SCD management has revolved around the acute painful crises. However, it became increasingly recognized that chronic pain is a significant problem for a large proportion of the sickle population and that it is these patients who are high users of the inpatient service with multiple and prolonged hospital admissions. This is not surprising since it is well known that chronic unrelieved pain can induce helplessness and depression (Thomas *et al.*, 1999; Tyrer *et al.*, 1989). These feelings of helplessness and depression in turn exacerbate pain and influence the manner in which pain is expressed. This distress causes exaggeration of emotional reactions in an attempt to gain adequate pain relief and to be believed by nursing staff and doctors. These reactions may appear 'over the top', thus confirming the staff's preconceived view of them as difficult and problematic patients.

Why Health Psychology?

SCD is a long-term condition (LTC) (Department of Health (DoH), 2008) and the essential element of LTC care is to support people to take a more active role in the decisions about their health and well-being. This means that services need to enable people with LTC to feel independent and in control of their physical health problem as well as to help people develop proactive care planning that includes using information to prevent disease progression. Health psychology is therefore ideal in this regard and has the best applied psychological models to achieve good outcomes for people with LTC. There are still only two full-time SCD-dedicated psychology services in the United Kingdom that are embedded within the SCD teams; ours and the one based at Central Middlesex Hospital. Other centres tend to use part-time clinical psychology input or refer patients onto a general liaison psychology service. Several documents recommend the involvement of clinical health psychologists in the care of people with physical long-term conditions and these have been utilized to guide the development of the GSTFT HPS service. These include 'National Service Framework for Long-term Medical Conditions' (DoH, 2005) and 'Organising and Delivering Psychological Therapies' (DoH, 2004).

Locating the HPS within the SCD team, improving communication between staff and patients, and increasing accessibility of health psychology for patients and staff were important features to establish from the start in order to address the areas of need identified by patients and staff.

The service is audited annually and these have revealed that our specialist health psychology input alongside the medical, nursing and social care at GSTFT is extremely valuable in reducing distress, challenging behaviour and the frequency and duration of hospital admissions, improving coping, confidence, self-esteem, and employment and educational activities. The following health psychology competences are utilized in the daily organization of the service; effective medicine management through psycho-education to improve adherence to medicines, behaviour change and health promotion. In addition to the practice element, the other elements of the HPS are consultancy, research and teaching and training. These are all important roles and responsibilities in the context of SCD.

The Nature of HPS

An important goal of the HPS is to ensure that it is a normal part of the SCD multidisciplinary package of care. The importance of normalizing it is to remove any stigma around psychology and enable patients to feel free to access the HPS. The health psychologist is a visible member of the multidisciplinary team (MDT) seen on ward rounds and in clinics, demonstrating a sense of availability and responsiveness. Being a visible part of the team ensures that the health psychologists are engaging with patients during times when they are unwell as when they are well and therefore get to learn about coping mechanisms first-hand. In this setting, the psychology team's opinion is actively sought by the other MDT team members. For example, during a consultant ward round, the health psychologists frequently offer a psychological perspective (i.e. on formulations and solutions) and feed back information about psychological, cultural, social, family, cognitive deficits and issues pertinent to concerns regarding treatment adherence and multiple admissions. There are three full-time psychologists within the HP team, two being health psychologists, and the third member a trained health and clinical psychologist. We are diverse in terms of age (senior, experienced and young adults) and culture (African Caribbean, English and Asian).

Locating the HPS within the SCD team led to significantly improved communication between staff and patients, and increasing the accessibility of psychology for patients and staff were important features to establish from the start and remains a key facet of the HPS today.

My Role within the Multidisciplinary Team

One of my important initial 'missions' was to ensure 'normality' in establishing the HPS, which was crucial because the SCD patients' past experience of psychological involvement had been through liaison psychiatry who had been called in to manage 'critical incidents'. This crisis management approach naturally led many patients to feel 'labelled' which ultimately caused distrust that was generalized to psychology (perceived by patients as an extension of psychiatry).

Ensuring normality and gaining trust were achieved through two main ways; firstly by undertaking a needs assessment of patients to learn from them the ways in which they believe a psychologist could help them. It was also very important to consult with MDT team members to get their views about what they thought I should focus on and they identified about 12 patients who had a history of frequent and prolonged hospital admissions, social problems and who displayed manipulative and challenging behaviour towards staff. Consequently these patients became my top priority in delivering psychological interventions.

I adopted an educational approach to staff and patients concerning the role of health psychology in the context of SCD as a long-term condition and provided a regular debriefing forum for nurses and doctors to deal with critical incidents with sickle patients as well as to help them reflect on their practice. This also helped them feel better supported and empowered in their daily management of sickle cell clients.

Altogether, these strategies helped to change the initial culture and to create a better climate of collaboration between the sickle cell team and the health care professionals caring for these patients. Initially there was reluctance on the patients' part to take up the service, however the education of patients and staff led to more patients accessing and self-referring to the psychological service.

An important aspect of the work was concerned with the introduction of behaviour contracts aimed at setting boundaries. These contracts are concerned with establishing agreement on code of conduct and highlighting the patients' rights as well as their responsibility in the management of their care. These are naturally developed according to the individual's needs, incorporating important clinical guidance for nursing and medical staff. This ensures that the patient receives appropriate treatment as well as a degree of consistency in the quality of care that is delivered.

Self-referrals

Over the past 13 years since the HPS began there has been a dramatic improvement in the awareness amongst the patients and their families and health care professionals of the importance of psychological support and its benefits in aiding coping with SCD. This has led to the patients coming to view the HPS as *their* psychology service and they access the service themselves through self-referral via telephone or email. The HPS offers a stepped-care approach and works on the premise that patients benefit most from psychological support when their concerns are identified early. Telephone-based therapy is offered especially when people are unwell and also for young people who are away at university outside of London.

We have two named patient representatives, one male and one female, whose main role is to represent the views of the patients. We seek their views around service development issues and they also attend the psychology-led support group and act as user representatives in that forum. Therefore, in addition to working closely with the sickle cell team, the HPS actively collaborates with patients and their families as well.

Neuropsychology Service

A neuropsychological component of the service commenced in March 2002. This service was created following the identification that some patients had great difficulty in understanding some of the more abstract concepts in psychological therapy, were forgetful of appointments and treatment regimes, showed problems with understanding information about their condition and treatments, and experienced angry outbursts because of difficulty in communicating their needs. Such problems with memory, comprehension and communication interfere with quality of care that the patient is able to receive and represent barriers to patients accessing the health services. It was hypothesized that some of the difficulties may be due to impairments in cognitive functioning (learning, memory and concentration) that result from strokes.

This led to the employment of a clinical health psychologist who can undertake neuropsychological assessments which has enabled previously unidentified but significant cognitive problems to be identified and addressed. The majority of the patients with cognitive problems are under 40 years old and therefore interventions focus particularly on helping patients to cope with cognitive deficits in the context of working or studying, liaising with employers and tutors, making referrals to others, and using the information to inform health care professionals about the patient's individual cognitive needs during consultations. This aspect of the service is in line with a number of guidance and briefing documents. For example, *The Royal College of Physicians' National Clinical Guidelines for Stroke* (2008) and the British Psychological Society's *Psychological Services for Stroke Survivors and Their Families* (2002) make numerous recommendations regarding the need to assess cognitive function and intervene appropriately. Accordingly neuropsychological assessment can:

- Identify areas of strength and difficulty in cognitive function so that recommendations can be made to the patient and relevant professionals about improving coping with cognitive demands of everyday life, work, studies, and communication; and
- Provide information about baseline cognitive function to which results of further assessments can be compared – a decline in function may indicate the occurrence of further silent strokes that have yet to be identified via other means.

Findings from the neuropsychology work are disseminated to other members of the team via reports, discussion in MDT meetings, and presentations at seminars. Findings can be used to enhance health professionals' communication with patients and enhance the process of informed consent.

An Evidence-based Approach to Service Development

The establishment of the current service was based on a randomized controlled study investigating the efficacy of cognitive-behavioural therapy (CBT) in the management of sickle cell disease pain (Thomas *et al.*, 1999). Ninety-seven patients from seven London hospitals, including Guy's and St Thomas' trust, were randomly allocated to a CBT pain management group, an attention placebo group or a non-intervention control. The CBT programme was based on the pain management programme used at INPUT (Guy's and St Thomas' multidisciplinary inpatient chronic pain management programme), but specifically tailored for use in SCD. Significant post-intervention treatment group differences in favour of the CBT intervention were identified for nearly all of the psychological measures. It was concluded that the CBT approach is effective for the management of SCD pain in terms of reducing psychological distress and pain, and improving coping but the positive effects diminished after 6 months (Thomas *et al.*, 2001). Consequently CBT is the main intervention utilized in the HPS. The number and frequency of the CBT sessions are dependent on the patient's need, and 6-monthly follow-up appointments are routinely offered in line with the evidence from the RCT.

Extension of HPS to Other Long-term Conditions

One way of measuring success is the extent to which health psychology is accepted and understood in other, related areas of medicine and the obvious benefits of the sickle cell HPS has led to requests for psychological input to other areas of haematology and also renal services. All these LTCs share much commonality with sickle cell disease, in that patients experience distressing symptoms, distress caused by dealing with uncertainty about the future, life-threatening issues, unpleasant symptoms, loss of control, changes in self-image and difficulties in maintaining relationships. In 2004 the HPS was extended to patients with other haematological disorders and haemophilia. Within haemophilia, the medical and nursing team's increasing acceptance of the role of health psychology in the daily care of patients has led to the development of dedicated full-time health psychology post in 2009. Consultation work based on the SCD HPS model and needs-led research undertaken within renal services in GSTT has led to the receipt of funding for the employment of a clinical health psychologist in 2009.

Psychologist-led Group Support

Psychologist-led group support was introduced at the start of service as a means of introducing health psychology to those patients who considered one-to-one support too stigmatizing and to increase the acceptability of the notion of psychological support. These weekly evening groups (between 6.00 p.m. and 7.30 p.m.) continued as a feature of the HPS utilizing a structured CBT approach and the broad aims are to reduce anxiety, depression and sense of isolation, to increase self-confidence and resources for coping with a serious chronic illness and to link people affected by SCD in order to share pertinent issues and to give and receive support. The groups have enhanced treatment options regarding psychological support as they have offered patients a wider choice, as some patients clearly prefer group to individual support and it's an extremely useful means of identifying patients who might benefit from more individualized support. Evaluations reveal that patients benefit in terms of reducing anxiety, distress and their sense of isolation as well as empowering patients to take charge of their own health.

Patient Information

The health psychology team provides patient information in 'carefully considered' language and is consistent with a recommendation of *The Psychological Management of Medical Patients* (Royal College of Physicians/Psychiatrists, 2003). The information leaflets that we have developed are aimed at facilitating the process of making informed decisions, and these leaflets present information at a level appropriate to the cognitive functioning of our patients.

Education of Staff

Good communication is associated with patient satisfaction, adherence to health advice, improved health outcome and fewer complaints and is an area included in the recommendations of *The Psychological Care of Medical Patients* (Royal College of Physicians/Psychiatrists, 2003). The HPS developed a Communication and Cultural Awareness Training Course for staff caring for sickle cell disease which utilizes a learner-centred 3-day workshop format that is based on the Maguire advanced communication skills model that has been shown to be effective in enhancing communication skills in cancer care (Maguire *et al.*, 1996). In the course, there is an emphasis on experiential learning, using role play with professional actors and specially commissioned videos to depict typically challenging scenarios. Evaluations of early courses revealed that professionals' confidence significantly increased at the end of the course and was maintained 6 months later (Thomas & Cohn, 2006). A similar course was developed for staff working with cancer patients (Thomas *et al.*, 2006).

The psychologists are also involved in SCD team education sessions for staff, and education days for patients (e.g. transition workshops) and the annual Sickle Cell Awareness Day. In addition to these formal efforts at enhancing communication, the psychologists also aid communication between staff and patients in other ways. We model communication styles when in team consultations with patients; we give specific advice to team members (e.g. when breaking bad news or addressing a drug dependency problem); and we facilitate conflict resolution meetings between patients and staff. In addition to teaching inside the hospital, I have made contributions to the specialist health psychology component on the following Applied Psychology professional training programmes:

- London Metropolitan University: MSc in Health Psychology
- University College London: DClin Psych
- Institute of Psychiatry: DClin Psych
- Salomons Canterbury Christ Church University: DClin Psych
- University of East London: DClin Psych

Health Psychology Placement

One of my goals is to demonstrate that there is a role for health psychologists within the acute NHS sector. We have offered supervised placements for MSc Health Psychology students since 1999 and Clinical Psychology trainees since 2001. Our service is highly valued and sought after by health psychologists in training, and this isn't surprising given that there are only a very small number of qualified health psychologists currently working as practitioners within the physical health settings of the NHS. One of my personal goals is make a small contribution to changing the clinical landscape to ensure that this situation is changed so that more health psychologists are working alongside both clinical and counselling psychologists.

Staff Support

Working with people with long-term physical illness can evoke powerful feelings of vulnerability in staff which can influence personal and professional lives (Altschuler,

1997) and close relationships between staff and patients that can occur when patients have been in hospital for repeated and prolonged admissions can get in the way of objectivity. We offer monthly support sessions to wards and accident and emergency nurses. In these sessions we invite staff to debrief from challenging situations, reflect on unhelpful styles of relating to patients, and learn alternative coping strategies. Evaluations have revealed that these sessions are valued by staff, are helpful in changing attitude towards patients with SCD, improve staff coping, and have an indirect beneficial impact on patient care (Thomas & Ellis, 2000). Staff can also refer themselves to the HPS for support and the uptake of this is enhanced by the efforts made by the psychologists to make themselves accessible and approachable. Since the inception of the HPS, in the past 13 years both medical and nursing staff have used this service largely to debrief from challenging and stressful clinical encounters. I have also provided coaching for staff and doctors and have had good outcomes around their membership examinations whilst I have successfully supervised a few nursing MSc and PhD students.

Guidelines and Protocols Concerning Patient Care

The health psychology team have developed the haematology suicide prevention management guidelines and, in collaboration with the rest of the clinical health psychologists in the Trust, I was responsible for the development of a trust-wide suicide prevention guideline.

UK Psychologists in SCD Group

The health psychologists facilitated and hosted meetings of sickle cell psychologists from across the United Kingdom and as a consequence we have formed a British Psychological Society Sickle Cell and Thalassaemia Special Interest Group. We had the inaugural conference on 15 July 2010.

Patients Living Longer: Accounting for Unmet Needs

Future health psychology services need to take account of the needs of an ageing SCD population. With advancing age there is a greater likelihood that chronic ischaemic damage to joints and vital organs will lead to chronic pain and disability and death. Consequently our vision for a health psychology service will build on the existing HPS service and incorporate the changing needs of the patients. For example chronic damage to kidneys can lead to renal failure and dependence on dialysis. Therefore, the HPS will be required to support patients whilst they receive bad news, adjust to and comply with treatment suggestions as well as diet and lifestyle changes.

Health Psychology Scoping Exercise

There is still, however, a lack of career structure for health psychologists within acute hospitals. I am a strong advocate for health psychology and within the trust I have been representing health psychology in a working party within our clinical and academic institutions. Our institution was identified as an academic health science centre in March 2010 and since then, a number of clinical academic groups have been established with a view to developing clinical and academic partnerships that can operate as vehicles to promote and enhance excellence in clinical care. Within the institutions there is a sizeable academic health psychology group, but hardly any health psychologists involved in patient care services. Therefore one of the aims of the health psychologists is to look at ways to integrate health psychology in the provision of care for all patients with physical health problems. However, anecdotal evidence suggests that there may be a number of barriers operating at clinical and managerial levels that are likely to frustrate and prevent the smooth integration of HP in provision of patient care. I achieved funding for one day per week to identify the barriers and to explore potential areas of opportunities for health psychology within GSTFT and our academic partner organizations. The specific aims are:

1. To gain an understanding of the varying perceptions of roles of health psychology;
2. To identify barriers to the integration of health psychology in patient care within secondary care settings; and
3. To identify patient care areas that would benefit from HP.

This work has since been completed and the findings have highlighted that clinicians have poor understanding of the differences between health and clinical psychology, however most people were of the opinion that clinical health psychology is extremely useful for people with physical health problems. Areas of need identified included the stroke unit, cardiac care, gastroenterology, diabetes care and childhood cancer. The barriers identified are largely financial.

Summary

At the start of the specialist HPS, patients with SCD were considered to be behaviourally challenging and high users of hospital services. Thirteen years later, health psychology interventions alongside medical and nursing care have resulted in a reduction in the frequency of hospital admissions and the duration of hospital stays, and an overall improvement in quality of life in these patients. These achievements are likely to be partly attributable to the prominent elements of the HPS, namely working embedded in the haematology team to make the service more psychologically minded, making psychology accessible to non-psychologists, and improving communication between health care professionals and patients. The success of the sickle cell HPS has led to requests for psychological input to other areas of haematology and also renal services.

Why I Love Being a Health Psychologist

Finally, I thoroughly enjoy my role as health psychologist for a variety of reasons. The work within our health psychology service is very diverse and covers inpatient, outpatient and outreach work. Working with patients from diverse cultural backgrounds has been stimulating and provides novel situations for testing out theories about health beliefs and illness representations in both the healthy people as well as those who are unwell. Working with a multidisciplinary team as a health psychologist provides many opportunities to influence patient care both directly and indirectly.

Key Debates in Health Psychology

New Ways of Working for Applied Psychologists and the Acute Physical Health Setting

New Ways of Working (NWW) for Applied Psychologists in health and social care was a joint initiative between the British Psychological Society (BPS) and the National Institute for Mental Health England (NIMHE). NWW is largely concerned with enabling psychologists to deliver effective patient centred care for all groups of patients and consequently it is concerned with the knowledge, skills and experience of applied psychologist in order to achieve this aim. It is also concerned with promoting flexible working of psychologists with other professions which goes a long way to enhancing career development and job satisfaction.

As well as having significant implications for universities, the report and its associated documents also provide important guidance about the ways applied psychologists need to develop their roles in teams and services that are changing quickly to respond to the justifiable demand from service users and carers for better access to psychological services. In addition, Lord Layard's (2005) proposal for Increasing Access to Psychological Therapies (IAPT) has clearly identified huge psychological needs that cannot be easily met by the current numbers of trained psychologists therefore new roles are being created. For example, graduate mental health workers and the low-intensity workers are currently working in various parts of the country. The IAPT programme has largely focussed on the mental health sector with little acknowledgement of the physical health problems. Within the acute physical health NHS setting, health psychologists have yet to enter the arena and currently the majority

---

of psychologists working in physical health are clinical psychologists. Within our institution here at Guys' & ST Thomas NHS foundation, NWW has been applied in limited capacity. Of the 27 psychologists working the trust there are currently, three health and two counselling psychologists being employed. Although the rest are all clinical psychologists, it is great to have health psychologists amongst the workforce. In my daily work within the trust, I strongly advocate for health psychology competencies as being wholly appropriate for patients with physical health problems. Our service has service-level agreements to take Stage 1 health psychologists as well as clinical psychology trainees to undertake placements, and this is a significant way in which to promote NWW and to ensure that health psychology competencies are impacting on patient care as well as providing psychologists with the opportunity to learn how to develop their roles within teams and acute physical services. Feedback from our MSc health placement psychologists suggests that this placement does offer a broad range of experience and is therefore very beneficial.

References

Barakat, L.P., Patterson, C., Weinberger, B.S., Simon, K., Gonzalez, E.R., & Dampier, C. (2007). A prospective study of the role of coping and family functioning in health outcomes for adolescents with sickle cell disease. *Journal of Pediatric Hematology/Oncology*, *29*(11), 752–760.

British Psychological Society. (2002). *Psychological services for stroke survivors and their families*. Division of Clinical and Division Neuropsychology Briefing Paper 19. London: Author.

Charache, S., Lubin, B., & Reid, C. D. (1989). *Management and therapy of sickle cell disease*. NIH Publications No. 84-2117. Washington, DC: National Institutes of Health.

Department of Health (DoH). (2004). *Organising and delivering psychological therapies*. London: HMSO Crown Publications.

Department of Health (DoH). (2005). National Service Framework for Long-term Medical Conditions. Retrieved from http://www.dh.gov.uk/en/Publicationsandstatistics/Publications/PublicationsPolicyAndGuidance/DH_4101902

Department of Health. (2008). *Increasing access to psychological therapies, long term conditions positive practice*. London: Department of Health. Retrieved from http://www.dh.gov.uk/publications

Edwards, R., Telfair, J., Cecil H., & Lenoci, J. (2001). Self efficacy as a predictor of adult adjustment to sickle cell disease: one year outcomes. *Psychosomatic Medicine*, *63*, 850–858.

Gil, K.M., Abrams, M.R., Phillips, G., & Keefe, F.J. (1989). Sickle cell disease pain: relation of coping strategies to adjustment. *Journal of Consulting and Clinical Psychology*, *57*(6), 725–731.

Gil, K.M., Abrams, M., Phillips, G., & Williams, D. (1992). A: sickle cell disease pain: 2 predicting health care use and activity level at 9 months follow-up. *Journal of Consulting and Clinical Psychology*, *60*, 267–273.

Maguire, P., Booth, K., Elliot, C., & Jones, B. (1996). Helping health professionals involved in cancer care acquire key interviewing skills: the impact of workshops. *European Journal of Cancer, 32A*, 1486–1489.

National Institute for Health and Clinical Excellence (NICE). (2005). Health needs assessment: a practical guide. Retrieved from http://www.nice.org.uk/aboutnice/whoweare/aboutthehda/hdapublications/health_needs_assessment_a_practical_guide.jsp

Royal College of Physicians/Psychiatrists. (2003). *The psychological care of medical patients.* London: Author.

Shapiro, B.S., Benjamin, L.J. Payne, R., & Heidrich, G. (1997). Sickle cell related pain: perceptions of medical practitioners. *Journal of Pain and Symptom Management, 14*, 168–174.

Thomas, V.J. (1996). A community-based cognitive behavioural pain management programme for patients with sickle cell disease: a pilot study. *Abstracts of the Llandudno Meeting, Journal of the Pain Society, 12*, 63.

Thomas, V.J., & Cohn, T. (2006). Communication skills and cultural awareness courses for HCP who care for sickle cell patients. *Journal of Advanced Nursing*, 480–488.

Thomas, V. J., Dixon, A.L., & Milligan, P. (1999). Cognitive-behaviour therapy for the management of sickle cell disease pain: an evaluation of a community-based intervention. *British Journal of Health Psychology, 4*, 209–229

Thomas, V.J., & Ellis, C. (2000). The benefits of psychological support for accident & emergency nurses caring for sickle cell patients. *The Nursing Standard, 15*(5), 35–39.

Thomas, V.J., Gruen, R., & Shu, S. (2001). Cognitive behavioural therapy in sickle cell disease: identification and assessment of costs. *Ethnicity & Health, 6*(1), 59–67.

Thomas, V.J., Rawle, H., Howard, J., Abedian, M., Westerdale, N., & Musumadi, L. (2009). Health psychology service for sickle cell disease: reflections on the service developments 11 years on. *Clinical Psychology Forum, 199*, 18–23.

Thomas, V.J. Richardson, A., & Cansino-Malagon, A. (2006). Communication skills and cultural awareness courses in the field of cancer care. *Cancer Nursing Practice, 5*(8), 23–30.

Thomas, V.J., Serjeant, G., & Hambleton, I. (2001). Psychological distress and coping in sickle cell disease: a comparison of Jamaican and British patients. *Ethnicity & Health, 6*(2), 129–136.

Tyrer, S.P., Capon, M., & Petersen, D.M. (1989). The detection of psychiatric illness and psychological handicaps in British pain clinic population. *Pain, 36*, 63–74.

20

Afterword

Mark Forshaw and David Sheffield

When we first plotted the outline of this book, we had ideas about how it would end up. In actual fact we are pleased to announce, now that all the contributions have merged into a fairly coherent whole, how right we were and how wrong we were. We were right in that the chapters show health psychology in all its diversity. Health psychologists are doing all sorts of interesting things in all manner of exciting ways. We were wrong because underneath all of this is a homogeneity that we did not predict would peek through quite so strongly. We are pleased because it is evidence of there being a tangible skeleton under the flesh of our discipline. We've been saying there is for years, and those of us involved in the development of the various training models worked hard to make sure that the backbone was in place, but over time it is possible for us to take that for granted, and for it to start to disappear from view. The chapters in this book just go to show how much we really all have in common.

Our roots are in research, and there is no shortage of examples of research in this book. On the one hand, the research that we are completing has become increasingly theoretical but we recognize that there is still some way to go before we have an evidence base. On the other hand, much of the research is practically orientated. Together it is clear that much of the research we are conducting is driven by real-world problems and our desire to solve them using models and theories. There is no sign yet of the weakening of our research base that some predicted might happen as the discipline evolves. Arguably, we have become more rounded professionals, but not at the expense of any of our skills and competences.

The change to regulatory processes, in particular the move to statutory regulation by the Health Professions Council, has led, for one reason or another, to some interesting consequences. The most pertinent, which we believe this book shows, is that we have entered an era where more and more of us feel comfortable using

Health Psychology in Action, First Edition. Edited by Mark Forshaw and David Sheffield.
© 2013 John Wiley & Sons, Ltd. Published 2013 by John Wiley & Sons, Ltd.

the term 'practitioner'. On the most superficial level, those of us who are HPC-registered are entitled to use the term 'practitioner psychologist'. This means that we are legally identifiable as practitioners. However, we think the change has worked deeper than that. We have begun to reflect on what practising means, and what a practitioner does. We have begun to recognize that *doing* health psychology, in whatever form, is practising. This includes research, teaching, training, consulting, providing interventions and so on. The list is familiar, of course; it is the list of competences. Thus, we come full circle. The regulated titles confirm what we do, and that is just how it should be: the dog *is* wagging the tail.

As the stories told in this book show, health psychologists rarely work in isolation. We are genuine multidisciplinarians, part of a wider community of academic and health professionals of all kinds, working together to find things out and to change lives for the better. This is probably one of our strengths, although it is something that has emerged from the work that we do, and possibly also from necessity. There simply aren't thousands of employment opportunities for health psychologists specifically. What we find, however, are jobs that we can do, and we are getting better at showing employers that we can do them. Our value is being recognized. By convincing others what we can do, to help the work of nurses, doctors, physiotherapists, neurologists and so on, we are becoming part of a wider health care team. Our multidisciplinary nature is a natural consequence of that.

Health psychology is still young, and shows few signs of becoming fixed or fixated. It is an evolving organism, and change is a good thing and a source of anxiety simultaneously. We must move with the times. However, change for change's sake is to be avoided at all costs. It is true that health psychology today isn't the same health psychology of 20 years ago. Nor should it be. We should not forget what makes us, but we equally should not be closed off to what we can still become. In this book, we find the roots of health psychology, its present and its future, cheek by jowl. What is clear to us, as the editors of this volume, is just how well those sit together.

Where Are We Going?

It is probably fair to say that every health psychologist has a slightly different opinion as to where the discipline is heading in the United Kingdom and beyond. These opinions reflect the variety of priorities, roles and responsibilities that different health psychologists have in their employment. Some of the authors of this volume are arguing for more time spent in patient work, some for more political and policy involvement and others for a strong evidence base derived from rigorous research (walking before running, as it were). Most trainees and those thinking about training typically say that they want funded training places, analogous to those available for clinical psychologists. We might not be able to position health psychology exactly where we want it just yet, and there is a long way to travel. We must never forget that clinical psychology in the United Kingdom is some 30 or so years ahead of health psychology in its history. The original professional division of the BPS that encompassed clinical psychology was established in 1958. We simply cannot expect to be in the same place, just yet, but we have all the characteristics of a credible profession, and a viable training model, and if it looks like a duck and quacks like a duck, then it's a duck. We owe it to ourselves, and new generations of health psychologists, to continue to work hard to publicize our value, as researchers and practitioners, to the purse holders and policy makers, to position ourselves where we should be. Only history, tradition and prejudices hold us back. None of these are good reasons for keeping intelligent, skilled people from plying their trade and contributing to society.

Index

Health Psychology in Action, First Edition. Edited by Mark Forshaw and David Sheffield.
© 2013 John Wiley & Sons, Ltd. Published 2013 by John Wiley & Sons, Ltd.

Index compiled by Terry Halliday